LEARNING FROM CHANGE

Issues and Experiences
in Participatory Monitoring
and Evaluation

Edited by

Marisol Estrella with Jutta Blauert, Dindo Campilan,
John Gaventa, Julian Gonsalves, Irene Guijt,
Deb Johnson and Roger Ricafort

INTERMEDIATE TECHNOLOGY PUBLICATIONS
INTERNATIONAL DEVELOPMENT RESEARCH CENTRE

First published in 2000 by
Intermediate Technology Publications Ltd,
103–105 Southampton Row, London WC1B 4HL, UK

and the International Development Research Centre,
PO Box 8500, Ottawa, ON, Canada K1G 3H9

A CIP catalogue record for this book is available from the British Library

Canadian Cataloguing in Publication Data

Main entry under title:

Learning from change: issues and experiences in participatory monitoring and evaluation

"Intermediate Technology Publications"
Includes bibliographical references and an index.
ISBN 0-88936-895-3

1. Economic development projects — Evaluation.
2. Community development — Evaluation.
I. Estrella, Marisol.
II. International Development Research Centre (Canada)

HD75.9L42 2000307.1'4C00-980337-8

ISBN 1 85339 469 6

ISBN 0 88936 895 3 (Canada)

Typeset by Dorwyn Ltd, Rowlands Castle, Hants
Printed in the UK by Cromwell Press, Trowbridge

Contents

Introduction

Part 1   Methodological innovations

Part 2   Learning with communities

List of figures

List of tables

Glossary of acronyms and abbreviations

ACIN	Asociación de Cabildos Indígenas (Association of Indigenous Cabildos of Northern Cauca, Colombia)
ACORD	Agency for Cooperation and Research in Development
ADB	Asian Development Bank
AERDD	Agricultural Extension and Rural Development Department (University of Reading)
AIM	Asian Institute of Management
AIT	Asian Institute of Technology
APAC	Aimag Poverty Alleviation Council
AS-PTA	Assessoria e Serviços a Projetos em Agricultura Alternativa (Training and Services for Alternative Agriculture Projects)
BATMAN	Barangay Training Management
CBO	community-based organization
CCDB	Christian Commission for Development in Bangladesh
CEDICAM	Centro de Desarrollo Integral Campesina para la Mixteca (Centre of Integrated Peasant Development for the Mixteca)
CEDRES	Centre d'Études, de Documentation et de Recherche Économique et Sociales (Centre of Economic and Social Study, Documentation and Research, Burkina Faso)
CEPCU	Centro de Estudios Pluriculturales (Centre for Pluricultural Studies)
CETAMEX	Centro de Tecnologías Alternativas de México (Mexican Centre of Alternative Technologies)
CIAT	Centre for Tropical Agricultural Research
CIC	Centro Internazionale Crocevia (Crossroads International Centre, Italy)
CIRDAP	Center for Integrated Rural Development for Asia and the Pacific
CIRES	Centre Ivoirien de Recherche Économique et Sociale (Ivory Coast Centre for Economic and Social Research)
CLT	citizen learning team
CM	community monitoring *or* citizen monitoring
CODESRIA	Council for the Development of Social Science Research in Africa
COMUNIDEC	Ecuadorian grassroots support organization, NGO
CONCERN	Center of Concern
CPC	community partnership centre
CSD	Centre for Social Development
CSM	community self-monitoring
CTA-ZM	Centro de Tecnologías Alternativas – Zona da Mata (Centre for Alternative Technologies – Zona da Mata)
DANIDA	Danish International Development Agency
DFID	Department for International Development
DFOs	District Forestry Offices
DoF	Department of Forestry
DPAC	Duureg Poverty Alleviation Council
EDA	Economic Development Authority
EE	empowerment evaluation
ELF	Education for Life Foundation
EMATER/PB	Empresa de Assistência Técnica e Extensão Rural/Paraíba (Enterprise for Technical Assistance and Rural Extension, Paraíba)

EZ/EC	Empowerment Zone/Enterprise Community
FAO	Food and Agriculture Organisation
FFW	food for work
FPR	farming participatory research
FSR	farming systems research
FUG	forest user group
GDF	grassroots development framework
GIS	geographic information system
GLC	general leadership course
GT	Ginabayang Talakayan (guided discussion)
HLS	household livelihood security
HUD	US Department of Housing and Urban Development
IAF	Inter-American Foundation
ICCO	Interchurch Organization for Development Cooperation (Netherlands)
ICDP	integrated conservation and development project
IDRC	International Development Research Centre (Canada)
IDS	Institute of Development Studies
IFAD	International Fund for Agricultural Development
IGF	income generation fund
IIED	International Institute for the Environment and Development
IIRR	International Institute for Rural Reconstruction
IoA	Institute of Aquaculture
ITK	indigenous technical knowledge
KJ	Key Judges (method)
KPAC	Khoroo Poverty Alleviation Council
LDF	local development fund
LFA	logical framework analysis
LFS	Livestock and Fisheries Section
LFSP	Livingstone Food Security Project
LGs	leader-graduates
LRs	leader-researchers
LWU	Lao Women's Union
M&E	monitoring and evaluation
MAE	Miniterio degli Affari Esteri (Ministry of Foreign Affairs, Italy)
MAF	Ministry of Agriculture and Forestry
MAP	Metodologías de Auto-Evaluación Participativa (Methodologies for Participatory Self-Evaluation)
McCAN	McDowell County Action Network
MIS	management information system
MLAL	Movimiento Laici per America Latina (Lay People's Movement for Latin America, Italy)
MPS	Maderas del Pueblo del Sureste
NEF	New Economics Foundation
NGOs	non-governmental organizations
Non-LGs	leaders not trained by ELF
NORAD	Norwegian Agency for International Development
NORRIP	Northern Region Rural Integrated Programme
NPAC	National Poverty Alleviation Committee
NPAP	National Poverty Alleviation Programme
NRSP	Natural Resources Systems Programme
NUKCFP	Nepal–UK Community Forestry Project
ODA	Overseas Development Agency
PAF	Poverty Alleviation Fund
PAME	participatory assessment, monitoring and evaluation
PAMFORK	Participatory Methodologies Forum of Kenya
PAPO	Poverty Alleviation Programme Office

PAR	participatory action research
PARC	Palestinian Agricultural Relief Committees
PE	participatory evaluation
PFU	Palestinian Farmers' Union
PIM	participatory impact monitoring
PLA	participatory learning and action
PM	participatory monitoring
PM&E	participatory monitoring and evaluation
PO	people's organization
PPM&E	participatory planning, monitoring and evaluation
PPRTH	Philippine Psychological Research and Training House
PRA	participatory rural appraisal
PREVAL	Programa para el Fortalecimiento de la Capacidad Regional de Evaluación de los Proyectos de Reducción de la Pobreza Rural en América Latina y el Caribe (Programme for Regional Capacity Building in Evaluation of Rural Poverty Alleviation Programmes in Latin America and the Caribbean)
PRIA	Participatory Research in Asia
PSSP	Pambansang Samahan ng Sikolohiyang Pilipino (Psychological Association of the Philippines)
REFLECT	regenerated Freirean literacy through empowering community techniques
REP	Research and Evaluation Programme
RP	range post
RRA	rapid rural appraisal
SAFE	Stop Abusive Family Environments
SDC	Swiss Development Corporation
SE	self-evaluation *or* auto-evaluation
SIDA	Swedish International Development Agency
SISDEL	Sistema de Desarrollo Local (Local Development System)
SM&E	self-monitoring and evaluation
SMART	specific, measurable, action-oriented, relevant, and time-bound
SP	Sikolohiyang Pilipino (Filipino psychology)
SPAC	Sum Poverty Alleviation Council
SPICED	subjective, participatory, interpreted, cross-checked, empowering, and disaggregated
STR	Sindicato de Trabalhadores Rurais (Rural Workers' Union)
SWOT	strengths, weaknesses, opportunities and threats
TAF	targeted assistance fund
TARO	Taller de Autoevaluación de Recursos y Oportunidades (Workshop on Self-evaluation of Resources and Opportunities)
T-PE	transformative-participatory evaluation
UNDP	United Nations Development Programme
UPAC	Ulaanbaatar Poverty Alleviation Council
UPWARD	Users' Perspectives with Agricultural Research and Development
USAID	United States Agency for International Development
USDA	United States Department of Agriculture
VGOs	voluntary group organizations
VMCs	village monitoring committees
WDF	Women's Development Fund
WN	World Neighbors
WWF	World Wide Fund

Foreword

As we embark on the twenty-first century, the words accountability, decentralization, democracy, diversity, ownership, participation and transparency are as common in development rhetoric as they are contravened in practice. *Learning from Change* shows how participatory monitoring and evaluation (PM&E) has the potential to make the rhetoric real. It establishes PM&E as one of the great remaining frontiers and challenges in development, with implications for learning and change which are at once methodological, institutional and personal.

Bringing together and analysing as it does varied experiences of innovators in South and North America, Africa and Asia, this book is a landmark. Its balanced, reflective and critical style cannot suppress the excitement. The discoveries of practitioners in different continents converge to suggest that where PM&E spreads and is sustained, much else can come to change: in the project cycle and activities; in the cultures and procedures of organizations; in professional norms and practices; in interpersonal relationships; and in gains to poor people. We have here seeds of a revolution in the theory and practice of development, with PM&E as both catalyst and clincher in reversing relationships of power, transforming institutions, and enhancing learning and adapting by stakeholders at all levels.

Learning from Change should be read by all development professionals, whether government officials, donors, academics, or others in civil society, who are concerned with improving performance to benefit the poor and powerless. It should inspire them to support pioneers of PM&E and to explore the potentials themselves. Those who ignore the themes and lessons of this book may be secure in their careers in the short term; and those in their fifties may even survive to a safe retirement. But they will be also be losers. For they will have missed not just the risks, but also the exhilaration and fulfilments of surfing a wave of the future.

Robert Chambers
August 2000

Preface

IN RECENT YEARS, participation has become a critical concept in development. In an earlier book in this series on participation published by Intermediate Technology Publications, Robert Chambers asks *Whose Reality Counts?* (1997) and argues the need to begin with the priorities of poor and marginalized people when planning and implementing development programmes. This book takes the argument one step further. Equally important as the question 'whose reality counts?' is that of 'who counts reality?' – that is, whose voices and knowledge are used to define success? Who benefits and who learns from the process of evaluating and tracking change? The book demonstrates that monitoring and evaluation – done in a participatory way – can be used to strengthen learning, accountability and effectiveness, and are a critical part of any participatory development process. However, as the essays and cases in the book also illustrate, these participatory processes are rarely straightforward, nor do they offer guaranteed outcomes.

Participatory monitoring and evaluation (PM&E) has been used in development for some time. However, until recently, there has been little documentation or analysis of how it works in practice, of its dynamics and impacts, successes and failures. While many people think it important, few can describe how it is *really* done. By bringing together 12 case studies from differing countries around the world, along with introductions and concluding syntheses, this book helps to fill that gap. The case studies and overview chapters give an in-depth view of PM&E practice, and some of its principles, approaches and challenges.

Where PM&E has been used in the past, it was often at the project level, and often for the purposes of giving the project donor an account of what had occurred. This book is important because it documents more recent and much broader uses of PM&E. While some of the cases illustrate the dynamics of the process amongst differing groups at a local community level, others show that PM&E is now being used on a much larger scale – with donors, institutions and governments. By thinking of PM&E as a learning process, involving many differing stakeholders, we can also see how it is used for empowerment, conflict negotiation, capacity building, collaboration, and new forms of mutual accountability and governance.

Finally, this book is important because of the collaboration it represents in itself. The book is the culmination of a project that has brought together practitioners and scholars, from differing sectors and from over a dozen countries in the South and North. The case studies and papers contained here grew from an international workshop on PM&E held at the training campus of the International Institute for Rural Reconstruction (IIRR) outside Manila, Philippines in November 1997. Non-governmental organization (NGO) representatives, government officials, academics, researchers and donors – representing 27 countries and 41 institutions –

gathered together for five days to share their experiences and to assess the state of the art in PM&E.

The idea for the Philippines Workshop arose from several meetings and discussions involving some of the contributing editors and others as early as 1996. In discussing significant gaps in the understanding of participatory approaches, the importance of more learning, documentation and exchange about PM&E was raised. IIRR suggested the idea of an international event to bring together practitioners to share experiences and to mainstream PM&E. It offered to take the initiative and responsibility for organizing and leading such an effort, in partnership with other groups.

An international steering group was formed including representatives from IIRR, the International Institute for Environment and Development (IIED, based in London, UK), the Institute of Development Studies (IDS, based in Sussex, UK), Users' Perspectives with Agricultural Research and Development (UPWARD, Philippines), Oxfam Hong Kong, Sikiliza International (Uganda), and the Philippine participatory rural appraisal (PRA) network represented by Kaisahan (Philippines). IDS and IIED commissioned literature reviews for presentation at the workshop. IIRR used e-mail to undertake pre-workshop exchanges and consultations and to begin to identify possible participants, with the help of the Steering Group. The group also selected the cases to be shared at the workshop after considering sectoral, geographic and gender representation criteria. The International Development and Research Centre (IDRC), through Fred Carden, made an early commitment to support the workshop with financial and other assistance. Swiss Development Corporation (SDC) was the second major donor. They responded at short notice and came in with critical support only a month prior to the workshop itself. IDS and the Department for International Development (DFID) in the UK and United Nations Development Programme (UNDP) in Manila provided strategic and complementary funding, allowing IIRR to move full steam ahead.

The November 1997 workshop was exciting and rich in its learning. For many participants, it became one of the first opportunities to share their PM&E concerns and experiences in an international gathering. Participants enthusiastically committed to a number of follow-up activities, including several documentation projects. The steering committee asked one of its members, Marisol Estrella, to co-ordinate production of a book which would further analyse some of the case studies and discussions from the conference. Since that time, she has worked enthusiastically with the authors and other co-editors to co-ordinate the development of this book.

The conference also led to several other publications and activities. Kiko Saladores and a team from IIRR documented the proceedings and issued an excellent in-depth report (*Workshop Proceedings*, 1998, IIRR). IIED published a special issue of *PLA Notes* (No. 31: 1998) drawing on several case studies and proceedings. Another team helped to summarize policy implications in an *IDS Policy Briefing* (12: 1998) (see Guijt and Gaventa, 1998), which subsequently has been translated into Spanish by IDS, with funding from PREVAL, a Latin American evaluation network based in Costa Rica. Background literature reviews were published as an IDS Working Paper (Estrella and Gaventa, 1998). IIRR has continued to gather examples of concrete PM&E methods for a manual, and organized a follow-up international training workshop on PM&E. In May 1999, several Latin American participants, along with IDS, held a workshop focusing more on the grassroots development framework and its innovations by NGOs in Latin America, and a more general Latin American PM&E conference is also being planned.

Today, across the world, PM&E is understood better than two years ago. Drawing upon lessons from the field, this book should further serve to inspire and guide policy makers, planners, academics and development practitioners in efforts to promote and to institutionalize participatory approaches to monitoring and evaluation. Equally important, the experience of working together in this neglected area of participatory work has enriched each of us who have been involved. We have learned and changed through the process.

Julian F. Gonsalves, IIRR and John Gaventa, IDS
August 2000

Acknowledgements

The efforts of many people contributed to a collaborative project like this one. First, thanks go to IIRR for organizing and hosting the November 1997 workshop in the Philippines from which this publication arose. Angelina Ibus persevered long and hard to prepare for the successful, though complex, international event. Mae Arevalo and Yvette Mercado also made important and strategic contributions without which the workshop could not have achieved so much. Dindo Campilan worked closely with the IIRR team in preparing for the workshop. Kiko Saladores led the process documentation and preparation of the Workshop Proceedings. Fred Carden of IDRC, Julian Gonsalves of IIRR, John Thompson at IIED and John Gaventa at IDS provided early support and guidance. Other members of the International Steering Committee played an important role in planning and implementing the workshop, including Jutta Blauert, Rene Clemente, Marissa Espineli, Irene Guijt, Deb Johnson, and Roger Ricafort.

In preparing this book, many others are to be thanked as well. Special thanks go to the case study writers who, from many parts of the globe, have patiently stayed in touch, and remained committed throughout the process. Thanks to IDS which helped to co-ordinate final production, including two writing and editing marathons in which Marisol Estrella came from Manila to work with Jutta Blauert and John Gaventa. Irene Guijt and Deb Johnson were especially helpful in reviewing and commenting on drafts through e-mail from other parts of the world. Linda Bateman, Jas Vaghadia and Alison Norwood at IDS have assisted in preparation of the manuscript, and Kath Pasteur helped to finalize the references and bibliography.

Most of all, thanks to the participants in these initiatives – some of whose work is now documented and ready to be shared. Through your experiences, we will all continue our learning.

Marisol Estrella, for the editors
August 2000

Introduction

1

Learning from Change[1]

MARISOL ESTRELLA

THIS BOOK IS a collection of experiences in participatory monitoring and evaluation (PM&E) from around the world. It allows different 'voices' to tell their story from their different perspectives, contexts, and settings. The purpose of the book is *not* to establish a singular definition of PM&E practice, but to pull together these experiences, review these efforts, and see what key issues and questions emerge.

This book focuses, above all, on the *process* of doing PM&E. Emphasis is placed not only on *what* is being monitored and evaluated, but more on *who* is measuring and *how* different concerns and interests are negotiated and represented. This process is shaped primarily by stakeholders – individuals, groups, organizations, and institutions – who directly and indirectly influence but who are also affected by the actions or development interventions of others. Stakeholders include, among others, beneficiaries; project or programme staff and management; researchers; local and central government politicians and technical staff; and funding agencies. The inclusion of many representatives of stakeholder groups is the 'axis' around which the PM&E process revolves, as people together analyse existing realities and seek points of action.

In many respects, *Learning from Change* is about the different lenses through which diverse groups and people are able to view, describe and act on changes. It is about changing the way we learn about the results and impacts of our development efforts. It recognizes the importance of people's participation in analysing and interpreting changes, and learning from their own development experience. This process of learning becomes ever more complex, as more stakeholders within all kinds of institutions become involved in monitoring and evaluation.

The book is a collection of 12 case studies that describe how different stakeholders have applied PM&E approaches across a range of purposes and contexts. The case studies have been selected from papers originally submitted at the Philippines Workshop, and together they represent inspiring examples from non-governmental organizations (NGOs), researchers, community-based organizations (CBOs) or people's organizations (POs), community leaders, government agencies, and funding agencies. While these case studies indicate the range of diversity in PM&E practice, they reflect experiences mainly in the field of development. They cut across different sectors, including agriculture, forestry, natural resource management, community development, organizational development and local governance. Many take place within the context of a development project or programme intervention, generally at the local or community level. All case studies except one (Rutherford) are from the South.

There are, of course, many other varied applications of PM&E in a number of other fields, sectors and areas of the world, that are not represented in this book. For instance, just as some development and academic institutions (e.g. NGOs, funders) are adopting organizational learning approaches, private businesses are adopting (and leading in the development of) learning-oriented approaches for greater social and ethical accountability (Boyett and Boyett, 1998; Edwards and Hulme, 1995; Zadek et al., 1997). PM&E is also applied in many communities of the North (MacGillivray et al., 1998; Parachini and Mott, 1997; Whitmore, 1998). There may be further experiences in other sectors, about which we know little, namely: health; education; urban settings; areas of conflict, emergencies and disasters; with women and marginalized groups (children, elderly, persons with disabilities), among others. Work is proceeding in these areas but did not form the focus of the discussions and case studies available for this book.

The book organizes the case studies into three thematic sections, although a number of cases cut across these themes. Part 1 describes experiences that innovate with various methods and approaches to PM&E. Part 2 focuses on community-driven monitoring and evaluation experiences. Part 3 looks at the implications of 'scaling-up' PM&E in terms of changing institutions and building more learning-oriented organizations. The concluding sections examine lessons and insights drawn from these case studies and other experiences, and pose challenges for the further development of PM&E practice.

This first chapter provides a historical background to PM&E, and outlines some of the key concepts and differences between participatory and conventional approaches to monitoring and evaluation. It attempts to clarify common terms and definitions of PM&E and describes how PM&E can be applied in a number of contexts and purposes. The purpose of the chapter is to raise issues and to identify questions emerging in the field.

Tracing the history of PM&E

The concept of PM&E is not new. PM&E draws from 20 years of participatory research traditions, including participatory action research (PAR), participatory learning and action (including participatory rural appraisal or PRA), and farming systems research (FSR) or farming participatory research (FPR). Some of these initial efforts to experiment with participatory approaches were supported by NGOs such as World Neighbors, Oxfam, Users' Perspectives with Agricultural Research and Development (UPWARD), the Agency for Cooperation and Research in Development (ACORD) and the Society for Participatory Research in Asia (PRIA) (see Armonia and Campilan, 1997; Bunch, 1982; Campos and Coupal, 1996; Howes, 1992; PRIA, 1981; Rugh, 1992).

By the 1980s, concepts of PM&E had already entered the policy-making domain of larger donor agencies and development organizations, most notably the Food and Agriculture Organisation (FAO), the United States

Agency for International Development (USAID), the Danish International Development Agency (DANIDA), and the UK Department for International Development (DFID),[2] the Swedish International Development Authority (SIDA), the Norwegian Agency for International Development (NORAD) and the World Bank (Howes, 1992; Rudqvist and Woodford-Berger, 1996). Outside the field of development, PM&E can also trace its beginnings in the private sector where there has been growing appreciation for individual and organizational learning (Raynard, 1998; Zadek *et al.*, 1997).

While interest in constructing PM&E processes is growing, it must be noted that there are still many local forms of PM&E that go unrecognized, as they are often regarded as commonplace practice and part of daily activity. Communities and CBOs have long been monitoring and evaluating their work (without labelling it as such), developing their own procedures for recording and analysing information, and using that information for making decisions. In one case study, researchers noticed that farmers in Bolivia and Laos already conduct and monitor on-farm experiments through direct observations and verbal sharing of information with other farmers (Chapter 4). Many of these local initiatives are carried out informally, and they provide rich potential for developing innovative approaches to monitor and evaluate change.

The interest in PM&E has grown as a result of several factors, including:

○ the trend in management circles towards 'performance-based accountability', with greater emphasis placed on achieving results and objectives beyond the financial reporting
○ the growing scarcity of funds, leading to a demand for greater accountability and demonstrated impact or success
○ the shift towards decentralization and devolution of central government responsibilities and authority to lower levels of government, necessitating new forms of oversight to ensure transparency and to improve support to constituency-responsive initiatives
○ stronger capacities and experiences of NGOs and CBOs as decision makers and implementers in the development process (Edwards and Hulme, 1995; Estrella and Gaventa, 1998; Guijt and Gaventa, 1998).

Integrating participation in monitoring and evaluation (M&E)

Interest in PM&E is also partly a reflection of the international development community's dissatisfaction with conventional approaches to M&E, particularly in the last decade. Arguments against the commonly practised 'top-down' approaches to M&E are discussed widely in the literature (see Feuerstein, 1986; Greene, 1994; Guba and Lincoln, 1989; PRIA, 1981, 1995; Rubin, 1995; UPWARD, 1997; Whitmore, 1998).

While there are many variations of conventional M&E, it has been characterized as oriented solely to the needs of funding agencies and policy makers. Many argue that conventional approaches attempt to produce information that is 'objective', 'value-free' and 'quantifiable'; hence, outsiders are usually contracted to carry out the evaluation for the sake of maintaining 'objectivity'. Stakeholders directly involved in, or affected by, the very development activities meant to benefit them have little or no input in the evaluation – either in determining questions asked or types of information obtained, or in defining measures of 'success' (Rubin, 1995: 20).

In response to these problems and criticisms of conventional M&E, new ways of monitoring and evaluating development interventions have evolved. These innovative approaches aim to make M&E more participatory and effective by including a wider range of stakeholders at every stage of the process. Although there are many variations of PM&E, there are at least four common features that contribute to good PM&E practice: (i) participation, (ii) learning, (iii) negotiation, and (iv) flexibility (Estrella and Gaventa, 1998).

Emphasis is shifted 'away from externally controlled data-seeking evaluations towards recognition of locally relevant or stakeholder-based processes for gathering, analysing, and using information' (Abbot and Guijt, 1998). Furthermore, PM&E can serve as a tool for self-assessment. It strives to be an internal learning process that enables people to reflect on past experience, examine present realities, revisit objectives, and define future strategies, by recognizing different needs of stakeholders and negotiating their diverse claims and interests. The PM&E process is also flexible and adaptive to local contexts and constantly changing circumstances and concerns of stakeholders. By encouraging stakeholder participation beyond data gathering, PM&E is about promoting self-reliance in decision making and problem solving – thereby strengthening people's capacities to take action and promote change.

In practice, the differences between conventional and participatory M&E are not so clearly distinguishable. There is a wide continuum of participatory and conventional M&E approaches. Participatory evaluations may engage outside experts, but in different roles and relationships to facilitate the inclusion of a wider number of stakeholders – on the premise that this will result in a number of ideas and perspectives. For instance, outside facilitators may play a critical role in helping to establish and design a PM&E system, in the actual facilitation of the process, and in analysing and learning from findings (see Chapters 2, 3, 4 and 7 in this volume). In some PM&E experiences, the project used pre-determined indicators for measuring 'success' (see Chapter 12), while others encouraged various stakeholders to measure change according to their own criteria and indicators[3] (see Chapters 3, 5, 8 and 9). During the Philippines Workshop, participants pointed out that both participatory and conventional approaches can and do employ qualitative and quantitative methods for data gathering and analysis; hence, the distinction between more or less participatory M&E does not lie in methods alone (IIRR, 1998).

Defining PM&E

Despite growing interest in the subject, there is no single definition or methodology of PM&E (see Box 1.1). The difficulty of establishing a common definition for PM&E highlights the diverse range of experiences

4

in this field, but also underscores the difficulty of clarifying concepts of 'monitoring', 'evaluation' and 'participation'. For example, the case studies featured in this collection do not make clear distinctions between monitoring and evaluation, and many of them use these terms interchangeably. The problem with clarifying definitions of PM&E stems partly from the discourse which surrounds the use of these terms. In the field of international development, monitoring and evaluation are terms that implicitly suggest particular meanings. Evaluations have been used by funding agencies primarily as a tool to control and manage the disbursement of resources to recipient organizations or beneficiaries. As argued by Carden in Chapter 13 of this volume:

> 'This approach to evaluation remains an important dimension of accountability for any donor agency . . . From the point of view of recipient organizations, evaluation has thus been viewed largely as a policing mechanism.'

Box 1.1: Terms used to describe PM&E practice

- Participatory evaluation (PE)
- Participatory monitoring (PM)
- Participatory assessment, monitoring and evaluation (PAME)
- Participatory impact monitoring (PIM)
- Process monitoring (PM)
- Self-evaluation (SE) or Auto-evaluation
- Stakeholder-based evaluation/Stakeholder assessment
- Empowerment evaluation (EE)
- Community monitoring/Citizen monitoring (CM)
- Self-monitoring and evaluation (SM&E)
- Participatory planning, monitoring and evaluation (PPM&E)
- Transformative participatory evaluation (T-PE)

The terms 'monitoring' and 'evaluation' can also take on different meanings when used and interpreted in the local language and context, which can make introducing PM&E problematic (see Chapters 10 and 12). At the Philippines Workshop, participants did not attempt to reach a single definition for PM&E (see Table 1.1). Defining 'participation' in the workshop proved to be problematic, as there were no set rules to determine *who* should be involved, and the *degree* and *quality* of participation throughout the process – a major issue to which we will return later in this chapter and again in the case studies and concluding chapters.

Multiple purposes of PM&E

Given that the approaches to PM&E are extremely diverse, it is perhaps more useful to group the range of purposes for which PM&E is being used,

Table 1.1: PM&E as defined by participants at the Philippines Workshop

Core concept	Definitions/Features
Monitoring	○ Knowing where we are ○ Observing change ○ Kilometre check ○ Regular ongoing assessment ○ Routine reflection ○ Feedback
Evaluation	○ Reflection process to look back and foresee ○ Assessment of achievements/impacts over a longer period ○ Learning from experience ○ Valuing ○ Performance review
Participation (in M&E)	○ Shared learning ○ Democratic process ○ Joint decision making ○ Co-ownership ○ Mutual respect ○ Empowerment

and in which contexts. This section discusses the differing purposes of PM&E and how these relate to each other. While there is nothing new about monitoring and evaluating change, the critical feature in a PM&E approach is its emphasis on *who* measures change and *who* benefits from learning about these changes. In PM&E, measuring change is used for different purposes, depending on the different information needs and objectives of stakeholders. These different purposes include:

○ to improve project planning and management
○ to strengthen organizations and promote institutional learning
○ to inform policy.

Determining what is to be measured and for what specific purpose (or purposes) will ultimately depend on recognizing and negotiating different stakeholder perspectives and interests.

Measuring change for differing purposes

Similar to conventional approaches, PM&E is generally used to measure changes resulting from specific interventions. The main difference is that in a participatory approach, stakeholders who are directly or indirectly involved in a programme take part in selecting the indicators to measure changes, in collecting information, and in evaluating findings. Measuring change can include tracking inputs, outputs, processes, and/or outcomes (impacts). It may also include monitoring intended and/or unintended consequences. This demonstrates what has been achieved, whether the needs of intended beneficiaries are being met over time, and whether the best strategies have been pursued.

6

In measuring change, PM&E provides information which is used to meet different stakeholder needs and objectives. Firstly, PM&E may be used for the purpose of *improving project planning and implementation*. As a project management tool, PM&E provides stakeholders and project managers with information to assess whether project objectives have been met and how resources have been used (Campos and Coupal, 1996). This helps in making critical decisions about project implementation and in planning future activities (PRIA, 1995; UPWARD, 1997). For instance, Sidersky and Guijt (this volume) describe how farmers in Brazil monitored on-farm changes that occurred as a result of a soil conservation programme, and how these results are being used to inform future interventions. PM&E may be introduced at any time throughout the project cycle, depending on stakeholder priorities and the resources available to establish the system, though others stress that PM&E should be made an integral part of the entire project cycle (see Estrella and Gaventa, 1998).

While there are a number of PM&E experiences in the area of project management, PM&E is increasingly being applied in newer contexts – including for the purpose of *organizational strengthening and institutional learning*. PM&E becomes a process that enables organizations and institutions, including NGOs, CBOs and POs, to keep track of their progress and build on areas of work where success is recognized. This helps to strengthen organizational capacities of self-reflection and learning, which, in turn, enhances the sustainability and effectiveness of their development efforts. For instance, the case study in Palestine illustrates how participatory evaluation served as a basis for strategic planning and programme development within a local NGO working with agricultural communities (see Chapter 10; see also Chapters 3, 11 and 13).

Institutional learning, in turn, helps strengthen institutional accountability. In this context, PM&E is regarded less as a means of reporting and auditing, and more as a means for demanding greater social responsiveness and ethical responsibility. Rather than being used solely by funding and government agencies as a way of holding beneficiaries and other project participants accountable, PM&E enables local stakeholders to measure the performance of these institutions and to hold them responsible for their actions and interventions. It is envisioned that if people are able to better articulate and advocate their needs and expectations, this will help ensure that their service delivery demands will be met. For instance, in several case studies, POs/NGOs and community residents are now working together with their elected leaders in formulating local development plans and assessing whether these achieve community development objectives (see Chapters 7, 8 and 9). But, also, NGOs/POs can develop their own accountability practice through PM&E approaches, by involving different groups of stakeholders (see Chapters 10, 11 and 13). In effect, PM&E can help build multiple accountability linkages across different institutional levels and stakeholder groups.

Another recent area of work in PM&E emphasises its potential role in helping to *inform policy*. For instance, in Colombia indigenous communities select their own development indicators (see Chapter 7). As a result, indigenous communities are better able to communicate local needs and compare these against the development priorities of local government offi-cials. In Mongolia, there are efforts to involve beneficiary groups in eval-uating a national poverty alleviation programme (see Chapter 12). Elsewhere, an evaluation of a national health programme in India, spon-sored by USAID and the national government, included beneficiary organ-izations in determining whether key objectives of the programme were achieved (Acharya *et al.*, 1997).

As the case studies show, PM&E is applied in a wide variety of contexts and combines these purposes to fulfil varying stakeholder objectives. Mea-suring change can take place beyond the project context, within institutions or organizations, for differing purposes. These multiple functions of PM&E are interdependent and often overlap. Determining the core purposes of the proposed PM&E system will essentially depend on different stakeholder interests and may well change over time.

Recognizing and negotiating different stakeholder interests

In order to identify what is to be monitored and evaluated and for what purpose(s), PM&E uses a process that tries to offer fora that allow different stakeholders to articulate their needs and make collaborative decisions. PM&E enables people to understand 'the views and values they share, work through their differences with others, develop longer-term strategies, and take carefully researched and planned actions which fit their contexts, pri-orities, and styles of operating' (Parachini and Mott, 1997). PM&E requires learning about people's concerns, and how different stakeholders look at (and, hence, measure) project results, outcomes, and impacts. How these differing (and often competing) stakeholder claims and perspectives are negotiated and resolved, especially when particular groups and/or individ-uals are powerless *vis-à-vis* others, remains a critical question in building a PM&E process (see Chapter 17).

Translating PM&E into practice

There are a number of questions raised in undertaking PM&E:

○ What are the key steps or stages in a PM&E process?
○ Who should be involved, and how?
○ How often should PM&E take place?
○ What tools and techniques should be used?

Although there is wide variation in the actual practice of PM&E, some common guidelines are emerging that help define how PM&E is established and implemented.

Establishing a PM&E process: steps, stages, and cycles

There are at least four major steps or stages in establishing a PM&E process:

○ planning the framework for the PM&E process, and determining objec-tives and indicators

○ gathering data
○ analysing and using data by taking action
○ documenting, reporting and sharing information.

The planning stage is considered by many to be the most critical to the success of establishing a PM&E process. This is when different stakeholder groups first come together to articulate their concerns and to negotiate differing interests. Stakeholders will need to determine their objectives for monitoring, and identify what information should be monitored, for whom, and who should be involved. In Brazil, knowing who will use the information was a critical step in determining what should be monitored and how results and findings would be applied (see Chapter 5). Often, however, stakeholders are left out of this initial planning process.

Once stakeholders agree on objectives, indicators for monitoring will need to be selected. In many cases, different stakeholder groups usually agree on a set of common indicators, while in other cases multiple sets of indicators are identified to address the different information needs of different stakeholder groups (see Chapter 3; see also MacGillivray et al., 1998). While there are no set rules to select indicators, one guideline is to use the acronym 'SMART': indicators should be specific, measurable, action-oriented, relevant, and time-bound. Another contrasting acronym recently offered is 'SPICED': subjective, participatory, interpreted, communicable, empowering and disaggregated (Roche, forthcoming). The acronym SPICED reflects a shift towards placing greater emphasis on developing indicators that stakeholders can define and use directly for their own purposes of interpreting and learning about change.

The next step is data gathering. A wide range of participatory methods are used for monitoring and evaluating information.[4] The case studies in this book provide further examples of innovative techniques for PM&E (see Table 15.1). Many of these methods have been drawn from participatory learning methodologies, such as PRA, which comprise a range of audio-visual, interviewing and groupwork methods. They can also include quantitative methods, such as community surveys and ecological assessments, which are made more participatory and accessible to local people (see Chapters 4 and 7; see also Abbot and Guijt, 1998; Rugh, 1992). Others have adapted methods used in the field of anthropology, including oral testimonies and direct observation (see Chapter 3; see also Feuerstein, 1986).

Once information has been collected, the next step entails processing and analysing data, although ideally data analysis should take place throughout the data gathering stage (Gosling and Edwards, 1995). The idea is to involve the relevant stakeholders in reflecting critically on problems and successes, understanding the impacts of their efforts, and acting on what they have learned. What becomes critical is how stakeholders actually use information in making decisions and identifying future action.

The final stage involves documenting and reporting information. This step serves as an important means of disseminating findings and learning from others' experiences (see Chapters 2 and 6). One important issue at this stage concerns ownership and use of information. Traditionally, information has often been removed from its original source and taken

9

elsewhere, usually to meet information requirements of funding agencies, government agencies and other outside institutions. This prevents local stakeholders from retaining ownership of the information and building their own knowledge base.

Figure 1.1 illustrates how participants at the Philippines Workshop described one possible sequence of steps in conducting a PM&E process, but there are other examples that portray how PM&E can be undertaken (see Chapters 9 and 15; see also Woodhill and Robins, 1998). These steps form part of what many describe as the 'PM&E learning cycle'. An essential feature of this cycle is the continuous process of reflection by stakeholders on what is being monitored and evaluated, where the process is leading them, and the lessons gained from their own successes and mistakes (Pfohl, 1986). In practice, there are no hard and fixed rules or steps on how 'to do' PM&E, because local circumstances or stakeholder needs change and thus alter how the PM&E process will proceed. At the Philippines Workshop, participants observed that the PM&E cycle is actually part of a series of loops, recognizing that the process is continually evolving and adapting to local contexts and information needs (see Chapter 10). Participants from the workshop further agreed that although the PM&E process may be cyclical, it does not necessarily start from the same beginning but rather builds on previous experience and moves forward as stakeholders learn what and how to evaluate (see Chapter 5).

Emerging issues

The literature and case studies reviewed contribute towards a more coherent body of knowledge about PM&E but also raise several issues about its practice regarding the need to:

○ clarify concepts of 'participation'
○ identify appropriate methodologies
○ develop and build on capacity for PM&E
○ scale-up PM&E and promote institutional learning.

Clarifying concepts of 'participation'

What most distinguishes PM&E from other more conventional approaches is its emphasis on the inclusion of a wider sphere of stakeholders in the M&E process. PM&E practitioners believe that the stakeholders who are involved in development planning and implementation should also be involved in monitoring changes and determining the indicators for 'success'. However, there still remains great ambiguity in defining who stakeholders are, who should be involved, and to what extent or depth they can or want to be involved (Whitmore, 1998). For instance, the M&E process may include beneficiaries as stakeholders, but still, in practice, pay little attention to marginalized groups, i.e. women, the poor, and non-literate.

Participants at the Philippines Workshop suggested establishing a common set of principles for PM&E, but what these core values will encompass, how these will be determined, and by whom, remains open to

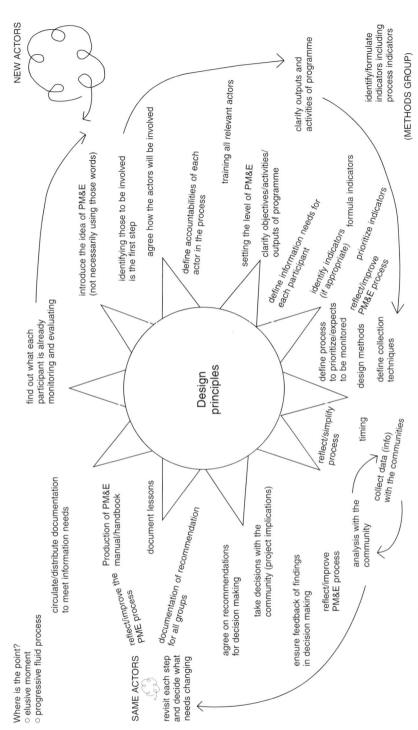

NEW ACTORS

introduce the idea of PM&E
(not necessarily using those words)

identifying those to be involved
is the first step

agree how the actors will be involved

training all relevant actors

clarify outputs and
activities of programme

define accountabilities of each
actor in the process

setting the level of PM&E

identify/formulate
indicators including
process indicators

clarify objectives/activities/
outputs of programme

(METHODS GROUP)

define information needs for
each participant

find out what each
participant is already
monitoring and evaluating

identify indicators   formula indicators
(if appropriate)

prioritize indicators

reflect/improve
PM&E process

circulate/distribute documentation
to meet information needs

Design
principles

define process
to prioritize/expects
to be monitored

design methods

define collection
techniques

Where is the point?
○ elusive moment
○ progressive fluid process

Production of PM&E
manual/handbook

document lessons

reflect/simplify
process

timing

reflect/improve the
PME process

documentation of recommendation
for all groups

collect data (info)
with the communities

SAME ACTORS

analysis with the
community

revisit each step
and decide what
needs changing

agree on recommendations
for decision making

take decisions with the
community (project implications)

reflect/improve
PM&E process

ensure feedback of findings
in decision making

Figure 1.1: *Sequence of steps in developing PM&E, as illustrated during the Philippines Workshop*

11

question. Part of the problem stems not only from the difficulty in identifying who participates, but also in determining *what roles different stakeholders can and should play at which stages of the process.* While the tendency is to emphasize the involvement of all stakeholders in all aspects of PM&E, this may not be realistic or desirable (see Chapter 14).

Identifying appropriate methodologies[5]

Translating PM&E into practice not only challenges concepts of 'participation' but also raises a number of methodological issues. These include issues associated with developing indicators, establishing new standards of 'rigour', combining different approaches and methods, and maintaining flexibility throughout the process (see Chapter 15).

While a great deal of documented literature on PM&E focuses on identifying indicators, the procedures for indicator development are not always clear or straightforward, especially when different stakeholders with different priorities and needs are involved. As PM&E is increasingly applied in different contexts, there is a need to develop new types of indicators to monitor important aspects of development that are not traditionally assessed – namely 'participation', 'empowerment', 'transparency' and 'accountability'.

Another issue pertains to establishing 'rigour'. It is often assumed that more conventional approaches are more quantitative and therefore achieve a certain degree of 'rigour', 'objectivity', and 'replicability'. By contrast, participatory approaches are said to obtain more qualitative information that is locally meaningful, readily useful and context-specific, but is said to be more 'subjective'. The question remains whether there are, indeed, inherent trade-offs in choosing more participatory approaches, specifically with regard to establishing 'rigour' (see Chapters 2, 4 and 5).

There has also been a great deal of emphasis on adopting a flexible approach to PM&E. However, this raises the question of whether maintaining flexibility in PM&E can provide information that compares changes on a continuous basis over time and that is applicable for making generalizations, especially when tracking processes on a larger scale and area of coverage. Further discussion is needed to explore the balance between ensuring flexibility and providing uniform information to allow for comparability and generalizability.

Developing and building on capacity for PM&E

Although many acknowledge that PM&E requires considerable time and financial investment, few experiences actually document the amount of resources needed to build and sustain a PM&E process over time. These resource requirements include financial resources, as well as human resources in terms of commitment, effort and capacities to carry out PM&E.

There is a further need to identify the types of skills and capacities necessary for conducting and sustaining PM&E. Key questions asked by participants during the Philippines Workshop with regards to capacity building included:

○ What type of capacity building is needed, for whom, and at what level (personal/individual, organizational/institutional, etc.)?
○ What types of skills, knowledge, changes in behaviour and attitudes are required in conducting PM&E?
○ To date, there is little documentation available on the best capacity building approaches for PM&E, which can include formal trainings and hands-on experiential learning (see Chapter 16).[6]

Scaling-up PM&E and promoting institutional learning[7]

As PM&E involves a wider range of participants, the stakeholders represented cut across different institutional levels and contexts. However, a key question is whether PM&E can be built into the standard operating procedures of formal institutions (Armonia and Campilan, 1997). Institutionalizing PM&E necessarily calls for changes in organizational cultures and procedures, but explicitly challenges higher-level institutions or organizations (i.e. funding and government agencies) to become more receptive to sharing decision-making power over limited resources (see Chapter 17).

There are two aspects with regard to scaling-up PM&E:

○ the scaling-up of micro-level information, e.g. information generated at the community or project/programme level
○ increasing the area of coverage by PM&E.

As PM&E is increasingly used to monitor and evaluate policy, this raises questions regarding how micro-level data generated from PM&E can be used to inform national and macro-level strategies and policies. Another scaling-up issue pertains to the area of coverage. Few experiences demonstrate how PM&E can be applied in large-scale development efforts, which cover a wide area and involve several institutional levels and a large number of participants. What type of PM&E approach, or combination of approaches, will be required to address the increasing complexity in scaling-up PM&E efforts?

Whether or not participatory M&E is successfully established will certainly depend on a number of factors, including the willingness and commitment of all stakeholders, the availability of time and resources, and a conducive external (institutional) environment, among others (Campos and Coupal, 1996). However, there is a need to identify the different contexts in which PM&E is applied and whether there are minimum conditions that need to exist before PM&E will be successful. Participants during the Philippines Workshop raised their own questions:

○ Would PM&E be as effective in project or programme contexts that do not initially incorporate a participatory approach in their original design and implementation?
○ Under what conditions can what type of PM&E approach be used?
○ What is the social, political, and institutional context of PM&E practice?
○ How does PM&E practice differ when applied across different political environments, i.e. from centralized to more decentralized systems of government?

○ When do we know that pushing for the practice of PM&E would be a mistake, e.g. by increasing vulnerabilities of already marginalized groups?

Tracking a moving target

This book provides an important contribution to our knowledge and understanding of PM&E practice. The case studies do not offer definitive conclusions but, rather, tentative lessons drawn from in-depth experiences in PM&E. Although we know more about PM&E, much documentation remains to be carried out about these experiences and the people involved in such processes. The value of documenting such experiences lies in the recognition that PM&E actually goes beyond measuring changes and is also concerned with building people's capacities to improve learning and self-reliance regarding their own development.

Part of the difficulty of documentation is that project- or programme-related work in a development context is usually ongoing and constantly evolving. As the development work matures and responds to changing needs and circumstances, so, too, the process of PM&E shifts and adapts. For many practitioners and advocates who write about their experiences, documenting such a fluid PM&E process has proven to be a challenge. In many of the case studies presented here, M&E work is ongoing; therefore, a case study can only capture glimpses of the entire experience, from which lessons are continuously being drawn. This means that by the time this book is published, many of these experiences may have already changed and evolved in their processes and directions!

As PM&E is increasingly applied in different contexts and in hundreds of development initiatives around the world, it gains multiple functions as people learn how to adapt, innovate, and experiment with participatory approaches. Because PM&E is an evolving field, this makes documenting PM&E experiences almost as difficult and problematic as 'tracking a moving target'. We hope this book can move us perhaps one step forward towards better understanding experiences in the field of PM&E – while also challenging us to continue to innovate and improve its practice.

Part 1

Methodological Innovations

2

Exploring Visions: Self-monitoring and evaluation processes within the Nepal–UK Community Forestry Project[1]

CLARE HAMILTON, RAJ KUMAR RAI, RAM BAHADUR
SHRESTHA, MAKSHA MAHARJAN, LEELA RASAILY and
SIBONGILE HOOD

Background

THE NEPAL–UK COMMUNITY FORESTRY PROJECT works with 1500 forest user groups (FUGs) in seven of the hill districts of Nepal. The project aims to increase the effectiveness of FUGs in managing their community forests on an equitable and sustainable basis. It is working together with the Department of Forestry (DoF) in handing over national forests to communities through the formation of the FUGs. However, in the process of transferring forest management to communities, it became evident that providing usufruct rights alone to forest users was insufficient to ensure equitable and sustainable management. Thus, there has been greater focus in providing FUGs with post-formation support,[2] so that they have the necessary skills and knowledge to undertake forest management responsibilities. The project is building capacity within both the District Forestry Offices (DFOs) and other district-level organizations to support FUGs in developing appropriate institutional and forestry management systems. The project strives to develop partnerships with these other organizations,[3] as the DFO has insufficient capacity to meet the increasing demand for FUG formation and post-formation support.

FUGs are the first legally recognized community groups in Nepal. They are given usufruct rights to small parcels of state forest, on condition that they manage the forest sustainably. FUGs must adhere to their operational plans and constitution agreed upon during the handover, unless they formally have these amended by the District Forest Officer. Operational plans mostly entail the management of natural forest and mature plantations. To increase the benefit flows from their forest, income-generating activities are being introduced. These are based on non-timber forest products, including cardamom, ginger, bamboo, resin, fibres and medicinal plants. As the FUGs generate income from their forest, they are encouraged to engage in community development activities, such as improving water supply, sanitation, irrigation or providing credit for users.

The project team (composed of the UK Department for International Development (DFID) and the DFO staff) are encouraging the FUGs to develop an internal learning cycle based on a continuous process of planning–action–reflection, that would enable FUGs to assess and improve their own performance. Self-monitoring and evaluation (SM&E) has been considered an effective tool to support the institutionalization of the internal learning cycle. Establishing this learning process assists in better targeting of post-formation support, as FUGs gain the capacity to analyse their own needs and then feed it into the bottom-up planning[4] process already in place in the project area. In the long term, this learning process will reduce the FUGs' reliance on external institutions. There is increased understanding amongst DFO staff that enabling FUGs to conduct monitoring and evaluation themselves would not only promote community self-reliance but also help make the monitoring and evaluation (M&E) process more locally relevant and effective. Amongst other partners (i.e. district-level organizations) still unfamiliar with community forest management, the SM&E process develops understanding of what their role could be in supporting FUGs.

One of the factors that may hinder FUGs' ability to promote change,[5] both in terms of institutional development and forest management, is the absence of a common vision between forest users in the FUGs. The FUGs tend to be dominated by the more literate and resource-rich élites who comprise the influential minority in the communities. They are asked to sit on user group committees, to communicate with outsiders and to attend DFO trainings. Because they have greater access to information, this minority group makes the key decisions within FUGs. The disadvantaged forest users, who are generally poor and non-literate farmers, have become marginalized as the FUGs fail to provide for their needs in favour of the interests of local élites. In order for these less advantaged users to participate more actively in decision making within the FUG, it is necessary to provide a forum that allows *all* forest users to express their views and needs, and to negotiate a set of common objectives or goals for their institution.

In order to make information more accessible to disadvantaged forest users, the creation and use of visual materials are stressed, facilitating communication within FUGs. In the context of SM&E, developing visual-based indicators[6] is seen as one way of encouraging greater discussion amongst all forest users, including less literate groups. The creation of pictures by the user group is a levelling exercise in which all the participants draw the pictures and so develop equal ownership of the process. The pictures are effective for clarifying underlying issues, as forest users continuously revisit and refine their understanding and interpretations of the visual indicators.

The SM&E process at the FUG level also has to take into consideration the potential friction between achieving 'scientific rigour' and ensuring participation. On the one hand, there is a recognized need for a SM&E process that is sufficiently sensitive to change – demonstrating trends and impacts – in order to inform decision making. On the other hand, three major factors need to be considered in order to sustain local participation within the SM&E process:

o the process should be structured in such a way that ensures participation of the different interest groups[7] within the FUG
o the process must be easy to facilitate (because local facilitators are themselves inexperienced in participatory techniques)
o the process should not be time-consuming (as the DFO staff are overstretched and forest users are mostly poor farmers who, for much of the year, are engaged in agricultural activities).

In this context, the Nepal–UK Community Forestry Project has been experimenting with a number of participatory methods for SM&E. These methods are based primarily on the use of pictures to facilitate better understanding and communication within FUGs, especially amongst less advantaged FUG members. By building up the forest users' and the committees' understanding of the process, SM&E becomes one way of empowering disadvantaged forest users and also exploring and establishing a common vision within FUGs. Four methods are described below:

o the 'FUG Health Check', a participatory monitoring and evaluation (PM&E) tool developed by the project team
o the 'User-generated Pictorial Decision-making SM&E' that builds on a literacy methodology
o the 'SM&E Information Management Tool', a process using participatory learning and action (PLA)[8] techniques to situate the SM&E in a planning cycle, and most recently
o the 'FUG Planning and Self-evaluation System' based on the Health Check with user-generated indicators and pictures.

The FUG Health Check

The FUG Health Check aims to allow Range Post (RP)[9] teams to develop an understanding of the support needs of the FUGs, as well as to enable forest users themselves to better understand the different aspects of their FUG (institutional or group management, forest management, community development, etc.). The Health Check is used at two levels:

o at the government administrative level, whereby RP teams assess the strengths and weaknesses of the FUGs and how they can be strengthened
o at the FUG level to encourage discussion and debate amongst forest users about their existing resources and their institution.

The RP team facilitates these discussions. The Health Check has a pictorial version that has been effective in provoking discussions within different user groups, promoting greater participation of the non- or semi-literate users.

The FUG Health Check method – including the indicators and the pictures or codes representing the indicators – is a tool developed by the project and DFO staff. Although in the long run the project team hopes to encourage more FUG input in developing the tool, at present the Health Check is primarily an RP tool. The RP team uses the Health Check as a format to

evaluate the FUGs – often with minimal consultation with the users themselves. One key obstacle to securing FUG input is the limited facilitation
capacity (that is, time and skill) of the RP team. Four broad categories of
indicators are covered by the Health Check:

o the forest resource management
o social and institutional development
o awareness and flow of information
o skill development and learning processes (see Box 2.1).

Box 2.1: Four themes of the FUG Health Check

o **Forest resource management**
The effect of the FUG's management plan on forest condition is
assessed using the following indicators: canopy density, regeneration, and tree age. The RP team, together to some extent with the
FUG, look at the forest protection system, whether there is active
management and whether forest products are made available to the
users.

o **Social and institutional development**
The group's strengths and weaknesses in terms of community development activities, fund mobilization, participation in decision
making, gender and equity issues, conflict management, networking and independence are all assessed.

o **Awareness and flow of information**
There remains much room for improving the flow of information and
communication within FUGs, and the Health Check aims to identify
how communication fora can be improved. The indicators considered include the FUG's awareness of forest rules and regulations, how the members share knowledge and experience and their
understanding of 'what their Forest User Group is' or the 'Community Forestry Process'.

o **Skill development and learning processes**
This last category highlights the need for the FUG to be continually
developing their skill base. The indicators examined include
whether the FUG has developed new forest management skills,
income-generating activities, or group management practices.

For each of these categories, different aspects of community forestry are
represented and discussed, and then assessed on a three-point scale – namely
poor, fair or good – which are depicted in the visual format by sad, content
and happy faces (see Figure 2.1).

Several areas need special attention in using the Health Check method.
First, the indicators used in the process cover relatively broad issues related
to community forestry and therefore may not accurately reflect the FUGs'
reality or be sensitive to changes occurring within the FUG.[10] Second,

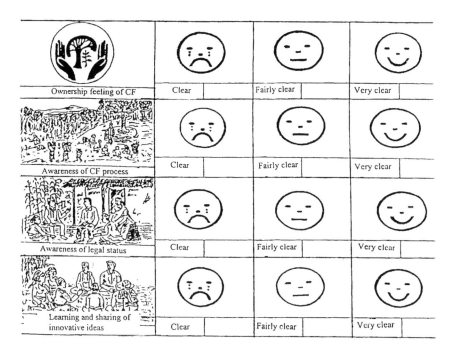

Ownership feeling of CF	Clear		Fairly clear		Very clear
Awareness of CF process	Clear		Fairly clear		Very clear
Awareness of legal status	Clear		Fairly clear		Very clear
Learning and sharing of innovative ideas	Clear		Fairly clear		Very clear

Figure 2.1: *The pictorial Health Check*

skilful facilitation is essential to prevent the process from becoming mechanical and dominated by the vocal minority within the FUG. Even when the tool is best used, with the whole FUG together (and otherwise with perhaps a few representatives), it is difficult to elicit the perspectives of different interest groups within the FUG and provide space for them to negotiate their needs. Third, because an external team developed the indicators and pictorial formats used in this process, discussions with the FUG need to ensure that forest users *themselves* decode and interpret visual indicators, so that they develop a common understanding of the conceptual issues the pictures represent. Finally, the FUG needs strong encouragement to adapt the indicators and pictures to suit their own information needs.

While with good facilitation the Health Check can encourage reflection within the FUG, no common vision amongst forest users is developed at present, thus reducing the strength of the learning tool in provoking institutional change within the FUG. It appears that the Health Check process is contributing more towards strengthening RP planning and therefore leading to stronger capacity building at this level rather than at the FUG level. Thus, unlike the other approaches outlined below, we consider this approach to be a PM&E tool. As the DFO staff and other partners develop better facilitation skills, the FUG Health Check may eventually be applied more as an SM&E tool by the FUGs themselves.

Over the past two years, the Health Check has been used by the District Offices for their annual review, when the best FUGs are identified for the annual district competition. The FUG assessment helps RP teams gain a greater understanding of the issues at the FUG level and what types of support they require (see Box 2.2).

The user-generated pictorial decision making in SM&E

Another SM&E method was developed to increase women's participation by encouraging them to assess their involvement in forest and group activities. This method was tried in two FUGs where women had been attending a literacy class that used REFLECT techniques.[11] By the end of the literacy class, the women had become skilled in developing pictorial materials. They created a visual SM&E format to assess their involvement in household and community-level activities such as 'Who makes the major decisions in buying and selling livestock?' Similarly, in forest-related activities, women use the visual formats to assess: 'Who makes decisions about harvesting different forest products?' and 'Who does the actual work?' (see Figure 2.2). From this assessment, they became aware as a group of how they are excluded from making decisions that have direct impacts on their livelihood.

Although this method is limited to analysing decision making, women acquire ownership over the process of analysis because they have developed the indicators and pictorial formats themselves. Their sense of ownership over the process has meant that the tool is effective in empowering them to strengthen their role in decision making. While the method focuses on who is excluded and who included in decision making, it may not reflect how the decisions are actually made, i.e. whether the decision making is consensual or one group continues to dominate. In addition, the tool does not involve other interest groups within the FUG. Therefore, although women have taken a more active role in decision

Community Forestry Harvesting				
	Household head	Male	Male/Female	Female
Collection of Grass				
Collection of Fuelwood				
Collection of Poles				

Figure 2.2: *The user-generated pictorial tool for decision making in SM&E*

making within the FUGs to promote their interests, the tool does not currently support other resource-poor groups in advocating for their needs to be addressed.

Of course, it is not easy to separate the impact of developing the monitoring tool from that of the literacy classes with regard to improving women's role in decision making. However, in the process, women have become considerably more vocal in FUGs (see Box 2.3). They have also established a group to give them greater autonomy over their income generation and savings activities. Women are now considering how to adapt and expand the tool beyond decision-making analysis, but they have not yet repeated the process to reassess changes in their role in decision making within the FUG and in the household. Because the process has been developed and used primarily by REFLECT animators[12] and their women's groups, the sharing of this approach with other FUGs has been limited.

SM&E in information management

The project team has realized that to promote institutional change within FUGs, monitoring and evaluation has to be more firmly grounded in the

Box 2.3: How women challenged the FUG Chairman

In discussing the FUG's fund, the women of Ochre FUG realized that they did not know how much money there was, how it was generated nor how it was being used. They decided to call the FUG Chairman and have him explain the funding procedures of the FUG. However, one woman consulted with her husband and learned that there was a discrepancy between what her husband knew and what the Chairman had told the women about the amount of money in the fund. The women later brought it up as an issue in the next assembly during which the Chairman was forced to account for the missing funds. The Chairman stated that there were no receipts but argued that the missing money had been spent on community development. Since then the Chairman has refused to attend assemblies. While the issue of missing funds remains unresolved, women were able to point out the need for a more transparent accounting system within the FUG.

internal learning cycle that links reflection and analysis of the FUGs' present situation, to goals formation, and to action planning and implementation. Therefore, a workshop for a FUG was held using PLA tools to provide a venue for analysing the current situation of the FUG and for developing goals and action plans. The workshop focused on improving communication within the FUG, and forest users' understanding of their legal agreement with the forestry office (namely, their forest operation plan and their constitution). The situation analysis, goal formation and action planning formed the foundation of a SM&E exercise, where trends can be identified over time through changes in the maps and diagrams produced (such as assessing increases in forest products with changing management or greater linkages with line agencies and non-governmental organizations (NGOs) as the FUGs start to demand services).

The process involved a number of other organizations with an interest in developing capacity for SM&E. They included a local FUG network and an NGO, who helped facilitate the workshop along with RP staff.

The workshop worked though the following steps:

○ creating two resource and social maps, one depicting the current situation and one a future 'ideal' to form the goals of the FUG
○ identifying activities that need to be undertaken in order to reach the ideal vision of the FUG and prioritizing these proposed activities through pairwise ranking
○ institutional analysis through comparative analysis of their management and communication practices (their constitution) and through Venn diagrams to identify current and ideal links and support from other organizations
○ developing a pictorial seasonal calendar to visualize their forest operational plan, showing the management practices needed to reach the ideal and the periods when harvesting could be allowed (see Figure 2.3). Pictures of each proposed activity were then placed on their resource

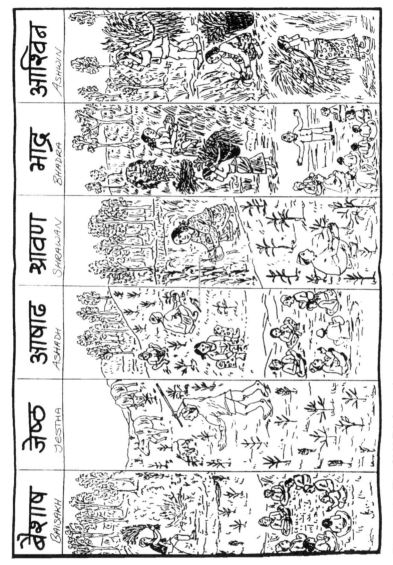

Figure 2.3: *The SM&E information management tool*

map in the appropriate forest block, reinforcing the concept that management differs with forest condition and with the provision of different products.

The workshop was effective in improving communication and management within the FUG, allowing the needs of the resource-poor to be articulated and addressed (see Box 2.4). It also enabled external organizations to identify how best they can support the FUG. However, the relatively inexperienced facilitators (the FUG network, NGO and RP staff) felt that the workshop was complicated, as many tools were used. Furthermore, the disadvantaged user groups within the FUG found the number of exercises confusing and time-consuming (the workshop lasted for three morning sessions). Whether the workshop has strengthened users' capacities to conduct future SM&E and internalize the learning cycle will only be clear in a year or two, when the FUG has had a chance to repeat the process.

Box 2.4:   The poor want grass not timber

During the workshop of the Chapgaire Tushepakha FUG, it was clear that the users felt they derived very little benefit from their community forest. Users pointed out that the committee placed greater emphasis on protecting the forest so that it would produce maximum timber yields. However, during the goal-formation exercise, resource-poor women prioritized their need for grass rather than timber. As a result of the discussions, the FUG agreed to make the production of grass a priority for the coming year and decided to contact the agriculture office about the possibility of planting Napier grass within their community forest.

The FUG Planning and Self-evaluation System

The latest development within the project area builds on the basic format of the pictorial Health Check, whilst incorporating learning from the other processes.[13] The process was developed through joint discussion and planning between the project team and an FUG. To ensure the various perspectives are fully incorporated in developing the evaluation system, the FUG was divided by *toles* (or hamlets, often according to caste or ethnic group), with each *tole* initially developing their own goals and indicators, assessing the FUG's current status, and identifying priority areas. It is considered an evaluation rather than a monitoring system as the FUGs do not consider the detailed progress of activities, but rather evaluate their overall performance against their goals.

The *toles* defined their goals by considering what their 'ideal' FUG would be like in ten years' time. These goals formed the basis for developing indicators. The indicators were then coded as pictures and arranged in a matrix to be scored by users. Scoring is based on a four-point scale, represented by phases of the moon, with each *tole* assessing what stage their FUG was at (see Figure 2.4). The *toles* then identified and prioritized three goals they felt should be addressed first.

	NOT STARTED	STARTED	LITTLE LEFT	FINISHED
"OUR FOREST" – OWNERSHIP FEELING		★ BAHUN GAUN		∿ RANICHHAP O GAIRI GAUN
THERE IS GOOD INTRA-HOUSEHOLD COMMUNICATION		O GAIRI GAUN	∿ RANICHHAP	+ SATHIMURE
THERE IS SUFFICIENT FIREWOOD FOR ALL		[O SOME GAIRI GAUN WOMEN]	∿ RANICHHAP	O GAIRI GAUN △ MAGAR GAUN + SATHIMURE ★ BAHUN GAUN □ DANDA GAUN ≠ CHAUTARA
THERE IS FAIR DISTRIBUTION OF FIREWOOD			△ MAGAR GAUN	★ BAHUN GAUN

Figure 2.4: *The user-generated SM&E tool*

The indicators from the different *toles* were then compiled and categorized by the facilitators, with exact repetitions removed and gaps identified. The categories identified usually were:

o forest management and condition
o forest products
o group management
o communication
o community development activities
o income-generating activities.

The *tole* assessments were then compiled for each category. This was presented to a forum of the FUG committee and to either *tole* representatives or the general assembly (all users), who reviewed the indicators, *tole* assessments and priorities, and agreed on a strategy for addressing the issues raised and for conducting future SM&E (see Box 2.5).

Box 2.5: FUG decentralization

During the final meeting, the Dhungedhara Thulo Pakha FUG decided to elect *tole*-level subcommittees to co-ordinate each *tole* in deciding which goals they would prioritize – such as providing wood for those far from the forests, or toilets for those without – as well as how they would carry out the SM&E exercise in the future with committee support. By decentralizing to *tole* level, greater collaborative participation of the different *toles* is ensured. For instance, decentralizing responsibility helped involve the new *tole* subcommittees when it was time to select trees for harvesting from the forest. The *toles* identified how much firewood each household needed, sent volunteers to help in tree selection for harvesting, and took responsibility for distributing the firewood. This was considered a significant improvement from users simply waiting for the FUG committee to act and provide services. Many women commented that they were now more aware of their responsibilities in forest management and of the benefits derived from working in *tole* subcommittees.

One of the major benefits of this process was the high level of ownership gained through planning with the FUG and developing the whole SM&E system in small groups (see Box 2.6). Using pictorial indicators promoted greater discussion and therefore better understanding amongst both literate and non-literate members. By contrasting the *tole* assessments, the

Box 2.6: Ownership means change

FUGs gain ownership over this decentralised SM&E approach because they are able to develop and adapt it based on changing circumstances and their own specific needs. For example, during the Dhungedhara Thulo Pakha exercise, users decided to change their indicator scoring matrix by replacing the happy, content and sad faces to four stages of the moon. Users felt that this change made their scoring system less judgmental and more accurate: i.e. the moon's absence better indicated that users have not started to address an issue, rather than implying users were unhappy because a sad face was used for scoring. Using a four-point scale also prevented an easy middle compromise, encouraging more discussion.

In the Ochre FUG, the committee decided that in one *tole*, the men and women should be separated, so they could see whether women more freely expressed their views when alone. During the FUG goal-formation, it became clear that the women – more than any other interest group – prioritized increasing forest product availability from the forest and near their homes.

perspectives of different interest groups within the FUG became apparent. In one pilot, the FUG decided to address this issue of differing perspectives by establishing *tole* sub-committees to address the different priorities of forest users. Careful facilitation is needed in order to negotiate the differing interests of the various users within FUGs (see Box 2.7).

Box 2.7: Creating space for negotiating interests

In developing indicators, there was a need to negotiate amongst different interests of forest users in the Dhungedhara FUG. One indicator, namely that 'there should be enough fuelwood for all', was challenged by a woman who proposed that a better indicator would be 'there should be fuelwood near the house'. However, the latter indicator would only primarily show benefits gained by women and by women living at a distance from the forest. It was eventually agreed that there should be an indicator for availability of forest products near the houses, as well as ones for specific products from the forest.

Second, in assessing the indicators, 'fair distribution of timber' was considered to have been achieved by a vocal group of participants, until this was disputed by several individuals who asserted that some users got larger trees than others. Through group discussion, users finally agreed that the indicator should be placed at the 'new moon phase' (i.e. at the initial stage). Users decided that until households were more involved in selecting their own trees, the FUG committee would be open to criticism despite their efforts to be fair.

These experiences show that the process of negotiating different interests often takes place between the powerful and more vocal interest groups, who usually dominate decision making, and the disadvantaged interest groups. As disadvantaged users are given opportunities to articulate their views and needs through discussion, they are often supported by others with converging interests. The negotiation process involves promoting one's interests and having an influence in decision making.

The indicators selected by *toles* reflect the level of understanding of the FUG regarding different aspects of their institution (i.e. forest management, decision making, good leadership, etc.). In areas of weak understanding – for example, in institutional analysis and timber yield regulation – the indicators suggested are also weak, in that the indicators remain broad and less specific, thus making them more difficult to evaluate. Outside facilitators themselves need to have a strong understanding of institutional and forest management issues to guide the FUG in the development of sufficiently detailed indicators. The assessment process, which uses the four phases of the moon as a scoring criteria, is not likely to be very sensitive to changes from one year to the next, and may not provide sufficient information to inform decisions in forest management.

Quantification of some of the indicators could be introduced later to make indicators more sensitive to tracking changes and to guide decision making within the FUG. This may take the form of a self-monitoring process.

Due to the simplicity of the process, it takes little time for facilitators and user groups to gain confidence in using the method and to build capacity in continuing this internal learning system. FUG members acquired ownership over the process and hence felt a greater sense of responsibility in using findings from the evaluation for future planning and action. However, a considerable amount of RP staff time is involved in developing the system in a large FUG; with fewer *toles* this is quicker, but still requires investment of limited RP human resources. This has implications for how the process can be shared or 'scaled up'. Capacity to facilitate can be built during one self-evaluation event in a number of institutions other than the RP, including the FUG itself; each can then support the development of the process in FUGs elsewhere.

Emerging issues

SM&E based in an internal learning cycle

It is clear that developing the SM&E process is an important strategy for building learning-oriented FUGs and thus more sustainable institutions. Based on the experiences described above, the users develop a stronger sense of ownership when they are involved in creating and adapting their own SM&E system. This, in turn, strengthens the foundation for an internal learning cycle within FUGs and hence builds their capacity to better manage community forests in an equitable and effective manner. The process raises users' awareness about the potentials of their FUG institution and encourages their greater involvement, so they then exercise stronger influence in decision making. However, FUGs need to have a clear understanding of what the SM&E process aims to achieve from the beginning and to have a common vision by which to assess their institution. Finally, the information produced should contribute directly into future planning and activities of the FUG.

Balancing participation, facilitation and 'scientific rigour'

Because of the inadequate resources of the DFO and the relative inexperience of other organizations at the field level, the SM&E process will only be widely spread if it is easy to undertake, i.e. if it is possible to develop confidence in facilitating the exercise in a day or two. Likewise, due to the above limitations, there must be mechanisms built in to ensure participation and to highlight the distinct perspectives of the various interest groups – as the skill of the facilitator can not always be relied on. These factors favour a simple process that does not go into too much detail.

However, if the SM&E exercise is to develop understanding and analysis of changes, it must be sensitive to them. To develop FUGs' ability to manage their groups equitably and their forest productively and sustainably, they need to have sufficient data in order to make informed decisions (i.e. knowing how to adjust their practices better). None of the processes developed above have included quantification of the indicators. To introduce this may require the FUGs and the supporting institutions first to become comfortable with the tools as they stand. The data needed to quantify the indicators and develop statistical analysis for studying changes and trends is, however, largely available, since the FUGs are legally required to keep an extensive set of records. The quantification need not demand a high level of numeracy. Appropriate methodologies could be introduced such as using the 'thumb rules' developed by the project to define forest off-take rather than growth models. However, even the most basic quantification – i.e. the number of months a household's allocated fuelwood lasts – would need careful facilitation to allow the full participation of non-literate user groups in the analysis.

The level of data analysis should, however, be appropriate to the different stakeholders' information needs. Where there is a significant difference in data requirements between the FUG and other stakeholders, the other stakeholders may have to conduct their own sampling and data collection (see below in the section 'Systems development').

Using visual materials

Based on the experiences described above, it is clear that using visual materials encourages both literate and non-literate users to explore and clarify concepts. The users' ability to express themselves is heightened when the idea is also visually presented. Developing these materials with the users gives them confidence to adapt them as necessary. It has yet to be seen how far this will spill over into other areas of communication within FUGs who have used these pictorial formats; however, a few FUGs are now using the visual indicators to explain concepts in their own trainings and assemblies.

Negotiating between interest groups

The extent to which disadvantaged user groups are empowered through this process depends on the quality of their participation within the FUG. They need space in which to negotiate the inclusion of their interests in the FUG. This negotiation of interests occurs at two stages within the M&E process:

(1) in developing the indicators
(2) in evaluating their FUG against these indicators.

In the process of applying SM&E, forest users have gained confidence in pressing for indicators that represent their interests and perspectives (see Box 2.7). By presenting their interests in formalized discussions, any conflicts are deliberated and often resolved. The FUG Planning and Self-evaluation System is a more effective tool than the other SM&E methods in providing a forum for negotiating interests because decentralization to *tole* level ensures that different perspectives are sought and included. However, the process of negotiations has occurred in all four SM&E methods discussed above, as forest users together discuss and prioritize their needs and common objectives.

Sharing

The project has made a considerable investment in developing these approaches of SM&E. It has played a key role in creating an environment where experimentation could take place. To ensure that the processes move beyond project-supported pilots, sharing experiences of the SM&E process needs to be encouraged and built into the learning cycle from the very start. Inviting other partners to be involved in the development of the SM&E process promotes ownership and strengthens capacities, which allow these partners to support future development of SM&E within FUGs elsewhere. However, there are not always active NGOs or community-based organizations (CBOs) in the area to form partnerships with. But FUGs themselves, having developed their own facilitation capacity, have shared the approach with neighbouring FUGs in networking meetings. In one case, a FUG now offers to facilitate the FUG planning and self-evaluation process for a small fee, which compensates them for their time.

System development

Most of the processes described above focus on building an internal learning process at the FUG level, although the FUG Health Check has been used at both the RP–DFO and project management level (see Box 2.2). Integrating different levels of the SM&E process would open up channels for communication between these actors and help establish learning feedback mechanisms from one level to another. However, there are a number of challenges to institutionalizing such an innovative approach to M&E.

For instance, stakeholders at the project and DFO levels (including the DoF and the UK's DFID) remain interested in performance-related M&E activities that are externally defined, as opposed to a learning-oriented M&E process that would allow user groups to gain ownership of M&E activities.[14] Promoting SM&E processes will entail higher level institutions – in this case, the DFO, RP and project team – to give away control to forest users in deciding how best to monitor and evaluate sustainable forest management. However, if higher level stakeholders are unable to accept the level of rigour considered appropriate by the FUG, then they may have to collect data themselves which will likely duplicate and run parallel to the M&E process of FUGs. Thus, institutionalizing an integrated PM&E process may require a few years of piloting to gain sufficient credibility and recognition among stakeholders at higher institutional levels.

A combination of the Health Check and the FUG Planning and Self-evaluation methods could be used to establish a more integrated PM&E system involving different institutional levels (the FUG, the RP–DFO, the DoF centre and the project, among others). However, there would need to be some degree of standardization of the indicators and the methods used for assessing them, to allow comparability at the district and project levels. This could be achieved by agreeing on a minimum set of indicators, which would cover the information needs of DFO and project-level staff for evaluating the impact of their services. Establishing this minimum set of indicators will require setting an appropriate level of 'scientific rigour' in order to gain official recognition. This will entail assessing, in quantifiable terms, trends in forest conditions and management, as well as the impacts on local livelihoods. However, to sustain local participation, the process should still enable FUGs to adapt SM&E methods to suit their needs and interests, as long as FUGs assess themselves in a consistent manner (i.e. monitor the agreed minimum set of indicators). The potential pitfall of a much more integrated PM&E system is that the process might become mechanical and extractive, and be seen as a 'blueprint' rather than as part of an adaptive and dynamic learning cycle internalized by its users.

SM&E has been found to be most effective when the institutional members (e.g. the users of the FUGs) share a common vision and are not preoccupied with maintaining power structures that allow an influential minority to have a stronger voice. As has been described above, creating a common vision is incorporated in the latter approaches (the SM&E Information Management and FUG Planning and Self-Evaluation System). While there may be no obstacles to establishing common goals within the DFO and the project, hierarchical relations within Nepali institutions may prove inimical to the SM&E process by maintaining power structures and thus discouraging others from openly expressing their views to superiors. Within the FUG, the presence of an external facilitator can mitigate against the influence of FUG political hierarchies. As we begin applying similar methods in the supporting institutions, these power relations become more difficult to negotiate.

Sustainability of SM&E

Finally, it may still be too early to assess fully the impact and sustainability of the SM&E processes. Only over time can it be observed whether FUGs are continuing to use and develop their SM&E process, whether they are able to use their analysis to plan effectively to reach their vision and whether they continue to ensure the participation of disadvantaged users. However, our experiences so far show that FUGs are clearly 'learning how to learn' which has had a positive impact in terms of empowering them to initiate changes. Furthermore, from these processes external organizations and institutions have a greater understanding of the capacity and needs of FUGs, and therefore are better able to provide and target their support.

3

Seeking Local Indicators: Participatory Stakeholder Evaluation of Farmer-to-Farmer Projects, Mexico[1]

JUTTA BLAUERT, with EDUARDO QUINTANAR[2]

'This is how it is in all the communities when one arrives: people listen, see the slides, and so they feel motivated. But then in practice, in the field, it is not so easy . . .'

(Mixtec farmer-extensionist)

THE ABOVE CONCERN about his work was expressed by a Mixtec subsistence farmer who is also employed as an agricultural extensionist in Oaxaca, Mexico. His words speak about the potential success but also the daily limitations of farmer-to-farmer extension work. While such farmer-led initiatives are promoted as alternatives to the destructive practices of the Green Revolution approach, little is publicly discussed of the daily and personal issues experienced by those directly advocating sustainable agriculture. Currently, sustainable agriculture and soil conservation projects (particularly farmer-to-farmer extension approaches) still face many questions about their impact and social dynamics – in spite of their recognized success and obvious need. The work reported on here addresses some of these problematic issues with regard to participation and team dynamics in such a context.

Participatory evaluations of farmer-led projects: issues and opportunities

Innovative, joint-stakeholder evaluation processes to measure impacts and to ensure social accountability and economic–environmental relevance of farmer-to-farmer extension work are gaining importance. Several trends in development and agriculture research make it possible to focus greater attention on adapting participatory evaluation methodologies for assessing such farmer-led initiatives:

○ Analysts are acknowledging the limitations of 'blueprint' tendencies of project monitoring and evaluation (M&E) frameworks (e.g. logframes and externally determined indicators).
○ Much evaluation work in agriculture still focuses largely on quantitative indicators and provides little insight into qualitative changes in social relations between project staff and between different stakeholders (see Avina et al., 1990; Gubbels, 1994; Hiemstra et al., 1992; Okali et al., 1994; Uquillas, 1993). Traditional indicators of economic validation and bio-physical impact alone are now recognized as providing inadequate measures of sustainable development (MacGillivray et al., 1998). For

instance, achieving and measuring technical success in extension or soil conservation work have proven insufficient in resolving basic conflicts between different stakeholders.

o Much project-impact analysis still ignores the social forces driving the failure and success of any project. Impact assessment usually does not address social dynamics and learning between, and by, the people who 'make the project happen' (or not happen): the project staff themselves, management, and local participants as well as non-participants.

This chapter addresses at least some of the issues highlighted in developing a participatory stakeholder evaluation approach. Key questions guiding this project are shown in Box 3.1.

Box 3.1: Key questions for learning about farmer-to-farmer projects

o What is the potential and actual participatory and democratic nature of these projects, given their declared objective of offering alternatives for successful livelihood strategies for resource-poor farming communities?

o What can be learned from the successes and mistakes of processes *within* these programmes in terms of contributing to the professional and institutional evolution of participants and staff (whether non-governmental organization (NGO) or community-based organization (CBO))?

o Who measures and appraises changes occurring within these projects, and whether they are impacting (or not) on the sustainability of the project work of the community at large? How would this work be conducted?

o Which indicators for change can be used, and how can they be established and 'translate' such experiences to regional, national and international levels?

o For which actors are results needed, and how do they perceive the organization's work?

o Which methods are appropriate for which stakeholder to design indicators, monitor them and use that information in a systematic way so as to enhance communication of lessons learned?

The experience presented here covers work undertaken over eight months between February 1995 and March 1996 with the Mexican Centre of Alternative Technologies (Centro de Tecnologías Alternativas de México, or CETAMEX), an NGO based in the semi-arid Mixteca highlands in the state of Oaxaca, southern Mexico. The first lessons have subsequently been incorporated into the work of another NGO, Maderas del Pueblo del Sureste (MPS), based in the tropical lowland region of Chimalapas, also located in the state of Oaxaca. Both organizations practise the farmer-to-farmer approach in their agricultural work, and work mostly with indigenous subsistence farming communities.

The project reported here was designed to develop a participatory evaluation methodology that would feed into ongoing work of the NGOs, farmer-extensionists, and village participants. It focused particularly on the joint evaluation of participation and human well-being within a project – both objectives of the farmer-to-farmer approach of agricultural and rural development. Work was undertaken in two separate phases. The first phase was conducted with CETAMEX by working together with farmer-extensionists and villagers to develop a stakeholder-based evaluation methodology. The purpose was jointly to adapt methodologies that would allow the different actors – farming families, communities, farmer-extensionists, NGO funders, outside researchers, etc. – to evaluate (separately and jointly) the socio-political, environmental and economic processes and impacts of CETAMEX's farmer-extension programme. The first phase involved trialling of methods as well as field training of NGO staff and villagers and first exploratory evaluations to help design indicators for future use. Similar work was undertaken also with other stakeholders. During the second phase (from March 1996 onwards), the farmer-extensionists have been applying some participatory appraisal methods with communities and, since 1998 have started to apply participatory indicator design in their social forestry programme in collaboration with a local NGO and a forestry adviser.

This chapter focuses on reporting lessons from the first phase of the work – that of developing the stakeholder evaluation methodology and identifying indicators for participatory impact evaluation.[3] The methodology looks at the work and behaviour of the farmer-extensionists themselves, as much as at the technical aspects of the programme's work. We begin by providing a background on the local organization and the regional context. We then present an overview of the methodology to show how farmers and extensionists used impact-evaluation methods. Indicators identified by external and internal stakeholders of the project are then presented. Finally, we briefly discuss the utility of the different methods and approaches tested, and their relevance with regard to establishing a stakeholder-based evaluation process. The chapter does *not* present an evaluation of the farmer-to-farmer project, or the organization itself; we are reporting on a process of methodology development and capacity building for the purposes of institutional learning only.

CETAMEX and its work

CETAMEX[4] is a Mexican NGO supported by World Neighbors, an international development agency known for its keen support of participatory approaches to extension work and evaluation (see Bunch, 1982; Holt-Giménez, 1995; Johnson, n.d.; Rugh, 1994). CETAMEX in this region of Mexico trains and organizes – and is staffed mostly by – local farmer-extensionists and has been operating in the state of Oaxaca since 1982. At the time of fieldwork, the programme team comprised 14 local, indigenous farmer-extensionists who provide advice on reforestation, nursery, agro-ecological production techniques, and nutrition to groups and individuals in 36 villages; in 1996 they were working directly with some 450 farmers and their communities. Locally-trained farmers, who are both women and men, in turn have trained over time many other farmers from other organizations and villages in Oaxaca, drawing on the same farmer-to-farmer, agroecological techniques.

The extensionists are small-scale farmers and former migrants who have not had formal, technical agricultural or forestry training, but rather have received an 'on-the-job' training from CETAMEX project co-ordinators and advisers. Farmer-extensionists bring to their work their own knowledge and that of their neighbours about local resource management and agricultural production. This experience is shared systematically with other farmers in the district through village agriculture groups, and through regional organic agriculture projects, organized through parish and diocesan institutions operating in the capital and in outlying villages. Technical advice is provided by the CETAMEX team to other farmers for free and aims to improve farmers' nutritional levels, economic self-reliance, sustainable natural resource management, and autonomous collaboration at the village level.

Through CETAMEX, farmer-led agroecological projects have been promoted since 1982. The organization has often responded to requests by local parishes and groups within the regional diocese that have supported such farmer-to-farmer projects. However, this increasing demand has also been accompanied by critical developments. Applied research and technical advisory work, for instance, have been problematic: participants and interested community members are unable to share their views effectively, or shy away from collaborating in a project such as this which does not offer direct financial incentives, and which is perceived to be an externally driven one, due to negative experiences with governmental programmes or NGO projects in the past. Contradictory or duplicating research, advice and technology development work are common.

Designing a stakeholder evaluation methodology

M&E has been a continuous part of the CETAMEX programme. The farmer-extensionists hold monthly meetings during which each farmer reports on their experiences over the previous month. This data is summarized every six months into evaluation reports sent to the main funder. These are not complicated reports, but reflect a mostly quantitative, technical assessment of the programme: they detail the number of seeds, trees, or fields sown, the terraces/contour bunds built, the number of farmer participants, etc. A yearly evaluation is held inviting all participants from the communities to the programme's offices in the regional market town. Again, the emphasis of these annual meetings has been on presenting quantitative summaries, with the villagers participating in planning the programme activities for the next year in terms of quantitative aims.

Although they recognized the merits of the farmer-to-farmer approach, CETAMEX began to observe that the level of local participation and the commitment and effectiveness of programme staff were declining, which the programme's in-built M&E system could not adequately account for. Hence, there was increased interest amongst programme staff in learning more about participatory evaluation approaches that would represent differing stakeholder perspectives and assessments of the programme. The aim, therefore, was for the outside research team to assist in the design and testing of a stakeholder-based evaluation methodology in order to better inform farmer-to-farmer extension practice.

The external research team for this work on participatory monitoring and evaluation (PM&E) was composed of a rural sociologist, a social scientist with environmental resource management training, a social anthropologist and a scientist with agricultural and forestry expertise. They worked together in different phases and distinct team combinations, both with CETAMEX staff, and without them. However, two farmer-extensionists from the team of 14 took on the lead responsibility in field and workshop work throughout this process.

Combining methods for stakeholder evaluation

Developing the evaluation methodology was set within a social auditing approach, which assesses the social impact and ethical behaviour of an organization or project in relation to its aims and those of its stakeholders (Zadek and Evans, 1993; Zadek and Raynard, 1994). Stakeholders here are not only the organization and its 'beneficiaries' but also other external institutions and non-collaborating community members, or even other NGOs. Social auditing is based on the concept of establishing multiple stakeholder indicators and assessing the social, economic and agro-ecological impacts and sustainability. The approach takes into consideration different perspectives, which are represented by various indicators and other information. The guiding principles of social auditing – inclusivity, completeness, comparability, continuous improvement, regularity, external verification and disclosure – are considered to be central to ensuring that beyond the sheer indicator definition, learning and changes take place within an organization from processes of consultative and analytical joint evaluations.

The overall approach of the study was then to use a combination of participatory methods that would allow an adaptation of the social auditing process to fit the particular context of this organization and its socio-economic context. The objective was actively to involve farmers and other project stakeholders from villages, and to incorporate views held by people from other institutions beyond the NGO project staff or the communities. The action research approach sought to encourage stakeholder analysis, and to analyse social dynamics within the projects and changes in power relations as a result of the projects. The social auditing approach principally, then, provided a framework for reflection with the project staff on accountability and systematic organizational learning, for which three key methodologies for evaluation were used to adapt social auditing processes to local conditions:

o conventional social science research using methodologies common to ethnographic work (semi-structured interviews, oral histories), to focus more on the perspectives of individuals within the projects and the surrounding communities, as well as on the history of the organization and of village agricultural groups

○ methods from participatory rural appraisal (PRA) which were adjusted to local contexts, to analyse the views held by the various stakeholders (at micro and macro levels), to appraise the social dynamics within the projects, and to identify qualitative and quantitative indicators of different stakeholders (Chambers, 1992; Pretty *et al.*, 1996)

○ the grassroots development framework (GDF) or the 'cone' developed by the Inter-American Foundation (IAF) (Ritchey-Vance, 1998; Zaffaroni, 1997), to integrate the variables and indicators of various stakeholders.

The following sections present some of the first experiences and lessons, and trace how a social audit process could be initiated within a farmer-to-farmer project.

Defining stakeholder objectives

In practice, social auditing uses an operational set of core indicators defined by different stakeholders and relies on a process of negotiating their adoption for monitoring and evaluation. However, before defining these indicators, monitoring and evaluation objectives first need to be clarified.

During a workshop session, the project team defined the objectives of this methodology development project. The setting of these objectives required identifying and addressing different personal perspectives within the CETAMEX team: the co-ordinator was concerned about extensionists' performance, but did not want to learn much about internal decision-making processes, while some extensionists were concerned about internal communication and issues of group formation within their team rather than with considering each other's performance by expressing opinions about each other.

Testing methods for indicator development

The next step was to test the participatory methods (discussed above) for identifying stakeholder indicators. Method trials were conducted through workshops and fieldwork in collaboration with two farmer-extensionists, the whole CETAMEX team, village participants, as well as other external actors (i.e. outside institutions, donors) in individual sessions. In testing methods, the project team designed the following steps for indicator development, drawing directly from the social audit approach that guided the work:

(1) Select currently available indicators for these areas, according to existing programme use and literature.
(2) Define stakeholder groups.
(3) Select stakeholder groups to be consulted.
(4) Develop indicators with different stakeholder groups.
(5) Test these across different stakeholder groups for appraisal of their resonance and effectiveness.
(6) Prioritize indicators 'offered'.

(7) Carry out fieldwork to gather data for the indicators.

(8) Create lists of indicators for full evaluation use – indicators with specific resonance for different actors, i.e. choose three key indicators for each stakeholder group.

(9) Collate data, analyse and present results in a visual fashion to different stakeholder groups.

(10) Identify recommendations for the programme.

Seven indicator areas were initially proposed by the research team, but these were eventually narrowed down with CETAMEX to four indicator areas, based on the objectives set out by the group as shown in Table 3.1.

Table 3.1: Indicator areas

Changes to local and regional, political and sectoral practice and policy
including level of dependence on external resources, involvement of local people, growing local institutions, changes in policy and practice.

Dissemination impacts: extension to other localities/regions
including both horizontal and vertical linkages with other projects, agencies and NGOs beyond the region.

Changes to the role of individuals in the project
including primarily the co-ordinator, outside advisers and immediate project participants, and the families of NGO staff.

Changes in the institutional structure
including within and beyond the actual project.

The programme staff decided to focus on changes in roles and attitudes within the organization itself, the impact of extension work (form of dissemination), and on changes in local political spheres – in this case, participation by different stakeholders in the programme's work. The local team also wanted to appraise the level and nature of participation in their practice, although they felt more secure in focusing on the technical side.

As noted earlier, indicators are increasingly demanded for quick information about operational aspects of project work, and refer usually to something measurable, e.g. numbers (percentage or share), rates (e.g. infant mortality rate) or ratios – output indicators. But in appraising the work with CETAMEX, indicators were sought that referred also to more intangible and less quantifiable things (e.g. take-up by non-participants, women's involvement at home, self-confidence of younger farmers in their technical knowledge). Therefore, indicators that emerged from local people's criteria were identified, and these gave weight to events, processes, relationships and leadership development.

Initially, organizational records were scanned for past M&E experiences, and current indicator use recorded and discussed with the collaborating extensionists and other staff. Then, together with the CETAMEX team, ten main stakeholder groups were identified (although some groups were later added as interviews exposed 'hidden' or less 'visible' stakeholders): farmer-extensionists, programme co-ordinators and advisers, funders, village farmers' group (the direct 'beneficiaries'), users of technology, non-members of village groups (informal beneficiaries), non-participants in villages, public sector institutions, researchers, NGOs working in sustainable agriculture, and church staff. The selection of stakeholder groups beyond the immediate beneficiaries was essential from the perspective of social auditing, i.e. to ensure that the project staff learned from the perspectives of different people affected by the project, as opposed to consulting only participating farmers. This approach to evaluation responds directly to accountability issues – to the wider community, beyond the 'beneficiaries' – and the need for developing a sense of ownership of the project by local people and institutions.

Having identified the range of different institutional and individual actors who affect and are affected by the project, the programme team then prioritized three stakeholder groups to be consulted for indicator development in this trial phase: farmers (participating and non-participating), farmer-extensionists (and their wives), and funders.

There were two main methodological approaches used for identifying stakeholder indicators: organizational ethnography and PRA.

Organizational ethnography

Organizational ethnography differs from ethnographic studies of whole societies in that it describes groups with more clearly defined boundaries while also considering them within a wider external context (Rosen, 1991). The study sought to seek out inter-relationships – the (implicit and explicit) rules and norms emerging and changing within a group of farmer-extensionists and within agricultural groups set up by participating farmers in different villages – in order to understand and explain various forms of participation and individual and group evolution, and barriers thereto.

The key tool used was semi-structured interviews, to construct individual oral histories of farmer-extensionists, and their experiences and involvement in relation to CETAMEX. To this end, previous farmer-extensionists and current staff (as well as members of agricultural groups) were interviewed. The external research team conducted these interviews, at the request of the staff. The main objective of the interviews was to obtain extensionists' criteria for individual and team self-evaluation, examining the basis of individual motivation and growth, as well as the wider organizational change they had experienced within CETAMEX. Following each interview, care was taken to respect confidentiality but also to involve farmer-extensionists and villagers in a number of reflective exercises on their own analysis. These exercises used PRA tools, such as Venn diagrams for analysing social dynamics, as well as group reflection and sharing.

Based on their personal histories, 'interviewees' identified criteria for becoming involved in soil conservation activities and their expectations of such initiatives. Several farmer-extensionists pointed out the importance of the programme's dependability – its constancy over the years in terms of providing a sense of identity, purpose and income – as the basis for their involvement. Their criteria for evaluating their initial interest in the programme was one of quick appraisal depending on: for whom work would be carried out, who would benefit from the training, and how much work would be conducted in the villages, or on an individual's plot.

It became clear that there existed a dilemma between the individual farmers who expressed personal interest and excitement at experimenting with new technologies, knowledge creation and learning processes, and the wider community who for many years had felt concern about the programme. Non-participants were accusing participants of 'betrayal' for working with a project, or an organization (CETAMEX), that improved agricultural production and addressed health issues but was not formally part of the community's own institutions.

This critique in itself is nothing new to farmers and migrants, or, indeed, to many rural development projects. Yet, after 13 years of work in this area, there still has been no resolution to this conflict nor any adjustments made in the programme. The struggle over this dilemma rests squarely on the local extensionists who face dual pressures: from their own conscience and personal convictions, and from their neighbours. The opportunity to visualize the tensions and concerns experienced daily by the staff – through dialogue, visual methods and reflective workshops – was considered to be a great relief for them, a space to acknowledge weaknesses in their work but also to develop new, more participatory ways for planning and assessment that involve the wider communities with whom they work.

Participatory rural appraisal

PRA methods helped to identify the evaluation criteria of farmer-beneficiaries, CETAMEX staff, funders and other stakeholders. Table 3.2 lists the PRA methods used to identify criteria, more specific indicator areas and the indicators themselves. The aim was also to train CETAMEX staff and villagers in PRA tools that could be used later to measure progress against those indicators.[5]

Table 3.2:   Examples of indicator areas and PRA methods used – Phase 1

Indicator area	Method
Extension impacts (visible and invisible)	○ Farm profiles and flow diagrams: Systems of advisory flows ○ Seasonal calendars (dynamic changes over years – e.g. changes in agricultural inputs, yields and risks) ○ Social mapping ○ Trend analysis (quantification with local materials, maps)
Extensionist's skills	○ Matrix ranking ○ Evaluation wheel (self-evaluation by farmer-extensionist, by village group, workshop participants, programme team)
Technology (relevance/impact)	○ Matrix ranking ○ Social map ('invisible' technology uptake)
Ecological change (resource availability)	○ Trend analysis/timelines ○ Social maps ○ Resource maps
Project dynamics (internal and external)	○ Matrix ranking ○ Venn diagrams

For instance, social mapping of group dynamics and flow diagrams were found to be used most keenly and creatively by extensionists in appraising the team's internal dynamics and visioning for their organization's future. Critiques, concerns, but also visions, about desired future changes regarding internal communications, favouritism, factions, etc. could be voiced – or visualized – in such a way. Using matrix ranking, extensionists could name their own criteria for assessing each other's performance, and listen to the villagers' own criteria. For instance, discussions based on matrix ranking allowed extensionists to listen to women farmers' criteria for preferring the vegetable crops that had been promoted; but the extensionists also learned that the women's appraisal pointed out the programme's neglect of working with local crop species already managed by women. The extensionists hence learned to apply a tool for encouraging women's assessment of extensionists' work, as well as for bringing out their own reflection on their work and group relations.

The advantage of using PRA methods for identifying indicators is that the techniques can be clearly directed at the line of enquiry, focusing on criteria and developing indicators with a group, which semi-structured interviews do not allow on their own. However, experience showed that it is best for local extensionists and some village group members themselves to have some familiarity with PRA, so that the tools are more effectively utilized. Incorporating PRA training workshops as part of the methods testing phases was seen as critical, with necessary continuous support and follow-up visits from CETAMEX staff. Farmers in the region need sufficient time to develop trust with outside researchers and local extensionists, and freely to articulate and share their views and opinions; the use of PRA tools in themselves does not magically create such trust, nor reveal significant insights by simply discussing the resulting pictures or scoring tables.

After the first period of introductory work, an evaluation exercise was held in parallel in three villages by the enquiry team comprised of villagers and farmer-extensionists, and facilitated by the external research team. Thus, for the first time ever, the extensionists divided into three teams, went into the villages where they had been working for many years, and carried out a multiple-stakeholder assessment of the programme, specifically focusing on the work and behaviour of each extensionist who had worked in that village. Based on the PRA results, the resulting comments from different village actors and groups were presented to village assemblies or authorities. Back in the office, the three teams gathered again to reflect on lessons and to propose necessary adjustments in the programme.

The different methods and steps for selecting indicators were flexibly applied across different social actors and contexts. These early trials referred to Steps 5 and 6, i.e. developing indicators, and testing methods with different stakeholder groups. Rather than leaving the programme team alone to prioritize indicators, the process allowed villagers also to learn by focusing initially on the PRA methods and 'daring' them to comment openly. As a result, several adjustments in programme activities were identified.

Table 3.3 summarizes some of the criteria and indicators selected by the three key stakeholder groups. One significant finding was that farmers prioritized social and economic well-being, types of technologies introduced and the performance of extension workers as more important than abstract notions of sustainability (e.g. resilience) or whether an impact was achieved at regional level. Figure 3.2 (the proposed PM&E framework or 'cone' for CETAMEX) also highlights how the resulting indicators by farmers and other actors clearly addressed issues of spiritual health, collegiality, physical well-being, and increases in productivity and self-sufficiency. Villagers and CETAMEX staff also emphasized self-esteem and democratic decision making within the team. Intangible impacts, and the processes underlying them, were clearly important to farmers.

Table 3.3: Selection of stakeholder criteria, CETAMEX

Funders	Extensionists and collaborators/advisers	Farmers
○ Learning opportunities ○ Agro-climatic conditions faced ○ Marginal areas ○ Small, feasible size ○ Widening impact ○ Alliance/network seeking ○ Health and gender awareness ○ Local vision and support ○ [Work with] Indigenous populations ○ Being able to speak the language of farmers	○ Owning the project ○ Sideways extension (number of experimental plots) ○ Impact of learning workshops ○ Changes in income/ wealth relative to others ○ Strength in defending technical experience locally ○ Changes in behaviour ○ Yields ○ Acquiring knowledge ○ Persistence ○ Results maintained over time ○ Commitment of extensionists ○ Simplicity in language and management of technology required	○ Erosion (control) ○ Nutrition and vitamins ○ Yields ○ Quality of crop ○ Labour, input ○ Variety in production (diversification) ○ Income ○ Ease of cultivation ○ Working together as a group ○ Creating independent income ○ [Not] leading to criticism by others[6] ○ Self-respect ○ Inducement to non-migration ○ Providing employment ○ Teaching something useful, practical

Phase 1 of the work with CETAMEX has so far only reached Step 6 for selecting indicators. Subsequent work (Steps 7 onwards) has also been designed for different stakeholder groups (i.e. villagers and project staff). For Steps 7 to 9, a systematic collection of different criteria and indicators is necessary. To that end, the external research team undertook to apply a tool for systematizing indicators, so as to enable the project team and villagers more easily to choose a set of indicators for conducting future M&E.

The 'cone': using stakeholder indicators to compare contrasting visions

The aim was to organize the initial stakeholder evaluation criteria into a conceptual framework that would present a general overview of selected indicators, without losing the specific meaning given to each indicator area.

Source: Inter-American Foundation/IAF

Figure 3.1: *The logic of the 'cone' – categories and variables*

The indicators were loosely combined and integrated using the 'cone' framework (see Figure 3.1), so that the set of mixed stakeholder indicators addressing different dimensions of impact and process of the project, could be presented visually – and thus aid M&E.

The GDF or 'cone' developed by the IAF is a conceptual framework that attempts to represent both the quantitative and qualitative aspects of programme work (see Ritchey-Vance, 1998; Zaffaroni, 1997). It focuses on three levels across a continuum of tangible and intangible impacts: individual and family, organizations, and society. The purpose of this framework is to allow comparisons across a number of projects using fixed categories and variables, but also to present specific indicators reflective of stakeholders' particular priorities and contexts.

Two main steps were followed to integrate stakeholder indicators into the 'cone' as follows.

Loose collection of criteria for evaluating CETAMEX

The first step was to collate the different criteria identified according to stakeholder groups (e.g. Table 3.3). However, since it would be impossible to evaluate a project using indicators responding to all these criteria (and more), two approaches were considered for indicator selection:

○ focus groups prioritizing three out of their own list of criteria, and then defining indicators for these, and the project team responding to each of these sets

○ grouping external and internal indicators first in the framework that respects the systemic form of the underlying approach to sustainable agriculture.

The latter was done in this case, at least with criteria available from fieldwork and workshops (Figure 3.2).

Categorising variables and criteria

The criteria identified by stakeholders, and the indicators subsequently selected, were then arranged according to the six categories designed for the cone (Figure 3.2). The 22 variables used by the IAF were maintained but made more specific to this programme, by associating a key objective of the organization's mission statement (e.g. 'to contribute to change in technical practice by the wider society in the region').

What is critical then is the need to refine how these indicators are measured, using which methods. Figure 3.2 and Table 3.4 present sample indicators only, to show which criteria and indicators emerged by working with different stakeholders; this is *not* a final evaluation framework for CETAMEX, but serves mainly as raw material from which the exact indicators for the annual evaluation and ongoing monitoring can be drawn.

Learning from stakeholder perspectives

The indicator search often revealed more about the stakeholders themselves – the outside professionals, farmer-extensionists, and farmers – than about the actual impacts of the project. This was clearly intentional, to aid CETAMEX staff in evaluating their work within a broader context. Perceptions by external stakeholders about CETAMEX obviously vary. The interest in extension styles led to most of the methodological tools being used to seek criteria for appraisal of the work and 'ways of being' of farmer-to-farmer extensionists.

Research and public sector professionals who were interviewed commented on CETAMEX only with regard to its technical work. This is partly explained because CETAMEX has worked in relative isolation from other institutions (apart from church networks) in Oaxaca. However, several external stakeholders did voice their concern over leadership styles and efficacy in conducting the programme. They stated that 'one can be technically very capable, but still be authoritarian', which referred in particular to the CETAMEX co-ordinator, whose working style is known in the region to be abrupt with non-church institutions.

On the other hand, both funders and church-related stakeholders share values with CETAMEX in terms of their participatory approach to rural

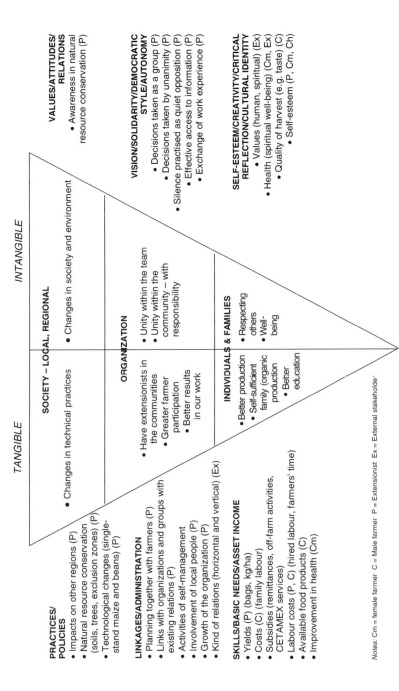

Figure 3.2: *Tangible and intangible indicators: Internal and external factors – CETAMEX 1996/7*

Notes: Cm = female farmer C = Male farmer P = Extensionist Ex = External stakeholder

45

Table 3.4: Categorization of sample indicators

Category 1: Policy environment (society) (local, regional, national), tangibles

Variable	Criteria definition	Sample indicator
Practice: *Change in technical practice by wider society of the region*	○ Impact over more distant regions in the state	○ Number of soil conservation techniques practised ○ Number of 'A' apparatus built ○ Hectares of plots on which farmers use them for building contour bunds
	○ More natural resources conserved	○ Number of trees planted ○ Tree mortality
	○ Changes in technology (single-cropped maize, beans in rows) in similar agro-ecological and social contexts	○ Number of smallholder communities that have adopted single-cropped maize

Category 4: Organizational culture, intangibles

Variable	Criteria definition	Sample indicator
Democratic style within the organisation:	○ Decisions taken by the group	○ Of the total of decisions taken: how many were taken by the team, and how many votes were there
Unity within the team and the community: with responsible behaviour	○ Decisions taken unanimously	○ Of the total of decisions taken: how many were taken unanimously, how many by majority vote
	○ Access to information	○ Whether everyone knows the work of their colleagues ○ Whether everyone knows the budget of the organization (in and out flows) ○ Whether all know what is happening, and why, in the decision making processes and with regard to training issues
	○ Disagreement* not expressed at time of decision	○ How many decisions, and in which areas, have been taken over the last year in this way?

* Silence here implies disagreement – when people do not express an opinion, this usually implies that they do not agree but do not want to contradict a decision taken by others development activities. Unlike other external actors who are perhaps more critical of the programme, these supporters in general praise the persistence and consistency of the work conducted by programme staff. Their evaluation criteria are based mainly on political interests in working with poor farmers and their families for change, as well as recognizing value in how extensionists identify themselves still as farmers rather than as technical advisers, in order to stress the importance of local knowledge and non-hierarchical relations within the villages.

Farmers from 'beneficiary' villages were very cautious and polite, as is so often the case, when the evaluation methodology was being developed. They generally avoided open criticism or conflict; hence, using ranking techniques with farmers often produced findings that were 'flat' and less meaningful. For instance, in the presence of farmer-extensionists or the collaborating nuns, farmers identified criteria for evaluating certain technologies that were almost a literal repeat of what had been taught to them in technical courses, and had to be disaggregated further with them to invite independent opinions. PRA tools helped in making this articulation somewhat less threatening, by allowing an opinion to be expressed on paper, on the ground, or to a mixed group of 'questioners'. Yet, some of the PRA tools were limited in their utility for monolingual and highly shy women where village men would insist on being present, and matrix ranking required some confidence building first because participants remained reluctant to openly express their opinions so as to avoid potential disagreements and conflicts. Theatre and conventional focus groups may have been more effective, though often requiring professional translation for team members as well as for external researchers.

The process revealed that farmer-extensionists demand of each other and of themselves just as much as communities expect of them with regard to their work. Extensionists emphasize imparting practical knowledge and honesty in carrying out their work: they say, 'praxis is worth more than theory' and 'a bad extensionist hangs around with his friends, drinks, but gives a report that shows he has worked'.

Finally, while the 'cone' framework helped systematize some of the criteria and indicators selected by the various stakeholders about the work of CETAMEX, it cannot tell a complete story of the organizational learnings that the CETAMEX team underwent during these trials. The ideal of the farmer-to-farmer approach means that being an extensionist also involves learning how to run one's own organization, following World Neighbor's approach to self-sufficiency and self-management by local people. Although the programme at the commencement of this work had not openly addressed issues of its own organizational growth, internal communication and leadership, considerable conflicts existed and were eventually visualized in terms of internal groupings, financial administration, gender relations and recognition of skills as well as political institutional relations. The methodological approaches used in this work helped to offer insights into how people within the project – and the families within wider communities – have been struggling with the challenge of changing institutional, or indeed organizational forms, such as CETAMEX and how the skills of the extensionists have evolved. The search for indicators and participatory evaluation led, in the end, to reflection and even negotiation of differences over concerns about accountability and democratic organizational rules and procedures.

Conclusions

A few of the lessons learned during this first trial phase with CETAMEX are highlighted here. The work in Mexico provides three key findings for PM&E practice:

♦ *PRA in the context of PM&E can contribute to institutional learning when set within an approach that systematizes the learning, e.g. through social auditing or the 'cone'.*

Because much data is generated by PRA work, it is more useful to combine PRA with a framework such as the 'cone' to organize information and clarify understanding. The social audit approach also offers a systematic way of structuring stakeholder consultations, and, when combined with PRA methods, can ensure that the 'hidden' stakeholders, such as family members and non-participants, are included and their opinions are expressed (e.g. through Venn diagrams and social maps).

Since intangible processes and impacts are not easily measured, the PM&E approach needs to be flexible yet systematic enough to track changes and report these using quantitative and/or qualitative formats (as done in social audit reports). This may require using conventional questionnaires while also relying more on participatory tools, such as PRA or organizational ethnographies.

♦ *PM&E takes time, which challenges people's commitment to and sense of ownership over a project. The methodological steps and the perceived 'value-added' benefits of such activities therefore need to be highly concrete and specific in order for participants to engage in the process.*

Our first experience in testing methods showed that some tools would not be appropriate for farmers' monitoring, simply because they will require considerable time investment from a project that offers little immediate financial return.[7] Organizations will also need to have gained some familiarity with using participatory tools or received appropriate training – which can be costly and time consuming. Nevertheless, focus group discussions have helped not only to save on time in identifying and analysing stakeholder criteria and indicators, but also saved on computerized data analysis for evaluation purposes.

Ultimately, PRA tools are useful in triggering participatory discussions and analyses rather than providing answers in themselves. Praxis still has to show whether farmers and farmer-extensionists will use PRA and other participatory tools in the future to construct the kind of evaluation system that makes most sense for the organization and that captures the types of change processes they want to see functioning in their communities.

♦ *For M&E to lead to organizational change for improving performance and impact, appropriate leadership qualities and human relations within*

48

the organization are required in order to address emerging conflicts and sustain efforts; M&E methodologies alone are not enough to enhance participation and effective learning, but social auditing provides a framework for organizations wishing to engage in change processes.

The first lessons in testing methods revealed that self-evaluatory tools can best be used by programme staff or village groups to improve extension work by looking at internal group dynamics, changes in work styles over time, local participation and limits to farmer adoption of technologies. However, avoidance of addressing power issues relating to leadership issues, external relations, internal communications, and reward systems, within the organization can constrain effective learning, particularly with regard to sustaining participation within the organization or project. The process of participatory evaluation and indicator development can itself trigger conflict and division within an organization, as various perspectives of assessments are brought in. This will require conflict management skills and strong leadership to harness or shape potential divisions or conflict into a learning process.

In this context, social auditing provides a systematic and principled process of enhancing organizational transparency by shared learning and reflection on change processes in the organization. This approach can give a systematic structure to the process of using the highly qualitative work of organizational ethnography, and the often very broad information obtained through PRA-based work. Rather than just the outputs of an M&E system, the social auditing approach allows organizational and individual learning to occur throughout the process, from the design of the M&E cycle through to the analysis of indicator results.

These lessons, drawn from the work with farmers and their technical advisers in Oaxaca, are only the starting point in establishing a process that we hope will better communicate success and challenges in promoting farmer-to-farmer extension. Future work needs to consider other village participants and non-participants indirectly involved and affected by these farmer-led projects, since they may have additional tools for voicing *their* evaluation of such initiatives and could therefore contribute towards strengthening farmer-extension work.

4

Adapting Participatory Methods to Meet Different Stakeholder Needs: Farmers' Experiments in Bolivia and Laos[1]

ANNA LAWRENCE, GRAHAM HAYLOR,
CARLOS BARAHONA, ERIC MEUSCH

Introduction

INCREASING INTEREST AMONG DONORS in linking natural resource management with poverty alleviation has motivated concerns to fund research that builds on experiences of non-governmental organizations (NGOs) in participatory technology development. The goal of such research is to develop sustainable agricultural technologies appropriate for heterogeneous environments occupied by poor farming communities. Another research objective is to improve understanding of the processes involved, their outcomes and wider applicability. Partners in this type of research project are often state research institutions or extension departments, which are typically bureaucratic but are wide reaching. The research is likely to involve a range of stakeholders, especially when the research is initiated by external actors responding to identified local needs. Stakeholders include donors, researchers, local institutions, and farmers with particular interests or direct involvement in the research. Stakeholder interests and the state institutions that support the research become significant factors influencing the process of developing agricultural technologies, monitoring performance, and evaluating impacts. For instance, donor interests pressure researchers to produce generalizable results of farm trials in order to apply research outputs more widely.

Another important factor affecting technology development research is in the nature of the technology itself. Previous attempts to involve farmers in the evaluation of technologies generally dealt with simple change, for example, evaluating the impact of introducing a range of crop varieties (e.g. Ashby, 1990; Joshi and Witcombe, 1996). However, many of the technologies appropriate for sustainable or low-input agriculture involve more complex changes that affect management of the whole farming system.[2] One implication for monitoring and evaluation (M&E) involving more complex changes is that it may be difficult for one farmer to compare several interventions simultaneously, because systems changes as a result of introduced technology may affect the whole farm.

This chapter describes two projects – one in Bolivia and the other in Laos – that deal with these particular challenges in monitoring and evaluating impacts of new technology: those of addressing donor needs, state–institutional contexts, and farming system change. The projects were collaborative initiatives carried out by local research institutions, external researchers, NGOs, people's organizations (POs), and individual farmers (see Box 4.1).

Box 4.1: The projects and institutions featured in this chapter

Participatory improvement of soil and water conservation in hillside farming systems, Bolivia

This is a collaboration between the Agricultural Extension and Rural Development Department of Reading University (AERDD), UK, and the Centre for Tropical Agricultural Research (CIAT), Santa Cruz, Bolivia. CIAT is a government research institution which aims to have a farming systems approach to research, most of which is currently conducted on station. CIAT does not strictly carry out extension but is involved in technology transfer through its close links with NGOs and producer organizations in the department of Santa Cruz. It has experience with on-farm trials, but these are designed and controlled by technicians, and farmers' perspectives are not formally taken into account in the evaluation of such trials. This project aims to strengthen soil and water conservation practices in the temperate valleys, through information exchange and support of farmer experimentation. It is CIAT's first experience of supporting trials that are designed entirely by farmers and that involve farmers in the evaluation.

Addressing technical, social and economic constraints to developing rice–fish culture in Laos

This project is co-ordinated by the Systems Group of the Institute of Aquaculture (IoA), University of Stirling, in collaboration with staff from the Livestock and Fisheries Section (LFS), Laos and the Lao Women's Union (LWU). The LFS in Savannakhet Province is at an early stage in its institutional development and is currently supported by the Asian Institute of Technology (AIT) Outreach Project to strengthen its capacity to work with farmers to develop and manage small-scale aquatic resources. Staff have no concrete experience with research, and do not have a national or local research system from which they obtain technical recommendations. Therefore, the LFS would like to strengthen its own institutional procedures for formulating and testing recommendations. The IoA project is working with the LFS and interested farmers to investigate and address farmers' constraints to raising fish in rice fields and to emphasize women's role in technology development.

Both projects are funded by the Department for International Development (DFID), UK.

The project context in Bolivia and Laos

Each project is characterized by its environmental diversity and the lack of available technology appropriate for the ecological zone (see Table 4.1).

The complexity of the local environment led researchers to propose a participatory approach for developing farming systems based on farmers' own knowledge and priorities. The project methodology adopted is similar for both projects, which facilitate a two-way learning process between farmers and technical researchers, and acquire government institutional

Table 4.1: Features of the projects in each country

Features	Bolivia	Laos
Other collaborators	NGOs	LWU, a government organization with representation at provincial and district level, and members in all villages
Project technical focus	Soil and water conservation	Rice–fish production
Project area	Rainfed semi-arid hillsides, Andean foothills	Mostly rainfed, lowland rice fields, strongly seasonal rain
Diversity of project area	Range of slopes and altitudes in each community, wide range of climates among communities	Range of climates, drainage systems, topography and population density
Environmental risks	Drought	Drought and floods
Situation analysis	Needs identified by local institutions; RRA and PRA assessments, also drawing from available literature.[3] These defined the scope for information exchange workshops during which farmers designed experiments	Needs identified by local institutions and farmers; RRA and PRA tools used to prepare a more detailed situation analysis (because little information existed), and to define institutional support for experiments.[4]
Availability of appropriate technology	No previous study of indigenous technical knowledge (ITK); soil-conservation practices not tested formally in the zone; appropriate species and practices not known	One ITK study; FAO recommendations inappropriate to rainfed, seasonal rice production
Approach chosen for trial design	Experiments planned by farmers at a workshop after sharing experience with other farmers and NGOs	Experiments planned by individual farmers in fields through discussion with researchers
Approach chosen for PM&E	Workshops for information exchange; flexible, informal PM&E approach initially, later more formalized PM&E to improve institutional and donor learning	PM&E formalized from the outset to suit institutional experience and fulfil requirements for institutional development
Indicator development	Inferred informally through interviews with farmers hosting formal on-farm trials. Listed by groups of farmers in workshops	Identified through group discussions with farmers and researchers, and use of resource flow diagrams to show systems change

support in designing trials based on local and scientific knowledge. The projects differ in terms of:

o their institutional contexts
o their project design (one is oriented towards production and the other towards resource conservation)
o ease of communications
o contact between local research institutions and NGOs (see Table 4.2).

Table 4.2: Characteristics of the partner research institutions in each country

Characteristics	Bolivia	Laos
Partner institution	CIAT (a departmental government agricultural research institution)	LFS (a provincial government support service for livestock and fisheries)
Institutional structure	'Matrix' of interdisciplinary and inter-zonal teams; non-hierarchical	Hierarchical, but with considerable autonomy at local (district) level
Commodity base	Whole system	Livestock (especially veterinary) and fish
Experience with diagnostic studies	Staff conduct RRAs in multi-disciplinary teams, often focused on a single commodity	None; staff conduct censuses of livestock
Usual sources of technology	Own research, some on-farm trials	Absence of national agricultural research system has led LFS to use their own judgment in order to propose recommendations for farmers
Experience with extension	Technology transfer to 'intermediary users' such as NGOs	Not systematized; recommendations made from officers' personal experience
Experience with PM&E	Researchers usually carry out formal assessments of farm trials, but have conducted informal assessments using farmers' criteria	None, but local staff are often farmers themselves and have a close understanding of farmers' needs and constraints
Ease of communication	Staff all contactable by telephone; local offices accessible by unpaved roads, taking up to six hours' journey	No telephones to remote districts; local offices accessible by unsurfaced road, sometimes more than six hours' journey
Contact with NGOs	Frequent, institutionalized	Infrequent

Appreciating knowledge of men and women

Gender issues remain a neglected aspect of rural development in both cultures. External researchers were concerned to highlight gender issues and recognize the different perspectives of men and women. In Laos, after a situation analysis was conducted, local government staff realized that several different opinions existed within the community, especially between women and men. In previous experiences, village consensus would be obtained but this usually followed the senior-male point of view. While external researchers viewed participatory monitoring and evaluation (PM&E) as an essential tool for learning more about women's experiences and views, local staff also recognized that men and women differed in their knowledge and attitudes, particularly about technology development.

However, neither of the collaborating research institutions is accustomed to consulting women farmers. Staff tend to assume that women and men share the same knowledge about farming, that men eventually discuss farming issues with their wives, or that women are not considered relevant actors in technology development. Aquaculture in Laos and crop production in Bolivia are generally regarded as 'men's work'. However, in each case, technology development is likely to affect women and men differently. Furthermore, in Bolivia and Laos alike, women are found to be much more closely involved in farming systems than technical researchers or extension workers expect.

In this chapter we compare these two experiences and consider the implications for developing a PM&E research process. We focus particularly on indicator development and the merits of using matrix scoring as a method for evaluating the impacts of new farming technology.[5] By looking at two projects from different cultures and institutional contexts, we can observe how evaluation tools are adjusted to local conditions and what participants have learnt from their use. We also further reflect on the wider applicability of information generated using a PM&E approach.

The methodology in practice

While both collaborating research institutions had little direct experience with PM&E, each adopted a project methodology that emphasized stakeholder participation. In Bolivia, the project involved farmers, scientists, and NGO development workers in identifying and sharing farming knowledge. CIAT's non-hierarchical structure has allowed its staff considerable flexibility in working with farmers, so field staff implicitly base their research on close knowledge of farmers' priorities. The PM&E process began with a research planning workshop during which farmers planned their own trials based on their own knowledge and experience of soil conservation. Because various project stakeholders are involved, different types of information were needed for the monitoring process. Local staff were quick to recognize the need for a participatory approach to M&E, because their close interaction with local communities made them aware of farmers' needs and experiences of previous farm trials, and conscious that farmers use different criteria to judge the success of a technology.

In Laos, because working closely with farmers is still a novel approach within the collaborating institution, researchers decided to integrate PM&E more formally into work plans to fit local institutional practice. The project focused on increasing fish production in rice fields, and intended to establish institutional linkages between external researchers (from IoA and AERDD), the LFS and the LWU at provincial and district levels. District-level staff were then supposed to work with farmers. From the outset, the knowledge and perspectives of the project stakeholders – including farmers, the various institutions, and researchers – were all considered important components of the research process. The local institutions (the LWU and LFS) had close contacts with the farming communities but little experience in sharing and recording information systematically together with farmers. LFS researchers had experience with data gathering but limited knowledge about local conditions, and they faced cultural and lan-guage barriers. After working closely with farmers in workshops, a parti-cipatory system was established for recording farm trials that would enable farmers to identify options for aquaculture development.

The process of developing indicators differed in each country, but in general the two projects used the following key steps:

(1) situation analysis, to improve understanding of the interlinkages in farming systems and to identify farmer perceptions
(2) discussions with farmers regarding individual experiences with systems changes as a result of incorporating new farming practices (i.e. soil conservation or fish culture)
(3) discussions with other farmers (individually or collectively) regarding their expectations of incorporating new farming practices
(4) indicator development together with farmers and researchers to show farming systems changes and impacts of new technologies
(5) refining of systems indicators in the field by involving more farmers
(6) use of matrix diagrams based on the identified indicators to rank and score changes.

In Bolivia work began with two to three farmers in each of the three communities; now work is continuing with ten farmers in each community and farm trials are planned for future seasons. In Laos the team is presently working with five to ten families in each of the six communities.

As researchers were interested in exploring the effects of new tech-nologies on farmers' livelihood systems, they decided to adopt matrix scor-ing for monitoring and recording information. Matrix scoring has been used in participatory evaluation of simple technologies, such as testing crop varieties (Ashby, 1990). As mentioned earlier, it is generally more difficult to make straightforward comparisons when whole farming systems inter-ventions are involved. Therefore, instead of comparing a range of tech-nologies with each other, these projects use matrix scoring tools to compare how farm household members perceive their farming system as a whole both *before* and *after* the trial. The intention was that such matrices would use the indicators defined by farmers to explore the changes throughout the farming system.

Changing indicators in Bolivia

In Bolivia the process of developing indicators was less formal and less systematically documented than in Laos. This was because of CIAT's more flexible institutional structure and limited staff experience with documentation. Researchers began by asking farmers to assess their previous experiences of conducting contour hedgerow trials. The process allowed researchers to determine indicators through semi-structured interviews with farmers. Farmers' assessments focused on their perceptions of change as a result of the trials. Outside researchers inferred indicators from these, which were then used to find out how farmers' perceptions changed during the trial. However, as will be discussed further below, the implicit indicators used by farmers changed in the process of applying the new technology.

At an early stage, when the contour hedgerows were still small, farmers identified criteria that were important to them:

○ time (labour) spent preparing the land for sowing (e.g. when the fallow or stubble is not burnt)
○ palatability to livestock or risk of losing hedgerows through browsing
○ compatibility with farming practices such as ploughing by oxen.

After eight months of growth, participating farmers and their neighbours began to notice how the soil was building up on the uphill side of the hedgerows, and how recent rain had left the soil around the trees damper than on the rest of the slope. Two new criteria were then added:

○ moisture retention
○ soil retention.

At this stage, more farmers began to express interest in establishing further trials. Initial caution regarding the potential negative impact on the farming system was being replaced by observations of potential positive impact. By documenting farmers' criteria for evaluating technology, researchers and farmers have improved their understanding of the role of soil conservation in the whole system. Identifying farmer's evaluation criteria also proved useful to researchers, who were then able to infer indicators based on these criteria and document how farmers' attitudes towards new technologies can change: initial doubts may give way towards greater enthusiasm for experimentation and identifying new production alternatives.

Later in the process, a research planning workshop was conducted during which farmers explicitly identified evaluation indicators. These expanded on the implicit indicators which researchers had inferred up to that point. The question posed to farmers was: 'How will I know if my experiment is working out well?' Farmers' evaluation indicators included:

○ dark soil colour
○ abundant vegetation
○ no bare soil
○ humidity in the soil
○ increased production
○ our neighbours copy what we are doing
○ water flow increases

o increased soil organic matter
o the soil will stay on the hillside and not wash away
o animals with increased weight.

Farmers' criteria indicated both causes and effects of improved soil fertility and conservation. The indicators themselves informed researchers that farmers understand linkages between soil cover, soil colour, soil organic matter, humidity, fertility and productivity. They also highlighted the fact that farmers prioritized the improving of fertility and crop and animal production over preventing soil erosion.

The process of developing indicators highlighted important differences in evaluation perspectives between men and women. Women were more concerned about the suitability of contour species for fuel and their palatability to sheep, while men emphasized species palatability for cattle over meeting fuel needs. Previous trials experimented with grasses and leguminous trees for creating contour barriers, which satisfied most male farmers. However, women's evaluation criteria revealed that women farmers were more interested in planting grasses and trees in pure pastures or plantations, highlighting their interest in livestock nutrition and fuel production.

More formal methods in Laos

In contrast with Bolivia, partner institutions in Laos had much less experience with participatory research or evaluation, and language barriers made communication amongst stakeholders more difficult. Consequently, the outside researchers initially played a greater role in establishing the PM&E process and supported project staff in developing tools. A more structured and formalized approach was adopted, partly because institutional staff were more accustomed to following fixed guidelines in conducting most of their activities. Project staff decided to use matrix scoring tools and work only with participating farmers with experience in fish production – to avoid the complications of recording information in larger group discussions. This more structured process helped ease language difficulties and staff's limited confidence in using flexible methods.

Since staff did not have much experience with semi-structured interviewing, the external researchers suggested adopting bio-resource flow diagrams as a tool for identifying local indicators of farming systems change.[6] Farmers involved in fish production drew diagrams to illustrate their farming systems before and after introducing aquaculture activities. Discussions with farmers revealed that biological and physical inputs and outputs changed, as did cash flow, labour and family nutrition. Figures 4.1 and 4.2 show two diagrams drawn by Mrs Nouna, from Nyangsoung village, who illustrated the complexity of her current rice–fish system (Figure 4.2) in contrast with her former system. This led to a realization that wild fish populations increased as a consequence of digging ditches in rice fields to help fish cultivation.[7]

Farmer observations of changes based on the systems diagrams were then used by farmers and researchers to identify criteria for evaluating

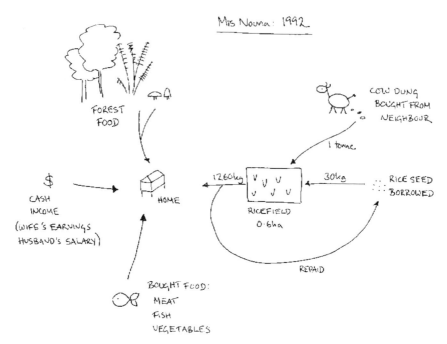

Mrs Nouna: 1992

FOREST FOOD

COW DUNG BOUGHT FROM NEIGHBOUR

1 tonne

CASH INCOME
(WIFE'S EARNINGS HUSBAND'S SALARY)

HOME

1260kg | RICEFIELD 0·6ha | 30kg | RICE SEED BORROWED

REPAID

BOUGHT FOOD:
MEAT
FISH
VEGETABLES

Figure 4.1: *Resource flows on Mrs Nouna's farm before introducing fish to her rice field*

rice–fish trials. Discussions in selecting indicators focused on weighing the benefits and risks of fish-in-rice – for instance, gaining or losing food, money, work, and land. Indirect effects, such as time saved looking for food, money saved from buying food, nutrition, rice production, and wild fish numbers, were also considered. Nine indicators were finally identified: time, investment, labour, land, rice production, wild fish yield, cultured fish yield, technical knowledge, living expenses. After interviewing other farmers, two more indicators were added: improved family diet and income (see Figure 4.3).

Selected indicators were incorporated into matrices for monitoring and evaluating results. The first attempt to use a matrix involved ranking the indicators, but was not very successful due to some confusion over its use. The second attempt used the conventional matrix scoring method, which local staff applied more successfully (Figure 4.3). Staff used matrix scoring with great enthusiasm during the situation analysis, and therefore had gained familiarity with applying the tool. They used stones to indicate their perception of the quantitative value of each factor (many, middle or few), both before and after the trial. The evaluation was only conducted *after* farm trials in order to look at changes of farmers' perceptions.[8]

Matrix scores indicate perceptions of large increases in both fish and rice production. The matrix was used during interviews with both men and women in each participating household. Matrix results suggest that men and women differed in terms of their assessment of the amount of labour

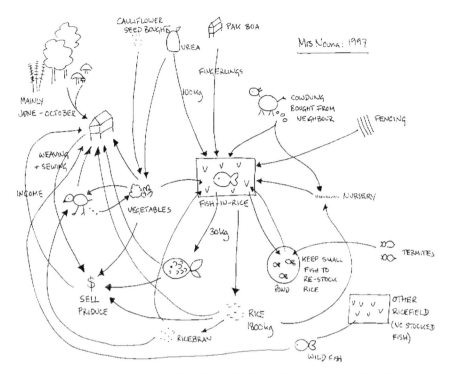

Figure 4.2: *Resource flows on Mrs Nouna's farm after introducing fish to her rice field, showing 'multiple simultaneous innovation' and a variety of factors changing as a result of the innovation*

required by the new technology (women usually indicated more) and perceptions of resulting fish yields (there were variable but no consistent differences between men's and women's views). Discussions provided further insights similar to those found in Bolivia: farming households (including men and women alike) prioritize indicators that represent risk or costs and, hence, are regarded as potentially negative, *over* indicators that represent potential benefit or positive impacts. As was the case in Bolivia, farmers' priorities may very well change if they perceive fish production to be successful.

Despite the more formal use of tools in Laos, the process helped to involve farmers actively in analysing changes on their farms. Local staff were particularly impressed by the effectiveness of using systems diagrams for technology evaluation, and have adopted the method in other research. Diagrams facilitated communication between researchers and farmers, who found it much easier to discuss experiences by using visual illustrations.

Scope for increasing stakeholder participation

In both projects, outside researchers (IoA and AERDD) and donors played a key role in promoting a participatory approach to evaluating technology. While partner institutions in Bolivia and Laos were both

province	....	
district	....	
village	....	
interviewer	....	
person interviewed	....	
date	....	

topic	before fish culture	after fish culture	comments
time			
investment			
labour			
land			
rice production			
wild fish yield			
cultured fish yield			
technical knowledge			
living expenses			
income			
food			
other			
other			

Explanation

1	many	10	xxxxx
			xxxxx
	middle	5	xxxxx
	few	1	x

2 Interview participants once only, after raising fish, and ask the importance of the topics both before and after raising fish. This comparison is to identify possibly differences between before and after

Figure 4.3: *Form for monitoring of fish-in-rice (Savannakhet, Laos)*

interested in using PRA methods, they initially did not regard 'participatory research' as going beyond the situation analysis or diagnostic phase. The process has encouraged a wider range of stakeholders to become involved and learn from the research process, including government and non-governmental institutions. This, in turn, has helped to widen project-reach and involve a greater number of participating farmers.

However, the team's experience suggests that it is mainly the research staff (from external and local research institutions) who may derive more benefits from the process than farmers. For instance, in Bolivia, CIAT researchers emphasized the need for evaluating trials with farmers using farmers' criteria. They felt that this process would help them carry out future research and extension work, and refine technology further. In Laos, there was incentive to build local institutional capacities, as local government research staff have limited experience in working closely with farmers, and wanted to learn more about using participatory research tools. As a result, researchers in Bolivia and Laos have learned a great deal about farmers' perspectives and priorities. They better understand local evaluation criteria and how these influence farmers' adoption or development of new technologies. However, in terms of providing direct benefits to farmers, it is not yet so evidently demonstrated that such a participatory process is useful.

During the self-evaluation of the entire research process (including PM&E), the research teams felt that greater farmer participation could still be achieved. For example, in Bolivia, involving women in the research process remains a challenge; both institutional and community perceptions hinder their more active participation and the fuller appreciation of their knowledge and recognition of their priorities. In Laos, focusing PM&E on participating farming households has meant that the technology impact on non-participating farmers has been ignored. Including non-participating farmers in the evaluation of farm trials would improve equity and provide information useful to international researchers and national policy makers concerned with agricultural development. In addition, local staff in Laos generally treated matrices merely as forms for recording information, rather than as tools for actually stimulating farmer analysis, recognizing different stakeholder perspectives, and assessing impacts on men and women.

Although there remain limitations to farmer participation, there is some indication that farmers can and do benefit from the PM&E process. For instance, in Bolivia, several farmers now use some of the indicators developed in documenting their own trials. Because of the more informal, personal mode of interaction between CIAT researchers and farmers, it has become rather artificial to document these indicators more explicitly into matrices. Instead, farmers participating in trials are designing their own evaluation forms to monitor indicators (such as soil loss, quantity of fodder produced, and crop yield) and to compare results before and after the trials.[9]

Using participatory indicators for wider application of results

The research process in Bolivia and in Laos led to farmer-designed and -managed experiments that involved several stakeholders with common aims but also with stakeholder-specific objectives. For institutional stakeholders (including donors), part of their interest in the research lies in the wider usefulness of findings for informing policy and recommendations in other comparable zones of the world (Lawrence *et al.*, 1997b). These include generalizing about farmer strategies, decision making, local M&E criteria and data gathering methods (i.e. the use of matrices). The next section focuses on how external researchers can use formal research principles and methods to address these stakeholder interests.

Who is carrying out the experiments?

Research objectives of these projects make clear that farmers play a central role as experimenters in designing farm trials, evaluating and comparing results, while researchers serve as facilitators and observers. These different roles and objectives, in turn, affect how research results are analysed and used by the different stakeholders. For instance, each farmer's experiment will yield information specifically relevant to the farmer in terms of the technology's direct benefits to his/her enterprise. Without external intervention, farmers are likely to monitor and evaluate results on their own but through more informal mechanisms (i.e. through daily observations). However, external researchers are interested in recording these M&E processes, and hence developing and using information gathering instruments in partnership with farmers. In Laos in particular, external researchers were eager to develop evaluation matrices which they used for recording relevant M&E criteria for each experiment and for formalizing the M&E methodology across farmers. Using M&E matrices can then later help external researchers to integrate results and make more formal/ quantitative comparisons.

Information collected in the matrices will, to some extent, allow external researchers to make comparisons across time and between farming strategies. However, the highly variable and risk-prone nature of the farming systems make direct comparisons between strategies difficult. Comparisons are less problematic when an individual farmer decides to conduct an experiment that tests at least two types of 'treatments'. This was not popular amongst farmers in Laos because fish culture technology is new and the main treatment – incorporating fish production into the farming system – was mostly adopted on a small scale as a single treatment in part of the landholding. In contrast, some Bolivian farmers have experimented with more than one treatment on the same farm, mainly by using different species for hedgerows and cover crops. The problem in comparing single-treatment experiments stems from the difficulty of separating the effects of local variability from the possible impacts of the treatments, as well as expecting that individual farmers will use similar criteria for evaluating treatments.

In other instances, comparisons are possible when a relatively large group of farmers decides to experiment with a relatively small number of treatments. Research results derived in such contexts can provide a general idea of the main effect of a treatment but also indicate how variable this impact might be. Analysing the variability of impact, especially in relation to individual farmer characteristics or recommendation options, might provide a sound basis for generalizations. In Bolivia we expect that by the end of the third year of the project, there will be around 50 farmers conducting experiments.[10] Depending on the results of the different treatments, CIAT could undertake an analysis of this sort in the mid-term. Replicating experiments would make findings amenable to using statistical techniques for establishing generalizations. However, our ability to measure variability will depend on the number of technologies adopted by farmers, the number of farmers conducting experiments, and the assumptions necessary in order to decide whether comparisons can be made (i.e. whether or not a farmer's strategy is similar enough to another farmer's strategy).

Representativeness

General statements can be made only if farmer participants adequately represent the farmer population and farming systems about which we attempt to generalize. But how can we ensure representativeness of farmers within a fluid, participatory research process? One way is to select farmer participants randomly at appropriate stages, but this may prove difficult – especially when aiming to carry out participatory research. Another alternative is to check after farmer selection whether farmer participants are representative of the wider population, using generally accepted characteristics (i.e. levels of wealth, ethnic composition, characteristics of the unmodified farming system, etc.).

Using ranks or scores?

In developing M&E matrices, the use of ranking or scoring will allow different types of analysis. Ranking is useful for identifying farmers' prioritization of criteria, but is less useful for making generalizations. Ranks contain less information than scores since they depend on the number and type of criteria determined by the participants in the ranking exercise. Consequently, it is difficult to use rankings of one group in combination with rankings produced by other groups, unless exactly the same criteria are imposed on the groups. This is a less desirable alternative, especially in the context of participatory research. On the other hand, scores have an advantage over ranks because scoring contains more information.[11] While ranks can be constructed from scores it is impossible to construct scores from ranks. Scoring allows the scores of different farmer groups to be combined and compared, with fewer conditions imposed on the participatory process.

In order to make generalizations or quantitative comparisons, measuring variability is important. However, group discussions that take place during participatory matrix scoring often tend to smooth out the variability of individual perspectives and experiences, resulting in group consensus or compromises. In Laos one way diversity and variability was ensured was to develop indicators based on group consensus but to ask each individual to evaluate their own experiments independently. The resulting sets of scores provide external researchers with a basis for further quantitative analysis, which will be useful in reaching wider conclusions about their own research questions.

In searching for ways to generalize about results obtained from participatory processes, research teams felt the need to use more quantitative measures and to take advantage of the pool of statistical ideas often used in other areas of research. The challenge lies in maintaining the real advantages of participatory methods, while at the same time incorporating principles such as replication, independent observations and representativeness that allow the use of statistical methods of generalization. Using matrices opens possibilities for arriving at a balance between these two research objectives.

Lessons learned

This chapter has identified some of the challenges presented by donor-funded participatory research projects:

○ taking into account different stakeholder needs
○ generalizing about project results and findings
○ developing appropriate participatory methods and institutionalizing participatory approaches within government research institutions
○ identifying indicators for measuring systems level changes affected by participatory technology development.

The next section elaborates on these challenges to PM&E research.

Usefulness of the PM&E process to different stakeholders

Researchers sometimes assume that asking farmers to evaluate new technologies is a process that is intrinsically useful to farmers. While our experience does not negate that assumption, it does indicate that participatory methods involving farmers in documenting change (even in using a shared, visual method such as matrices) may be of more value in facilitating communication between farmers and *researchers*, than in enabling farmers themselves to arrive at dramatic new insights. The more formal approach and forms used in Laos, in particular, limit the method in terms of providing in-depth, meaningful data. It becomes all too easy for government officials who are accustomed to collecting census data to fall into the mode of merely recording views without generating local analysis and reflection.

The method has also been invaluable to researchers in terms of drawing out the different perceptions between women and men. Through external facilitation, local staff were encouraged to compare the evaluation matrices of men and women. In both projects in Laos and Bolivia, government staff are now much more aware of the value of women's perspectives on the impact of new technology. Particularly in Bolivia, staff, despite initial reluctance, eventually appreciated the different views of men and women farmers and that each were equally valid. As a result, the value of women's knowledge of livestock forage preferences is now much more acknowledged by CIAT staff.

This raises the question of who is benefiting from the PM&E process. Our experience suggests that farmers may not immediately value nor derive direct benefits from indicators, forms and matrices used as evaluation tools, because many already have informal ways of assessing their own experiments. The tools are more useful in that they help extension agents and researchers better understand farmers' needs and perceptions, and the costs and benefits of farming experiments. Nevertheless, using participatory evaluation tools can place local staff and farmers in a better position to make decisions about new technologies on local farms. Overall, however, our experience shows that the process of learning from farmers' indicators and their evaluation of those indicators has been most valuable in helping outside researchers, e.g. in thinking about replicability, institutional appropriateness, and institutionalization.

Adapting methods for different institutions or cultures

CIAT and LFS have quite different institutional cultures, which in turn have implications for the way PM&E methods are used and adapted. CIAT staff in Bolivia tend to adopt a more informal, flexible approach to decision making and working. Because most of their time is spent in the field, staff have a very good understanding of farmers' perspectives and ideas about technology development and are quick to support them. However, CIAT staff are less interested in formal documentation and reporting. Matrices and forms have been introduced into workshops but are not widely used. On the other hand, LFS staff in Laos respond to a more centralized model of decision making and accountability and have adopted a more structured approach to documenting results. District staff wanted to record quantitative data and use forms for recording information, pointing out that farmers were able to quantify changes and values more often than PRA methods allowed them to. These observations led them to develop more structured methods, such as matrices, for monitoring and registering feedback.

While matrix scoring was promoted in both institutions, differences in institutional working styles necessitated that the tool be adapted and supplemented. Staff in Laos used matrices for recording information but found resource flow diagrams helpful in facilitating communication between farmers and researchers. Because of language barriers and staff's limited experience with open-ended group discussions, resource flow diagrams made it easier to identify farmers' evaluation criteria – which were eventually converted into indicators on the matrices. On the other hand, in Bolivia semi-structured interviews between farmers and researchers sufficed.

Potential for comparisons and applying the results elsewhere

The way research was conducted in Laos and in Bolivia, in turn, affected the potential for comparing and generalizing results. As mentioned previously, in Laos, local staff paid more attention to detail and documentation. In Bolivia, by contrast, while staff were enthusiastically committed to helping farmers, they did not see much value in filling in evaluation forms but invested in developing more personal interactions and informal discussions with farmers.

The Laos approach led to a data gathering method that was more amenable to statistical analysis and generalization than in Bolivia. Once sufficient data has been collected in Laos, it will be possible to link the results to factors such as gender, the agroecological system and individual wealth, and to draw conclusions on how these factors affect farming strategies. However, the validity of the data collected through the Laos form-filling approach has yet to be verified. Furthermore, while the more formal Laos approach led to meticulous quantitative documentation of farmers' evaluations, there was limited explanation of *why* different farmers rated change in different ways. By contrast, the more haphazard, informal approach in Bolivia – while perhaps more frustrating to donors and others seeking more systematic procedures – provided a better understanding of why farmers were developing technologies in a particular direction. Limited documentation in Bolivia, nevertheless, prevented the further sharing of experiences amongst other staff and farmers. These institutional differences are cultural – an aspect of PM&E which has been little explored but has significant implications for the way information is obtained and used.

Evaluating farming systems change

In both countries the research process made new attempts to explore the range of factors affected by farming systems development. Through resource flow diagrams and semi-structured interviews, farmers were able to identify indicators which pointed out systems impacts that researchers had been unaware of. For example, in Laos management of cultured fish can affect wild fish populations. In Bolivia, growing contour hedgerows for soil conservation could affect cattle nutrition, or be affected by browsing cattle.

Farmers' indicators were themselves a valuable product of the research. In both projects indicators revealed farmers' understanding of ecological and economic processes and interactions. In particular, indicators of success identified by Bolivian farmers (described above) show that they understand the role of organic matter in conserving nutrients, humidity and soil.

The use of indicators in a matrix improved comparability before and after trials and across farming households. However, the research team found it more useful to complement the more rigid matrix method with more open methods that helped reveal unexpected outcomes or benefits, even though results may be less comparable and generalizable. For instance, the more open-ended use of methods in Bolivia showed that indicators can change over time, as farmers' experiments produced results which farmers and researchers did not expect.

Towards institutionalization: building on participatory evaluation of technologies

In both projects, an iterative approach to the research process incorporated stages of self-evaluation and learning, which led to local staff defining their own needs for PM&E. In Bolivia, workshops to share the experience with other CIAT staff and a range of NGOs have helped to draw out stronger conclusions about the usefulness of the research, including those reported in this chapter. In Laos, a key feature of PM&E was that it incorporated methods that staff had learnt and used in conducting other PRA work, thus building their confidence and understanding in applying the tools more flexibly. In both countries, staff have strengthened their understanding and capacities to plan, monitor and evaluate new technologies together with farmers, and to apply what they learn in other aspects of their work.

5

Experimenting with Participatory Monitoring in North-east Brazil: The case of AS-PTA's Projeto Paraíba[1]

PABLO SIDERSKY and IRENE GUIJT
(based on discussions with LUCIANO MARÇAL DA SILVERA
and MANOEL ROBERVAL DA SILVA)[2]

Introduction

DURING A WORKSHOP to further simplify a proposed monitoring process, an agronomist working for the Brazilian non-governmental organization (NGO), AS-PTA,[3] argued, 'I want the monitoring to continue independently of us. What use is it to choose indicators and use complicated and expensive monitoring methods that will be dropped as soon as we pull out?' This agronomist is involved with a three-year action research project to develop and test participatory methodologies for monitoring and impact analysis of sustainable agriculture, in which AS-PTA is collaborating with CTA-ZM[4] and the International Institute for the Environment and Development (IIED).

This chapter draws on two years of work by AS-PTA in the dry north-eastern state of Paraíba. Although many questions continue to be raised, (and some are still unanswered), we have gained precious insights into the practical meaning of participation in monitoring and impact assessment. We have discussed and debated the quality and the use of information, tested methods, and identified and revised indicators, and – above all – deeply experienced the importance of a flexible participatory monitoring methodology. After describing the context and the project, we present an overview of the path we have travelled to date, sharing key observations of what participation – for us – boils down to in the practice of participatory monitoring and evaluation (PM&E).

The region, the partners, and the strategy

The region

The Brazilian north-east is a huge tropical region of over 1.5 million square kilometres, ranging from the vast sugar cane estates along the coast to the semi-arid interior. Sandwiched in between lies the Agreste, a zone that is home to Projeto Paraíba. As elsewhere in Brazil, land area is concentrated in large holdings, yet the majority of farmers are smallholders, more than three-quarters of whom have less than five hectares.

The Agreste is characterized by its immense environmental variation, with diverse natural flora and widely differing agricultural systems. In 1994, AS-PTA's environmental survey with farmers identified ten environmental micro-zones (Petersen, 1995). Six production sub-systems were also identified: annual cropping, permanent cropping, livestock, home garden, extractivism,[5] and small-scale irrigated agriculture. Each micro-zone, therefore, contains several types of smallholder farms, each facing specific problems that hinder economic viability and agricultural sustainability.

In these diverse niches, farmers grow maize, common beans, and cassava, often adding a patch of sweet potato, lima beans, banana, or potato. A very short rotation cycle is common, sometimes giving way to permanent cultivation, with only occasional use of organic fertilizers and even rarer use of other agro-industrial inputs. Small-scale livestock is an important supplement to diets and incomes. Amidst the enormous diversity, virtually all smallholders face the same two basic problems:

o intense pressure on scarce natural resources (particularly soil, vegetation and genetic diversity)
o a large drop in agricultural income with the disappearance of cash crops.

Addressing the latter is clearly the first priority of local farmers.

The partners

Projeto Paraíba started in 1993 and is a local agricultural development programme run by AS-PTA. Projeto Paraíba's work focuses on the municipalities of Solânea and Remígio. Project activities are carried out by a team of five agricultural professionals, in partnership with *animadores*[6] (motivators) who are active members of the municipal rural trade unions, the STRs.[7] The STRs are AS-PTA's main partners in the project. They are crucial to the sustainability of the work, as they will carry on with the agricultural experimentation, innovation, and dissemination activities once AS-PTA moves on to other municipalities.

Besides the unions, small local farmer associations and farmers' experimentation groups are increasingly involved. Few communities have well-organized associations but their number is slowly increasing. The latter have no formal structure as yet but meet to discuss specific agricultural innovations with which they are involved, such as integrated pest management in banana stands or pigeon pea inter-cropping. These groups are facilitated by the *animadores* or AS-PTA staff. Project staff also interact infrequently with the local university, Enterprise for Technical Assistance and Rural Extension/Paraíba (EMATER/PB)[8] (the state-level agricultural extension service), and other NGOs in the region.

Projeto Paraíba's strategy and activities

The project has two strategic goals to address farmers' basic problems:

o conservation and regeneration of natural resources, focusing on soils and biodiversity o revival of household income, focusing on diversifying cash crops, including the reintroduction of abandoned cash crops.

The main priority is improving production systems, with plans to tackle marketing and processing aspects in future. Work revolves around innovation development and dissemination. Innovations include technology development, such as new inter-cropping patterns or soil preparation techniques, but also social innovations such as establishing community seed banks. Time is also invested by the project team on institutional development of local organizations, continual planning, and networking.

Projeto Paraíba operates on the principle that it is farmers who will ultimately be the managers of ongoing innovation and change, and so farmers are involved in the whole process of technological development and implementation. However, the team also recognizes that not all farmers are equally interested and/or able to participate in all aspects of agricultural innovation. Therefore, Projeto Paraíba works with three different levels of farmer participation:

o a core of about ten farmers, the *animadores*, involved in strategic planning, farmer-based experimentation, data analysis, and designing/implementing the monitoring and evaluation process
o a group of about 80 men and women farmers, including community-association leaders and individual farmers engaged in joint experimentation. Practically all are also involved in key moments of monitoring, evaluation and planning
o activity-specific collaboration with the general farming *publicó* and community associations, covering over 30 communities and between 400 and 500 farmers, who are keen to adopt particular measures and with whom the monitoring/evaluation findings are shared.

Farmer participation has been central to Projeto Paraíba from the first step in 1993, when a participatory agroecosystems appraisal was conducted with 30 farmers and STR representatives to analyse the regional agricultural crisis and local coping strategies. This formed the basis for designing the focus of the project. Since 1994, a permanent participatory planning process has been in place, with annual seminars bringing together about 40 farmers to review progress and reassess priorities. Outputs from farmer-based monitoring and annual evaluations provide essential planning inputs.

Projeto Paraíba can claim a range of impacts (AS-PTA, 1997; Guijt and Sidersky, 1998). Most relate to more sustainable use and conservation of natural resources through developing and disseminating less destructive agricultural practices. Progress is occurring with strengthening social sustainability through more secure livelihoods and more cohesive social organization and collective action. The team feels that it is clearly on the right track with its participatory approach, without which progress would be much slower. However, while promising, these results are not yet overwhelming – neither in terms of their geographic scale nor local impact. To understand better what was actually happening as a result of Projeto Paraíba, the project team decided that participatory monitoring of project impacts was necessary.

Participatory monitoring in Projeto Paraíba

Why monitor?

Several reasons led Projeto Paraíba to undertake more systematic monitoring of impacts. First, annual evaluations suffered due to a lack of data or lessons to analyse. Early attempts to monitor fieldwork were mainly driven by AS-PTA staff, with little or no participation of other partners. While producing some results, it contrasted starkly with the participatory principles of its work and provided insufficient data. AS-PTA hoped that by involving more of the local stakeholders, more accurate and relevant data could be collected. Developing a participatory monitoring and impact assessment was also considered an important capacity-building process for the entire project team.

Second, accountability to donors also became more urgent, now that the project had passed its inception phase and had clear objectives and activities. A third reason was the desire of both AS-PTA and the STRs to influence regional and national debates about the future of more sustainable agricultural alternatives. Discussions with government researchers and extension workers, and commercial local banks, emphasized the need for solid data to convince them of the merits of agricultural alternatives.

Thus, the monitoring project aimed to develop – together with the STRs, different farmer groups (interest groups, seed banks, etc.) and other stakeholders (i.e. funding agencies) – a participatory monitoring system to allow the collection and processing of more useful information with, perhaps, less effort (Guijt and Sidersky, 1996) and certainly more relevance. Above all, the system would have to be one that was meaningful locally and could be sustained by local partners.

The PM&E process

The action-research process started in January 1996 (see Box 5.1). Periodic workshops attended by all the partners, and facilitated by IIED,[9] have been the 'backbone' of the process. The workshops reviewed the quality and usefulness of the work done and of the results obtained. At each event, the work for the following period was also planned. In between, fieldwork was carried out by the *animadores* and AS-PTA staff who collected and analysed data. Data has fed into the annual evaluation and planning processes of Projeto Paraíba.

Getting started

The first workshop was attended by more than 30 participants, including AS-PTA staff, the IIED facilitator, *Sindicato* leaders and *animadores*, and other farmers. This was followed by several smaller meetings and another large workshop in July. By this stage, it was clear that the key partners for designing the monitoring process were the two STRs and AS-PTA staff. Farmers' perspectives are represented by the STR.

71

Box 5.1:	Time-line of the process
January 1996	**First workshop:** Discuss what monitoring involves and agree on a process to design and implement a system
February – June 1996	Meetings by partners to clarify objectives to be monitored
July 1996	**Second workshop:** Design first practical steps – final choice of indicators, choosing data gathering methods (several of which are from participatory rural appraisal (PRA)), training on use of methods, frequency and timing of data collection
August 1996 – February 1997	First stage of data collection and analysis
February 1997	**Third workshop**: First review of work done, revision of indicators, frequency and methods
March – October 1997	Second stage of data gathering and analysis
October 1997	**Fourth workshop**: Second review of strategy, process, methods, results plus expansion of domains that are being monitored
October 1997 – June 1998	Third stage of data gathering and analysis

During this period, the following were agreed:

○ objectives of Project Paraíba as viewed from the perspectives of AS-PTA and the STRs, plus prioritization of objectives for monitoring purposes
○ key indicators for tracking progress, i.e. the information needed to assess whether objectives were being achieved
○ methods for collecting and recording information which suited the indicators identified and the local cultural context.

To allow time to build monitoring skills, we consciously decided to start monitoring only part of the wide range of project activities that include dissemination, technology development through farmer experimentation, capacity building and networking. We aimed to expand the monitoring programme gradually until all aspects of the work are included. Based on intensive discussions and negotiations over a six-month period, the project team prioritized *technology dissemination* for monitoring, as technologies affect farmers' lives more directly and immediately. Three technologies that were being disseminated were selected for the monitoring: contour planting, banana weevil control, and community seed banks. One *technology development* activity was also prioritized: cattle-fodder alternatives.

For all four project activities selected for monitoring, AS-PTA and the two STRs reviewed separately what they expected as short- and medium-term results and long-term goals and developed them into what we called 'objective trees'. We thus had three sets of four 'trees' that required merging.

From theory to practice

The second workshop started by merging the three sets of trees into a single 'objectives tree', one for each of the four activities.[10] The 'trees' were massive, some having as many as 17 objectives (see Table 5.1). As everyone realized that it would be impossible to monitor all the objectives, we then had to prioritize which were most important. We tried to limit ourselves to only two objectives per activity but it was difficult to reach consensus on this.

Table 5.1: Objectives and indicators per activity

Prioritized activities	Total number of objectives identified	Number of objectives prioritized for monitoring	Number of indicators to be monitored
Community seed bank support	11	3	5
Banana weevil control	9	4	7
Contour planting	7	4	5
Alternative fodder production and storage	17	2	5
Total	44	13	22

Indicators were then identified for each of the prioritized objectives. This was carried out in several stages. First, a trial run was conducted with one activity – contour planting – in plenary, during which we selected indicators. This helped everyone understand the process. We then divided into three sub-groups, each with representation by the different partners. Each sub-group took one of the remaining three activities under its wing. The question posed to find good indicators for the prioritized objectives was: 'What information would you need to be convinced that you are making progress in achieving that objective?' There were many suggestions and much debating in the sub-groups, until agreement was reached on one or more indicators per objective. These were then presented in plenary again and refined, adjusted, and clarified until everyone understood what information we were trying to find. Despite attempts to limit the workload, 22 indicators were still chosen to be monitored!

Methods were then found to collect data for each of the indicators, drawing on both conventional (i.e. individual interviews) and more participatory methods, such as participatory mapping. This, too, was an interactive process. The IIED facilitator suggested two or more methods per indicator, drawing from a long list of possibilities.[11] Many of these were tested on the spot in the workshop through simulations. Then the group discussed the feasibility of each and selected the most suitable ones, adjusting each method to better fit the indicator, staff skills, and cultural context. Some methods, including quantified impact flow diagrams, were tested with farmers (Guijt and Sidersky, 1996) but considered too complicated and discarded for the time being. Maps and diagram-based group and individual forms were selected as the best methods to apply in this early phase. Once the methods and indicators were clear, the frequency and scheduling of data collection and analysis were identified and everything was placed on a single 'monitoring calendar' with clear allocation of who was responsible for what.

From August onwards, the monitoring calendar guided the fieldwork for data collection and analysis. This effort took a considerable amount of time. Table 5.2 gives an idea of how data was gathered for assessing the seed bank activity. The picture was much the same for the other three activities.

Table 5.2: Participatory monitoring of community seed banks

Objectives	Indicators	Data collection methods	Fieldwork
Ensure poor farmers' have access to good-quality seed at the right time	Proportion of 'easy access' seed (from seed bank or farmers' own stock) compared to 'difficult access' seed (bought seed or 'sharecropping' seed)[12]	Individual interview form	60 farmers in communities with seed banks and 60 in communities without seed banks were interviewed by *animadores*
Lower expenditure on seed	Expenditure on seed for a seed bank member compared to non-member	Same form as above	see above
More community independence of seed companies through well-run seed banks	Seed returned after harvest, compared to seed borrowed	Seed bank control form	Improving the forms already used by community members responsible for seed bank
	Quality of stored seed	New method being trialled with university to test germination quality	
	Size of seed bank committee and participation of committee members	Indicator not monitored by team but intention is to encourage seed banks to do this themselves	

Reviewing the first round

Early in 1997 a third workshop was held with the *animadores*, AS-PTA staff and the IIED facilitator. The monitoring activities carried out were reviewed and results analysed (see Box 5.2).

Box 5.2: Checking the monitoring process

To evaluate the experiences, the team used four criteria to assess the methods and two to assess the indicator. These criteria were selected before the workshop by a small organizing committee consisting of two AS-PTA staff members, one *Sindicato* representative, and the IIED facilitator. They were discussed in plenary and adjusted during the workshop before they were used.

Method-related criteria

o the level of participation of farmers in the collection, collation, and analysis of the data, and dissemination of the findings
o time demand (for collection, collation, analysis and dissemination)
o the degree of difficulty of applying the method (mainly for collection and analysis)
o the potential for others outside the current monitoring group (e.g. farmers, community associations) to use the methods

Indicator-related criteria

o reliability of the information
o relevance of the final information (for different audiences: farmers, union, NGOs, donors, public agencies)

Methods were adjusted, tips exchanged about dealing with application problems, and the importance realized of always keeping the end-use of the information in mind. The team also recognized the importance of conducting immediate assessments each time a new monitoring method is used, to ensure ongoing learning.

Sources: Abbot and Guijt (1998); AS-PTA, CTA-ZM and IIED (1997).

Overall, the group concluded that farmer participation in data collection was high during this first period. But the same cannot be said for the data analysis, where *animadores* and particularly AS-PTA staff dominated and data was sometimes analysed later in the AS-PTA office. We realized that though the participatory monitoring process was an improvement on conventional, extractive monitoring, involving farmers in data analysis was still crucial if the information was to have some meaning for them.

The data gathered revealed interesting insights. The best example of this is the data on the impact of contour and *atravessado*[13] planting obtained with the participatory mapping exercises that were carried out in seven communities (AS-PTA, CTA-ZM, and IIED, 1997). Much to everyone's surprise, the data showed that downhill planting, which was thought to be widespread, had decreased dramatically in favour of more soil conserving practices. Notwithstanding the team's intense efforts over the past two years, everyone realized they could not claim responsibility for this great improvement. Several questions remained unanswered by the monitoring results including 'What other factor had caused the switch?' More importantly, was it still worth while investing time in training farmers on contour planting and should Projeto Paraíba drop this activity, or was the monitoring process fraught with ambiguous questions? The team decided to undertake a mini-appraisal in a sample of communities to understand better the situation regarding land preparation and to review that aspect of its work again.

Another finding was the limited progress with regard to monitoring farmer experimentation with alternative fodder production and storage. It struck us that the distinction between monitoring technology dissemination as compared with monitoring an experimentation process was significant. In the case of dissemination activities, the monitoring scope was clear and the approach straightforward: assessing the presence of each activity in a sample of farmers or communities, and the impact on farmers' lives. In the case of technology development, monitoring focuses on the progress of the proposed development process. Therefore, the area covered, the types of indicators, and the people involved will vary. It was clear that we needed a strategy to encourage each group to design and implement the monitoring of its own experimentation activities. Therefore, we set out a series of steps and discussion questions for the groups to help them define a useful monitoring system (Guijt and Siderksy, 1998; AS-PTA, CTA-ZM and IIED, 1997).

The high workload was confirmed as a problem by the *animadores* and AS-PTA staff alike. Out of the 22 indicators selected for monitoring, the team actually only monitored 17 (see Table 5.3), as some indicators and methods proved difficult to measure in practice. One example is 'production from banana stands where weevil control was being practised as compared with control plots with no weevil control'. Comparing production from different plots was considered too fraught with uncontrollable variables to produce reliable data.

Table 5.3: Planned versus actual monitoring in 1996

Prioritized activities	Indicators to be monitored	Indicators actually monitored
Community seed bank support	5	3
Banana-weevil control	7	2 planned; 3 new ones
Contour planting	5	5
Alternative fodder production and storage	5	4
Total	22	17

Some data was collected but was not systematised or analysed, probably because we had not developed a clear enough way of documenting and analysing the information. It is also possible that despite the participatory process, the *animadores* were still unclear about the usefulness of some information. In other cases, team members simply did not find the time. Despite these problems, few radical changes were made in the monitoring programme for the 1997 season. People felt that better integration of monitoring with everyday project activities would greatly enhance efficiency, thereby making it possible to monitor the same indicators. The easiest way to achieve better integration was only to undertake monitoring activities if the *animadores* had planned to visit communities or farmers for other reasons as well. We agreed to repeat the data collection and analysis for all the indicators monitored so far, as well as those that had been omitted.

At this stage, the data was already proving very useful for AS-PTA, who made ample use of it in the annual reports and in an external evaluation. Whether it was as useful for *Sindicatos* and experimenting farmers was unclear at the time. All that can be said is that, along with AS-PTA staff, the *animadores* showed interest in discussing more thoroughly the value of the dissemination activities that were the backbone of Projeto Paraíba. Overall, it strengthened the team's awareness that much more effort was needed in the area of participatory technology development before proceeding to the full-scale dissemination of the technological innovations.

Changes to match reality

The fourth workshop was held in October 1997. Attendance increased with the presence of newly elected *Sindicato* leaders from Solanea. This required a detailed summary of the work undertaken to date to bring the new people up to speed on events. Though their participation in the actual monitoring is unlikely, their support for the work of the *animadores* is crucial for long-term sustainability of the efforts (see the last section of this chapter).

A thorough mid-term evaluation of the work from March to October showed that reality had imposed some significant changes on the monitoring tasks. Although some tasks were still scheduled until January 1998, it was clear that the fieldwork in 1997 was not as similar to the 1996 work as we had expected.

There was progress in monitoring work with four farmer experimentation groups. The group working with yam as a new cash crop to be distributed via a seed bank made much progress: it defined its objectives, indicators and methods. Members then designed their own data-registration form, which was to be filled in by all seed bank beneficiaries. Although some farmers found it difficult to fill in the form and required help from the *animadores*, group members played an active role in data analysis. Data collected was brought together by AS-PTA and the *animadores*, organized and fed back to the group (in the form of tables, averages, etc.). This simple initiative resulted in a collective discussion on the results of the yam activities. Analysis and the interpretation of data involved not only AS-PTA and the *animadores* but also the farmers' group as a whole. Good progress was also made in the fodder production and storage experimentation group, but the other two had been too unsystematic to bear much fruit, and another four groups had yet to start discussing monitoring of their efforts.

There was significantly improved participation in the monitoring of the community seed banks. As mentioned above, data was collected, systematized with the local seed bank committee and analysed with the whole group (of all the committees together). This event provoked much discussion in the communities and in the seed bank committees, and was considered an important step in moving towards encouraging each seed bank to develop its own monitoring system, rather than participating in Projeto Paraíba's process.

Another interesting development was the complete change in the monitoring of contour planting. Since the 1996 monitoring results had cast doubts on the merits of this activity, training in contour planting had decreased considerably. Instead of monitoring the five indicators defined in 1996 (see Table 5.1), a totally different path was followed. AS-PTA staff and *animadores* undertook a participatory appraisal exercise in two communities. In-depth discussions with farmers on how they prepared their plots for sowing and whether contour planting was a useful alternative or not, led the group to better understand why many farmers were opting for contour planting.[14] It confirmed the accuracy of the 1996 monitoring data in one of the visited communities;[15] thus, the team agreed the need to rethink its entire strategic approach to soil conservation in the region. The monitoring from 1996 clearly had an important impact on this project activity, as the data forced the team to rethink its assumptions about the region and its strategy. It is exactly this type of internal learning that makes collective monitoring such a valuable process.

Indicators were reassessed, yet again, quite simply in terms of 'who was using (or going to use) the information'. If neither the STRs nor AS-PTA were interested, the indicators were dropped or modified. Discussions also included the question of widening the scope of the monitoring process. As mentioned before, the first steps with monitoring only touched on part of Projeto Paraíba's range of activities: innovation development and dissemination. The team identified four additional aspects of Projeto Paraíba's work which they wanted to monitor:

○ contribution to changing municipal policy towards more sustainable agricultural alternatives
○ improved participatory communication methodology with farmers
○ creating a new STR approach on rural regeneration and sustainable development[16]
○ developing strategic alliances for sustainable agriculture.

Everyone agreed that they would not repeat the process of identifying relevant activities, objectives, indicators and methods as was used for the activities of dissemination and innovation. This was partly out of a concern about the time involved but also due to the very intangible nature of changes related to these themes.

It was therefore decided to experiment with a methodology suggested by the IIED facilitator, one that was developed by the Christian Commission for Development (CCDB) in Bangladesh and Rick Davies (Centre of Development Studies, Swansea) (see Davies, 1998). In essence, this approach requires each STR and AS-PTA to discuss in separate groups what the *single most significant change* is for each of the broad themes during a given period, without referring to pre-determined objectives, indicators, etc.

They agreed to report their identified 'most significant changes' to each other every three months, thus giving four monitoring moments per year.

A trial run of the method was carried out, using the theme 'improved participatory communication methodology with farmers' and discussing the most significant change during the September to November period. General enthusiasm for this system was tempered by some doubts about the difficulty of assessing trends. As the themes were very broad, it was likely that the significant changes identified would vary from one monitoring event to the next, making it difficult to track if specific changes were sustained or not. Nevertheless, everyone agreed it was worthwhile testing it for the next nine months.

It's not as easy as it looks: First lessons from practice

While firm conclusions lie ahead, the work to date has been inspiring and revealing. In this final section we discuss some of the initial results and critical questions and problems, thus offering some words of advice and encouragement to others interested in the path we have travelled.

Participation shaping the process

The monitoring work started in January 1996 with the three key stakeholder groups who form Projeto Paraíba: AS-PTA, *Sindicatos* and farmers. It soon became clear that as individual farmers are not full partners in Projeto Paraíba as a whole (see Box 5.1), it therefore did not make sense to involve them in the monitoring design process at this stage. The four big workshops that were key moments of in-depth discussion were not able to include the 400-plus families who are involved in the sustainable agriculture work. Some farmers attended these workshops but in no way could they be considered representatives of 'farmers' as a distinct group. The monitoring process thus focused around the information needs of AS-PTA and the *Sindicatos*. This probably influenced the limited local interest in analysis during the first applications of the monitoring methods. If larger numbers of farmers drive the technology development and dissemination work, they are likely to find the monitoring of their own efforts more relevant than when the work is driven by only a few. However, achieving farmer participation in monitoring activities may be more difficult, especially when the group is not clearly defined and of a manageable size. For instance, involving farmers in data analysis may be possible if the group concerned is a part of a seed bank or a farmer experimentation group. But how does one obtain feedback when the concerned group is 'farmers' as a whole – each with individual, rather than collective information needs?

Over time, two new players appeared on the scene: community seed banks (with their committees), and farmer experimentation groups. These are slowly becoming new (and for the time being informal) associates of Projeto Paraíba. Their increasing participation in collecting and analysing monitoring data has led to discussions regarding their own objectives and what *they* might want to monitor and how. These needs were not incorporated in the original design of the monitoring system.

As these new players become more involved in Projeto Paraíba, the monitoring system will no doubt need to be reviewed yet again. For example, the community seed banks may well decide to prioritize other objectives and indicators that are not a priority for AS-PTA or the *Sindicatos*. This implies that the monitoring of that particular activity may be handed over entirely to the seed banks themselves, with AS-PTA and the *Sindicatos* monitoring only their involvement in the banks rather than the performance of the seed banks as a whole. However, this raises an important issue, as AS-PTA will still need some information for its advocacy work and accountability requirements on the impact of the seed banks. What will happen if this information is of no interest to all or some of the banks? Will AS-PTA have to produce this information itself then? Does this not bring the issue full circle – that is, with AS-PTA needing to monitor performance of the seed banks irrespective of local interest?

The institutional design of Projeto Paraíba as a whole is still evolving and the monitoring process must evolve alongside. The more these new players get involved, the greater the likelihood that different needs, objectives, and indicators will appear. The trend is towards a certain decentralization, or even fragmentation, of the participatory monitoring process. Many questions loom ahead. What could be the implications of this? Is this good or bad for the monitoring process as a whole?

Flexibility is crucial

Monitoring systems, with their obsession for pre-determined indicators, are generally viewed as static systems with fixed players. As discussed above, our reality has proven the opposite. When we started, few of us knew what a good indicator could be, what viable methods existed 'out there', how often data should be collected, and what kind of information was actually going to be useful for our aims (see 'Why monitor?'). By trial and error, we have slowly progressed towards a more relevant and viable monitoring system, with project objectives and indicators changing along the way.

For those interested in seeing trends for fixed indicators, this fluid process poses a problem. Any change to an indicator means reducing the possibility of producing a time series of data. Yet if a monitoring process is going to be participatory, in many contexts this means including those for whom monitoring and impact assessment are new, and accommodating an ever-changing combination of stakeholder groups. Such processes are likely to undergo similar changes to those we have experienced, as the people involved learn and adapt. A PM&E system has to be responsive to changing information needs, changing skills of those involved, and, indeed, changing levels of participation as new partners join and others leave.

A critical question appears to be whether the need for changes will diminish with time, as the partners become clearer about the kind of information that is important to collect and analyse, and the partnership itself matures. Overall, obtaining a time series of monitoring data should not be considered impossible. However, such a series may well only prove relevant or feasible for those indicators that are general but remain important enough over time irrespective of project activities, such as 'well-being of participating families' or 'local capacity building in planning agricultural innovations'. The CCDB work illustrates how monitoring can remain effective over time despite changes in the context. The secret to its success lies in the general level at which the nature of themes are defined, which contrasts with the specific objectives that AS-PTA is monitoring. Long-term objectives, such as 'poverty reduction', 'forming strategic alliances', 'influencing municipal policy' are less likely to change than shorter-term objectives, such as 'numbers of farmers planting along the contours' or 'amount of seed returned to the seed bank'. Yet the longer term and more abstract the objective, the more difficult cause–effect linkages will be – for example, that supporting of seed banks led to a reduction in poverty.

Useful information for whom?

The continual reviews of the monitoring system have improved data collection to the point where we feel the data quality is satisfactory. But for whom is the information useful? Who 'owns' the information and where is it currently located? Individual farmers, farmer organizations and NGOs do not have the same information needs and interests. For example, the number of farmers adopting contour planting is important information for AS-PTA and, perhaps, for the STRs. But it is hardly so for the individual farmer.

As discussed above, most of the data has been very useful for AS-PTA reports and project documentation.[17] With the *Sindicatos*, the case is slightly different. They are clearly interested in the data and, therefore, are tempted to say that it is a priority for them. However, we are under the impression that they have not used it independently of project activities. For example, the *animadores* and *Sindicato* leaders were delighted to see that the seed banks had made a big difference in farmers' access to seed, but to our knowledge, they have not made direct use of this information in a publication, an information panel for *Sindicato* associates or negotiations with the local bank manager. Unless the information starts to be useful for the STRs, and remains focused around Projeto Paraíba, the system may well collapse once AS-PTA moves to other municipalities.

It is too early to make conclusions about what this means for the sustainability of the monitoring system, as information that has not yet been used could suddenly become very useful. It may also be that it has already been used without our knowledge. What our experience has shown is the importance of seeing monitoring essentially as an information system, a system that needs to have a 'home' and that is only worth while if the information is shared (Rodenburg, 1995). Finding a sustainable 'home' for the process and ensuring that information is shared thus requires further work on our part.

Sustainable monitoring and impact analysis?

Our experiences with participatory monitoring and impact analysis have helped us to challenge some common beliefs. One of these is the ongoing search (with which many funding agencies are involved) for indicators that are universally applicable to tracking changes in sustainable agriculture projects. If indicators concern context-specific objectives, then logically it follows they will vary from one situation to the next. Our indicators make sense for Projeto Paraíba – and may well prove irrelevant in other contexts. Yet we feel that our general process of developing a monitoring system has wider significance and can be replicated.

We have experienced how difficult it is to achieve 100 per cent participation of all stakeholders in a PM&E process. Not all people want to be involved – and not all are needed. Related to this, we have been buffeted particularly by the very dynamic and unpredictable processes that the *Sindicatos* experience, with internal politics and regular elections forcing changes in the people involved. The fledgling farmer experimentation groups and seed banks have added to the ever-changing institutional context of the monitoring work. It has made us aware of the extra difficulty of setting up a monitoring system with partners who do not have a certain degree of institutional stability and maturity. However, involving this growing group of partners, has also helped us take one step further in realizing one of the central objectives of Projeto Paraíba: that of strengthening local capacity for project planning and institutional learning.

The luxury of three years' funding to explore this process and taking small steps at a time are unlikely to be available for other organizations. But it is a luxury that has helped us learn what others may also find useful. Above all, we feel that realism about what PM&E can deliver is key. Repeatedly asking ourselves 'for whom is this information useful?' has helped us keep our feet firmly on the ground.

Part 2

Learning with Communities

6

Strengthening Citizen Participation and Democratization in the Philippines: ELF's Impact Evaluation

ROY V. ABES

Background

THE EDUCATION FOR LIFE FOUNDATION (ELF) is a non-governmental organization (NGO) working to strengthen grassroots organizations for greater citizen participation and democratization. It aims to build a dynamic civil society that actively participates in public affairs, and can effectively negotiate with local government and other powerful players to ensure they are more accountable to community needs.

ELF's main project is the Philippine-Danish Folkschool (*Paaralang Bayan*). The school provides different leadership formation programmes for community-based grassroots leaders, through working in partnership with field-based NGOs, people's organizations (POs), and in some cases, local government units. The key principles that shape the leadership programme reflect ELF's focus on democracy and local governance, agrarian and asset reform, sustainable development, gender equality, and environmental protection. Participants for the leadership programmes are selected based on the recommendations of ELF's field-based partners.

Main components of the Paaralang Bayan

Paaralang Bayan supports five leadership training activities:

○ life history workshops: a five-day sharing of life experiences and lessons from prospective participants prior to the general leadership course (see below). This serves to assess training needs and integrate participants in the leadership course
○ general leadership courses (GLC): six-week courses covering topics related to leadership formation, namely: effective communication, negotiation, conflict management, organizational development, project development, culture, research methodologies (i.e. *Sikolohiyang Pilipino*, (SP) discussed below), gender, ecology, popular economics, politics, health, leadership, and empowerment

○ special leadership course: intended to meet the continuing educational needs of graduates of the GLC (also referred to as 'leader-graduates')
○ short courses on specific needs identified by communities, groups or organizations, which are open to anyone
○ a new distance-education programme, which has also been developed – initially for ELF-trained leaders.

In addition to these programmes, ELF also supports a popular economics programme which provides popular economics courses and other training activities to help leader-graduates successfully develop and implement socio-economic projects in their communities.

ELF has also established a Research and Evaluation Programme (REP) to develop participatory evaluation methodologies and strengthen the research skills of leader-graduates. The REP carries out participatory evaluation activities that enable ELF as a learning institution to theorize from its practice, and train leader-graduates to become researchers themselves and to learn directly from their communities.

Between 1992 and 1996, a total of 866 community leaders from 42 provinces, 211 municipalities, and 502 *barangays*[1] (villages) in the Philippines have participated in the GLC. This chapter describes the initial experiences of developing a three-year participatory impact evaluation of ELF's leadership programme. The findings and conclusions remain, at best, very tentative as ELF and its partners are still in the process of synthesizing and writing-up the results of the last three years of research. This chapter focuses on the first year (1996) and the process of designing the participatory impact evaluation.[2] It looks at the methodology and data gathering tools used, as well as the process of developing indicators for conducting subsequent evaluations.

Recognizing the value of participatory evaluation

Early on, ELF recognized the importance of evaluating its leadership programme, both as a learning tool for participants (community leaders) and as a means of ensuring that trainings were appropriate and addressed their needs. However, making sure that an evaluation adequately measured how much difference our programme had made locally was not an easy task. Our initial efforts to evaluate the programme remained largely undocumented and lacked systematic measurement. Attempts at evaluation occurred during group reflections immediately after trainings, during staff visits or reunions, and through anecdotes describing the positive impact of ELF leader-graduates on their organizations and communities. The stories were elating and encouraging, but we had no way of determining how widespread these impacts were – and if these were 'valid' and representative.

Aside from this informal evaluation, two systematic evaluations of the programme were undertaken during the first phase of the project cycle in 1995, in collaboration with funding partners, the Philippine Psychological Research and Training House (PPRTH), ELF staff, and several leader-graduates. The findings revealed that ELF leadership formation activities, such as the GLCs, influenced individual leaders positively, who, in turn, were able to serve their organizations and communities more effectively. While these studies provided positive feedback, we had no baseline information against which we could compare them from other community leaders who had not attended ELF's leadership courses. Hence, we could not easily learn what *difference* ELF's leadership programme had made to leader-graduates, their organizations and communities. Therefore, it became necessary to develop another way of evaluating the programme, in terms of establishing baseline data and comparison areas, and developing the research skills of leader-graduates so that they would play a key role in subsequent evaluations.

In parallel with our second project cycle phase (1996–1998), ELF initiated a three-year longitudinal impact evaluation. By involving leader-graduates, we were moving towards making evaluation a more participatory process. Their involvement was regarded as part of building their leadership capabilities, as the evaluation methodology can be used in their own organizations and communities. It involved other stakeholders as well, including ELF staff, PPRTH, and the communities of leader-graduates. We also worked with a comparison group, comprising community leaders who had not participated in any ELF course. The following lists the main objectives of the evaluation:

○ to determine the impact of ELF's courses on its leader-graduates
○ to determine the impact of leader-graduates on their respective communities
○ to involve leader-graduates as researchers, so that they can further build their competencies
○ to help individual leader-graduates to be aware of their own development by involving them in the study and sharing the results with them
○ to popularize and further develop indigenous methods and instruments for data gathering and analysis, in particular the SP methodology ('Filipino psychology', see below)
○ to contribute to theory-building on grassroots leadership in the Philippines.

So far, 23 rural communities (*barangays*) have taken part in the participatory evaluation (PE) process (14 in leader-graduate communities, 9 in communities identified as the comparison group). These are distributed across five provinces in the country, namely Bataan, Mindoro, Nueva Ecija, Pampanga and Zambales.

Stages of the participatory impact-evaluation

At the time this chapter was first drafted, we were just about to complete the second phase (1997) of the three-year evaluation process; therefore, only the findings from the initial phase (1996) were readily available. In the first year, ELF worked closely with PPRTH to design the participatory impact evaluation in terms of selecting the sample size, leader-researchers, indicators to be monitored, data gathering methods, and baseline data. In the second year, the leader-researchers worked on validating the baseline information with communities, following up training, and conducting a second round of data gathering to verify selected indicators. The final phase of the evaluation, which was still ongoing in 1998, has involved a third round of data collection and will provide a comparative review of findings over the last three years.

Each phase of the three-year impact evaluation began in the month of July and lasted for a month and a half (or about six weeks). The following describes in greater detail the stages of developing the PE process.

Preparatory stage

The first stage required careful planning, training of leader-researchers, and designing the PE process with them. We were unable to involve all the many hundreds of leader-graduates. Instead, we selected a sample of 24 leader-graduates and their communities from two GLC courses conducted in 1996. The leaders came from five provinces (Bataan, Mindoro, Nueva Ecija, Pampanga and Zambales). All leader-graduates were eager to participate, as they wanted to reflect on their own progress and identify possible areas for improving their leadership skills. An additional sample of 24 community leaders, who had not joined any of ELF's leadership courses, was selected as a comparison group.

Seven groups of people have been involved in the evaluation process, in many different ways. Table 6.1 shows the level of participation of different groups at different stages of the research. ELF is now working to enhance the role that all groups can play in the entire evaluation process.

Table 6.1: Level of participation of the different groups involved in the evaluation process

Stages	ELF staff	PPRTH	LRs	LGs	LG communities	Non LGs	Communities of non LGs
Planning	H	H	M				
Training of LRs	H	H	H				
Design	H	H	M				
Data collection	M	M	H	L	L	L	L
Data collection/ analysis and validation	M	H	H	L		L	L
Data presentation/ report writing	M	H	L				
Use of the evaluation findings	H	M	H	H	M	M	M
Assessment of the impact evaluation	H	H	H	M	L	L	L

Key: Group: LRs = leader-researchers; LGs = leader-graduates; non LGs = leaders not trained by ELF
Level of participation: H = High, M = Medium, L = Low, not involved

86

During the preparation stage, ELF and PPRTH staff along with leader-graduates selected criteria to assess the impacts of leadership courses. Two different types of evaluation criteria were chosen:

○ those that assess changes at the individual leader-graduate level
○ those that look at community-level changes (see Table 6.2).

Table 6.2: Selected criteria for evaluating ELF's leadership training programme

Individual level (leader-graduate)	Community level
1 Their notions and practices of 'democracy, citizenship, gender roles, community development, environmental protection, active and effective participation of community members in public affairs'	1 Community members' notions and practices of 'democracy, citizenship, gender roles, community development, environmental protection, active and effective participation of community members in public affairs'
2 their capacity to manage projects	2 livelihood and household income
3 their livelihood	3 level and quality of participation of community members in public affairs
4 their household income	4 level of government services provided in response to community action
5 their own perceptions of being a leader	5 capacity of grassroots organization to manage projects
6 personality characteristics, i.e. self-esteem	6 community members' perceptions of leader's capacity to manage projects
	7 community members' perceptions of leadership qualities in their leader
	8 community members' perceptions of their leader's personality characteristics, including self-esteem

Each of these evaluation criteria was to be assessed annually from 1996 to 1998. By obtaining baseline information in the first year based on these criteria, we hoped to be able to develop a three-year comparative assessment of the impacts of ELF's leadership programme.

In the preparation stage, both leader-researchers and ELF staff underwent training on participatory principles and SP, the methodology to be used for carrying out the participatory evaluation. As will be discussed further below, the Filipino cultural context was recognized as a vital factor in the evaluation process itself; hence, awareness of the concepts and methods of SP was an important prerequisite.

Participatory rural appraisal (PRA) techniques were also adopted, but would be used mainly in the third phase (1998) of the evaluation. PRA techniques not only serve as a validation tool, but also allow us to plan future activities with leader-graduates and help them to further enhance their leadership capability.

The PE process itself was regarded as further training and capacity building for the leader-graduates. The training initially provided leader-researchers with a theoretical background on evaluation research. This included training in using SP methods, qualitative data gathering, documentation, and analysis. However, the training also served as 'hands-on' learning, involving leaders in the actual planning, design, and implementation of the impact evaluation itself.

Linking data gathering to Filipino psychology

The data gathering methods were developed by PPRTH and the Psychological Association of the Philippines (*Pambansang Samahan ng Sikolohiyang Pilipino/PSSP*). They include:

○ guided discussions
○ story-telling
○ asking questions (*pagtatanong-tanong*)
○ observation
○ psychological assessments
○ surveys
○ interviews.

These methods and the norms for validating information used by leader-researchers take into account Filipino local culture and language.

Filipino psychology identifies eight levels of relationship that characterize how Filipinos interact with other people. These levels of relationship centre around the concept of 'insiders' and 'outsiders' and are viewed across a continuum (see Table 6.3).

Table 6.3: Eight levels of relationship in Filipino psychology

Outsider	Civility	(*Pakikitungo*)
	Mixing	(*Pakikisalamuha*)
	Joining/participating	(*Pakikilahok*)
	Conforming	(*Pakikibagay*)
	Adjusting	(*Pakikisama*)
	Mutual trust/rapport	(*Pakikipagpalagayang loob*)
	Getting involved	(*Pakikisangkot*)
Insider	Fusion, oneness, full trust	(*Pakikiisa*)

The relationships range from 'respectful civility' (*pakikitungo*) to 'oneness' (*pakikiisa*). To gather valid and reliable data, researchers have to cultivate at least the sixth level of relationship – that of mutual trust and rapport. Hence, researchers need to spend time in one area and become 'insiders' by staying and integrating themselves into the community: participating and being part of the natural flow and rhythm of life in the locality; being sensitive to and respectful of the values, traditions, norms, and taboos; and being truthful about the purpose of her or his stay.

Leader-researchers were assigned to visit different communities (other than their own).[3] A contact or 'bridge' person was initially required who could introduce the leader-researchers to the community and find a place for the researchers to stay. There, the leader-researchers usually stayed for about a week – during which data was obtained. Because leader-researchers already have a grounded grasp of realities at the grassroots, and in some cases may even speak the local dialect, it did not take long for leader-researchers to integrate themselves into the communities. Leader-researchers organized discussion groups and/or story-telling sessions, and even took part in the natural and regular discussions that are part of the oral tradition of information exchange in the communities. These sessions were generally open to the public and invited those people interested to join in the discussions.

Three tools of SP were used to obtain information. Because data gathering took place mostly through discussions, these were tape-recorded by leader-researchers and later transcribed.

(1) *Pagtatanong-tanong* (asking questions) was a local way of asking questions characterized by a casual approach and thus differing from formal interviews or surveys (in which one person usually asked the questions and another responded). In *pagtatanong-tanong*, both researchers and participants could ask each other questions. Both could equally decide on the process of *pagtatanong-tanong* – what types of questions were asked, and the appropriate time and place.

For instance, with regard to issues of democracy, some questions that were asked included: 'Can you recall events within your community during which you considered democracy to be absent/present? Can you describe them?' Regarding issues of citizenship, some questions included: 'What does a "good citizen" do?, What does a "bad citizen" do? What does the concept of "inalienable rights of a citizen" mean to you? What are the duties of a citizen?'

Leader-researchers also asked people how they perceived their community leaders: 'What do you think are the strengths of your leader? What do you consider to be her/his main weaknesses? What can you say about her/his style of leadership in the organization/*barangay*?' Certainly, how questions were formulated depended on the particular context or setting. Given the turbulent political history of the country under the Marcos dictatorship (1972–1986), several topics – notably issues of democracy – remained highly sensitive and were not openly discussed during the researchers' initial stay in the community.

(2) *Ginabayang talakayan* (GT) (guided discussion), was a semi-structured discussion between several people (usually about eight) focusing on one topic or issue. Before a GT session began, participants and leader-researchers first decided on a specific issue to discuss and on the objectives of their discussion. Some topics for discussion included issues pertaining to gender roles and the environment. Leader-researchers facilitated and encouraged community members to participate in analysing what was being discussed. A documentor was usually assigned to note down the main points of the discussion in front of everyone so that they were readable to all participants.

(3) *Pakikipagkuwentuhan* (story-telling), has been one of the favourite pastimes of Filipinos, especially in the rural areas. Similar to the process of *pagtatanong-tanong*, in *pakikipagkuwentuhan* both researchers

and community members participated in the discussions and took turns sharing stories about a particular theme or topic.

Data collation and analysis

Tape-recorded sessions of *pagtatanong-tanong, pakikipagkuwentuhan,* and *ginabayang talakayan* were then transcribed and data analysed by leader-researchers, using the Key Judges (KJ) method. This method clusters and labels the data, provided there is consensus from at least three people. Leader-researchers identified key findings and clustered information based on the evaluation criteria which they had selected earlier (see Table 6.2). An important outcome of this process was that it required leader-researchers to discuss among themselves and reach consensus on the findings, i.e. how data should be clustered. The process of data analysis allowed leader-researchers to learn from each other and to find out about community perspectives on leadership.

Based on the information generated from the communities, leader-researchers were able to identify a preliminary set of indicators, and establish a baseline for evaluating the leadership training. One important result of the first year of research revealed how communities defined their notion of 'democracy' (see Box 6.1).

Data validation

After collating the data, leader-researchers held community meetings in both leader-graduate communities and the comparison group areas (communities with no ELF training). Clustered data generated from *pakikipagkuwentuhan, pagtatatanong-tanong* and *ginabayang talakayan* sessions were presented to the community for validation. Leader-researchers explained how they analysed data, clustered information, and inferred indicators based on participants' responses (see Box 6.1). After data was presented, community members were given the opportunity to provide feedback, comments, and suggestions.

This stage of validating findings proved valuable because it allowed further analysis of the data. Community members gave additional input and ascertained whether the clustered information and selected indicators adequately captured their realities and perspectives. In some cases, even choosing or agreeing on the 'appropriate' word to represent an idea or concept stimulated further group discussion. The results of the discussions showed that leaders, even in comparison areas, found the evaluation to be a positive learning process. As one community leader commented, 'It is good to know these things. We had no time and opportunity to discuss these in the past because we were busy at work. But now, we are here and have a deeper understanding of our community.'

Report writing and sharing

By identifying indicators and establishing baseline data in the first year, we hoped to compare findings about the impacts of the leadership trainings

Box 6.1: How communities defined 'democracy'

The first phase of the research attempted to establish how communities in the five provinces defined whether democracy was present or absent in various contexts. Community members who participated in the *pakikipagkuwentuhan* data gathering sessions were asked to recall situations which indicated for them the presence and absence of democracy, within their families, their POs, and their community as a whole (see Table 6.4).

With regard to the family, the main indicator for democratic practice was independent decision making, i.e. children choosing their own college courses, family members voting on the basis of their own preferences. Another indicator was the absence of hierarchy between siblings, i.e. older siblings dominating younger family members, as is traditionally the case in Filipino culture.

With regard to their organizations, democracy was said to be present when members have freedom of participation, thought, speech, movement, consultation and decision making. Democracy was 'when things were going right with the organization', i.e. rules and guidelines of the organization were properly implemented. Democracy was said to be absent when there were problems with the leadership (i.e. inaction, conflict among leaders, skills and attitudes that are considered unbecoming in a good leader), lack of transparency in financial matters, lack of unity among members, among others. For community members, their leaders played a critical role in ensuring that democracy prevailed within their organizations. For instance, participants in *pakikipagkuwentuhan* sessions said that democracy was absent when leaders' assumed the sole responsibility for decision making, when the style of leadership was dictatorial, when leaders were not held accountable for their actions, or when there was nepotism or corruption amongst leaders.

With regard to the community or *barangay* in general, people's indicators of democracy included: respect for individual rights, communication between community leaders, and upholding of the laws of government. By contrast, people viewed undemocratic communities as characterized by: disrespect for individual rights and laws, political oppression (i.e. no free elections, leadership is dictatorial and exploitative), lack of transparency, and inequality (i.e. prices are controlled by those who have the capital).

over the next two years. We are now in the process of completing the third and last phase of the impact evaluation. Report writing for each year was initially undertaken by PPRTH, but it is now mainly carried out by ELF.[4] The reports are a compilation of what leader-researchers have written about their experiences, reflections, and insights into conducting the impact evaluation. The reports have focused on two areas: (i) findings of the research, and (ii) lessons from applying the SP methodology.

Table 6.4: Community indicators of democracy, based on *pakikipagkuwentuhan* sessions conducted in leader-graduate communities of Bataan, Mindoro, Neuva Ecija, Pampanga and Zambales

Local context	'When is democracy present or absent?'
Within families	Present: ○ deciding what course to study ○ voting based on individual members' preference ○ older siblings do not dominate younger family members Absent: ○ only parents make the decisions
Within people's organizations	Present: ○ freedom of participation ○ freedom of thought ○ freedom of speech ○ consultation in decision making ○ things are going right in the organization ○ rules and guidelines are being implemented Absent: ○ problems with the leadership ○ lack of transparency in financial matters ○ disunity among members ○ lack of freedom to exercise organizational rights ○ only leaders formulate projects and make decisions ○ style of leadership is dictatorial ○ officers refuse to admit their mistakes ○ nepotism amongst leaders
Within the overall community	Present: ○ members' rights are respected ○ community leaders exchange ideas among themselves ○ community members are treated diplomatically ○ laws of government are implemented Absent: ○ information is disseminated without the knowledge of community members ○ laws are not followed ○ elections are not free ○ politicians take advantage of ordinary citizens ○ prices are controlled by those who have capital ○ leadership is disunited ○ leaders are self-centred and dictatorial ○ government perceived to be exploitative ○ benefits and services do not reach the citizenry

Lessons and findings from the impact evaluation have been shared by ELF and leader-researchers in the annual Conference on Grassroots Leadership sponsored by ELF and its partners (NGOs, POs, and the academe). This wider sharing of the impact evaluation has served as an important basis for stimulating conceptual thinking and theory building on grassroots leadership. Communities and local NGO partners have also received copies of the preliminary evaluation reports. The information is now being used as part of their community profile and as learning material for improving leadership in their community.

Lessons learned

ELF expects in the future to learn more about the effectiveness of its programme for training leaders for democratization and development. More importantly, it hopes that the leaders and graduates will become more aware of their own progress and be able to identify areas for improvement. ELF plans to continue bringing the lessons and experiences from the evaluation to other exchanges with grassroots leadership practitioners and researchers from other NGOs, POs, and academics.

For the leader-researchers, leadership qualities have taken on an added dimension. Leader-researchers view their new competencies as directly contributing to their development as individuals, and as leaders of their organizations and communities. During a presentation at a grassroots leadership conference organized by ELF, the leader-researchers said the experience of looking into the lives of other leaders was like looking into themselves: 'We understand ourselves as leaders, our organization and community more now. It is just like "researching" on ourselves.' For the communities, the evaluation provided them with opportunities to discuss issues like democracy and gender which they had not discussed in the past.

Methodologically, the project is significant as it is the first longitudinal study to use the orientation and methods of SP. This makes explicit the link between the quality of data gathered and the relationship between researcher and participants, and implies that there are no shortcuts to good quality data.

An important and positive factor was the participation of leader-researchers in the evaluation process. Even though they come from different areas in the Philippines, leader-researchers are easily integrated into new communities and can understand the issues, concerns, and opinions shared by community members. The leader-researchers are able to gather data from fellow leader-researchers who might otherwise be uncomfortable with ELF staff or unfamiliar researchers. This further enhances the validity of data gathered.

Constraints

We have, of course, also experienced a number of constraints related to data collection, collation, and analysis. For example, due to the sensitivity of Filipino culture, discussions, conversations, and story-telling often took different directions in different contexts. The leader-researchers had to be creative in focusing the discussions to gain relevant information, without appearing discourteous to their hosts.

Also, tape-recorded discussions had to be transcribed manually which was a laborious process. For fear of losing relevant information, the researchers included data almost word for word. This led to an enormous amount of field data that had to be sorted. We learned that it is a skill to be able to summarize data into appropriate units for content analysis.

As many people were involved and as there were many steps in handling and analysing data (e.g. transcribing, coding, writing codes onto paper and sorting, grouping them together using the KJ method), some data loss was inevitable. This was mainly caused by processing within a limited time the voluminous amount of data generated through a not-so-systematic computerization procedure.

In the future, we plan to minimize the constraints on data collection by providing additional trainings for leader-researchers on facilitation, small group discussion and exercises on writing, summarizing, and synthesis. To address constraints on data collation and analyses, a full-time data-encoder and a more systematic approach to data handling will be needed.

The PE process is an important step for ELF's learning and sharing programme. ELF recognizes that the ongoing evaluation is focused on assessing the effectiveness of training activities, but further research is needed to evaluate the efficiency of these activities. ELF is now in the process of evaluating the SP methodology. Some of the questions we are trying to address pertain to how we can make the process more participatory, and what modifications are needed to make the methodology more useful in the lives of leader-researchers, their organizations, and their communities.

7

Monitoring and Evaluating Local Development through Community Participation: The Experience of the Association of Indigenous Cabildos of Northern Cauca, Colombia

RUBEN DARIO ESPINOSA ALZATE[1]

Introduction

SINCE THE MID 1990s, legislative reforms in Colombia have been enacted to decentralize state resources and promote participation in local development. By law, 20 per cent of the national income is disbursed to municipalities and indigenous *cabildos* (community authorities) which are now responsible for resource allocation and use.[2] The experience of the Association of Indigenous Cabildos of Northern Cauca (ACIN) shows how a grassroots organization can take advantage of the opportunities made possible by these legal reforms. The ACIN now exercises greater authority over its territories, and has adopted a participatory planning, monitoring and evaluation approach that proves the relevance of participatory approaches for indigenous communities to manage their own development processes, and to achieve their objective of strengthening local culture and their people's self-reliance. As a result, the ACIN is increasingly regarded as a legitimate 'partner' in development by the different social, institutional, economic and political forces that operate in the region.

This chapter summarizes the experience of the ACIN in designing and implementing a community-based monitoring and evaluation (M&E) system for their development plans and programmatic work. Details are given about the steps of process design, indicator development, monitoring and community validation processes.

The ACIN as an organization

The ACIN is a legal entity that represents 12 *cabildos* of Paez Indians, spread over seven municipalities in a region that is known for its sugar cane production and other industrial sectors. Based on the New Constitution of 1991, the ACIN is recognized by the state as an autonomous, public organization with the power to represent and negotiate with other public and private entities. In 1993, the ACIN had a membership of approximately 90,000 individuals, or 20,000 families, 60 per cent of whom belong to indigenous communities and 40 per cent are small farmers belonging to other ethnic groups. Together, they live in a territory that spans a total of 170,000 hectares and which constitutes an ecological and cultural unit.

Through their organization, the communities exercise real political power in the region. At the provincial level, their own law takes precedence; their political and judicial systems remain active and are locally recognized. National civil law does not apply and the judicial branch of the state may not intervene, even in the case of trials of non-indigenous individuals who commit crimes within the territory, unless the community so desires.

The ACIN is responsible for the administration and development of the provincial indigenous territory. As a result of decentralization policies, the ACIN now has greater access to state resources, which are being used to meet basic needs at the local level.[3] The organization is currently involved in developing their own systems of education, healthcare, natural resource management, and enterprise development. These programmes are designed to achieve equity, sustainability and regional self-sufficiency, in order to ensure the future well-being of the population. Activities include:

- agroforestry
- water conservation
- integrated management of small animals in schools
- improving food security through seed production and technology development
- commercial enterprises, including a dairy farm, a sugar mill, a marble- and limestone-processing plant, and a wholesale food business, among others.

These enterprises and activities are administered by staff from the organization, with professional and technical assistance from non-governmental organizations (NGOs), universities or others hired to provide training, technical assistance or advice. Decision making is undertaken in general community assemblies and councils of the *cabildos*. The ACIN itself employs five staff, with 100 to 150 collaborators at any given time.

The region

The territory under ACIN's jurisdiction is important in ecological, economic and political terms. The area spreads over snow-capped mountain peaks, moorlands, lagoons, forests (which are considered sacred places) and flat lands. As a major source of water, the territory irrigates 36 per cent of the nation's sugar production area and supplies water to important economic and industrial sites, including regional pipelines and a hydro-electric dam. However, 85 per cent of the lands are seriously degraded due to heavy settlement and land production. The area has always been attractive to private investors. There are large mineral deposits in the region, which continue to draw mining companies to the area. There is also an expanding sugar cane agro-industry.

Just as it is important in ecological and economic terms, the territory is also politically significant. As a result of the recent legal reforms, indigenous political representation has been strengthened both locally and nationally. In the last elections, the number of seats held by indigenous members in municipal councils increased from 12 to 28. At the national level, there are now two indigenous representatives in Congress. These are important political victories because political power in the region has traditionally been dominated by economic interest groups represented by the major political parties.

This changing political situation has gone hand in hand with the process of indigenous communities recovering land from large-scale farmers and regaining control of important economic activities in the region, including mining and trade. Industrial and agro-industrial companies increasingly recognize indigenous authority over the territories, and are building alliances with the ACIN to achieve mutual economic benefits.

The territory is also an important strategic crossroads where armed guerrillas, drug traffickers, and military and paramilitary groups operate. This has resulted in many deaths and massacres in the area at the hands of armed forces, including those of the state. As the main political authority in the region, the ACIN is presently supporting efforts to bring these groups to the negotiating table, but direct confrontations continue to occur.

Community development planning, monitoring and evaluation

The recent legislative reforms have not only strengthened indigenous control over its territories, but also provide a major opportunity to promote community participation in local development. In 1993, the ACIN embarked on a participatory process to formulate local development plans for each *cabildo*. This led to the design and legal recognition of 11 *cabildo* development plans for the 13 *cabildos* and one zonal (provincial) development plan for the whole area, which was designed to enable indigenous communities to manage their resources efficiently and to strengthen their cultural values.[4] As a result of this planning process, communities have defined their unique form of development: this includes education and preventative healthcare systems that incorporate the Paez' particular cosmovision and cultural practices, and their own concept of economic development based on self-sufficiency. The planning process also put in place a system for the monitoring and evaluation of development plans and projects, so that communities remain actively involved in their implementation, management and oversight. Proposals presented by the community served as the basis for formulating local government programmes, adjusting local development plans, and evaluating and adapting the ACIN's programmes and projects at the provincial level. In other words, the M&E process itself has become an integral part of local development planning.

The M&E system assesses all sectors of development (i.e. education, health, natural resources, the economy and institutional development), and where these sectors interrelate (i.e. the cultural–productive, the cultural–environmental, and the productive–environmental aspects) (see Figure 7.1), seeks to base learning on the overall objective of harmonious relationships between the environmental, socio-economic and political aspects of the Paez's life.

Communities themselves define the indicators for M&E, based on their own world views and cultural practices. The methodology used is simplified

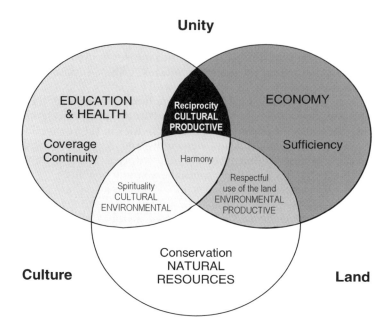

Figure 7.1: *Our development plan: expected fruits of our labour*

in order to work directly with the community and facilitate local understanding. The process enables communities to review the expected results of their development plans and projects, adjust their goals, formulate new strategies and projects, and learn how to record information systematically (which they carry out themselves). It allows communities to interpret, compare and analyse data based on indicators defined by themselves from the outset. In effect, communities assess their development at different levels, by looking at overall performance within the family and community, the organization, and local society in general (i.e. at the municipal and provincial level).

The entire planning, monitoring and evaluation process is designed and conducted primarily through a body known as the assembly. Each assembly is a community meeting of about 300 to 600 people, held over three days. It is a large gathering of men and women, adults and youth, children, leaders and government officials, and others who collectively take part in decision making. Assemblies are usually held in different localities each time, during which all *veredas* (communities) are represented. In general, each *vereda* sends no less than 12 community representatives, with two members representing each of the six sectors (education; health; institutional development; agricultural–environmental; sports, recreation and culture; and households). What is decided by the assembly is regarded as official and is adhered to. These decisions carry authority and are therefore respected and taken into account by community leaders, local governments, working committees and advisers. The assembly is used to inform, develop awareness, and train members of the community. It provides a forum for community discussions to define local priorities and goals with regard to life, health, education, policies, justice, natural resource management and the economy.

So far, development planning has been undertaken in 13 *cabildos* in seven municipalities of *la Zona Norte*, which included the M&E of a total of 11 local development plans. Drawing up the local development plans and establishing the M&E system were both lengthy processes. Local development planning initially lasted between two to three years, while developing the M&E system took about a year. The development plans were drawn up over 14 three-day assemblies, with one assembly held every two or three months. The following section focuses in particular on the M&E of local development plans and projects.

Different levels and steps in M&E

The M&E process undertaken by the organization involves three cyclical levels (see Figure 7.2):

○ a three-year evaluation cycle of the local development plan
○ an annual evaluation cycle of local development projects
○ a monthly monitoring cycle of project activities.

At each level, the M&E work is conducted in a series of stages or steps.

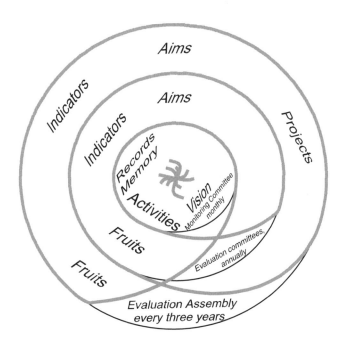

Figure 7.2: *Cycle of monitoring and evaluation*

First level

At the first cyclical level, local development plans which have been drawn up are evaluated every three years. The three-year evaluation cycle corresponds to the period of governance of the local administration, because every three years a new administration is elected, and development plans evaluated and adjusted. M&E at this first level occurs in several stages and takes place in four assemblies for each *cabildo*. Before the assemblies are held, a *consejo de planeación* (planning council) is selected by community representatives and is approved by the municipal mayor or governor of the *cabildo*. The *consejo* is represented by two members from each sector and co-ordinates the M&E work, including gathering information and documenting agreements reached in the assemblies.

The entire process is held in each *cabildo* or municipality that is monitoring and evaluating its development plan, and lasts for four months. In some cases, the M&E work was initiated during the first quarter of the three-year period beginning in 1995, while others began M&E work during the final months of the three-year period in 1997, which has then carried over to the next period. In total, 44 assemblies (four assemblies for each of the 11 development plans being monitored and evaluated) have been held. During the first assembly, the community defines or revisits its vision of the future or what it would like that future to be, and establishes development criteria by comparing present and past situations. Visual representations are used to provoke discussion amongst the different sectors and to reach consensus on the community's vision of its future. For instance, the present situation is analysed by reproducing data from using geographic information systems and other information on maps and models, which are small, three-dimensional scale models of the local area. These visual aids are used to define boundaries, land use, coverage of services and any other information regarded to be necessary for decision making. The first assembly is also used to revisit the existing local development plan, identifying the achievements, strengths and weaknesses of each sector – based on the goals they had set out to achieve for the next three years.

The second assembly involves identifying expected results by sector, based on the vision and development priorities defined in the first assembly. From each *vereda*, and each of the six sectors of work, representatives are present throughout the four assemblies so as to ensure continuity. The expected results or achievements are prioritized and grouped into categories and variables, and indicators are selected for each. This work is undertaken by posing thought-provoking questions to the participants both in general plenary sessions and smaller groups. For instance, one such question raised may be: 'If this is your vision of the future, what concrete results do you hope to accomplish or achieve over the coming three years?'

After the second assembly, a workshop is held by the *consejo de planeación*, which reviews the indicators formulated by the assembly and converts them into questions. These questions are then used to develop surveys in order to collect baseline information. The surveys are answered collectively in large group meetings held in each *vereda*, with guidance from *consejo* members. Once the surveys have been filled out, the information is systematized and summarized in tables that show expected results, the corresponding indicators, monitored information, and achievements attained.

In the third assembly, the surveyed information is presented. The indicators are compared against the goals previously set, and additional goals are identified for the period that the local administration or municipal council will be in office (three years). Participants analyse the information in working committees set up to represent each sector. Information is then transferred on to bar graphs or histograms to indicate achievements and the new goals. Based on these figures, the assembly is able to compare the local situation across the different sectors.

The general analysis and findings of the third assembly are brought to each local *vereda*, where the community analyses its own situation and may even compare their performance with that of other *veredas* or the municipality. To conduct their own analysis, local communities receive summary reports containing visual information (i.e. bar graphs) that details the expected results and their respective indicators. The entire process of analysing data in a general assembly and then in local communities helps ensure that the goals and findings are verified and receive broad-based support from the communities.

In the fourth assembly, the local development plan, the goals, and activities are revisited and adjusted based on the evaluation findings and analyses. Goals are prioritized by the assembly, looking at the strengths and weaknesses that help or hinder the achievement of these goals, and strategies identified to attain prioritized goals. Development projects, which should support the local development plan, are then formulated with the help of the *consejo* and sectoral representatives from the community. These projects are then presented to the assembly for approval.

Throughout this entire M&E process, the *consejo de planeación* plays an important role, co-ordinating M&E work, providing facilitation support, etc. In between each assembly that is held, they conduct workshops and training activities in various localities. However, the *consejo* works together with a range of other individuals and groups who have helped in developing the M&E system. They include: a professional educator, a medic, an agronomist, a recreation specialist, an expert on family/ household issues, a statistician, a map maker, and two planning co-ordinators. Community teachers, promoters (*promotores*), and leaders have also contributed. All of these individuals have assisted in some way in designing a participatory M&E (PM&E) process and have helped to select appropriate goals and indicators, data gathering instruments, and methods for analysing data.

Second level

The second level outlines the process for monitoring and evaluating the projects which have been approved by the assembly. Specific goals and expected results are defined for each project. Indicators are then identified, and a baseline study is carried out. The methodology used to conduct M&E at this level is the same process used for the local development plans at the first level (i.e. through assemblies, workshops, etc.). Projects are evaluated each year by the management committees responsible for their implementation. These committees comprise community leaders, *promotores*, the direct beneficiaries of the project (community members), the technical and professional personnel involved in the project, local NGO representatives, and representatives from other participating institutions, as well as public officials from *cabildos*, municipalities and the ACIN. The annual evaluations are usually held in two or three workshops, which last for three days each.

Third level

Project monitoring and continuous recording of data take place at this third level. Monitoring is conducted monthly and is carried out by the same management committees in charge of project implementation. The committees conduct workshops that allow them to collect monitoring information as well as to provide trainings to support project-related activities. They also carry out field visits and present periodic reports to the *cabildos*.

Results and findings from project M&E become part of the community's collective 'memory' which kindles and affirms their vision of the desired future. For the communities, the future is created by learning from and better understanding past experience: 'the future comes from behind, it is like a river.' Every three years, the assembly comes together with outgoing and incoming authorities to re-examine this 'vision'; it reviews and readjusts the expected results of development plans and projects, and once again begins a new cycle of planning, monitoring and evaluation. The M&E process itself is continually being reviewed and improved as the programmes and projects of the ACIN are implemented. The next section looks more closely at how communities select indicators and how results are viewed at both local and national levels.

Defining indicators and viewing results

As discussed earlier, indicators are defined to monitor and evaluate local development plans as well as development programmes and projects of each sector. The process for defining indicators uses an adaptation of the grassroots development framework (GDF) (see Figure 7.3) developed by the Inter-American Foundation (Ritchey-Vance, 1998; Zaffaroni, 1997; see also Chapter 3 of this volume).[5]

Indicators are selected to evaluate two main areas of work: (i) the development plans and projects; and (ii) the institutions involved in their implementation. The indicators defined are culturally meaningful and help communities assess the *quality* of their development plans and projects. Three expected results are identified; indicators are then selected for each expected result (see Figure 7.4).

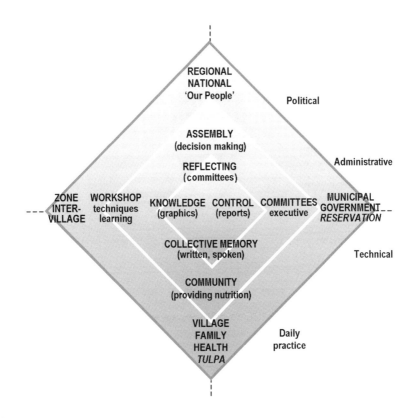

Figure 7.3: *Categories and variables of the development framework, ACIN*

The first expected result is the strengthening of local spirituality, religiosity and the cosmic vision of the community's relationship with nature. This is viewed in terms of improving education, health and natural resource management. The second looks at the concept of reciprocity, which is achieved through forms of communal work, such as the *mingas*, and the collective distribution of the means of production and profits. Values of reciprocity are also used to assess the content of educational programmes and local health conditions. Thirdly, the respectful use of land is considered by assessing indigenous production systems, such as the *tul* (i.e. agroforestry, indigenous irrigation systems, etc.).

However, at the core of defining these goals (or 'results') and their respective indicators is the concept of harmony which communities regard as the ultimate expected result. In other words, 'harmony' is the desired state of well-being, signifying equilibrium and describing the harmonious relationship between nature, spirits that inhabit nature, people, and the community. Hence, ideas of unity, land, and culture form the central elements of the ACIN and the communities, and therefore must be incorporated into all development plans, programmes and projects.

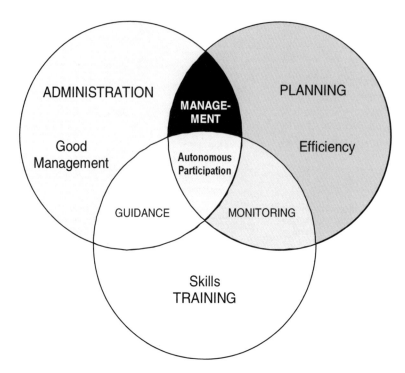

Figure 7.4: *Expected fruits of our labour – our institutions*

Box 7.1 provides some examples of indicators and results defined for agroforestry programmes.

Selected indicators are also designed to assess the institutions that influence how plans, programmes, and projects are formulated and implemented. These include the ACIN, the local government (*cabildos* and municipalities), and private business. Three different aspects of institutional development are assessed, namely administration, orientation and planning, monitoring and management. The indicators listed in Box 7.1 address the categories identified in the development plan (see Figure 7.1) such as coverage (*cobertura*), sustainability (*permanencia*), efficiency or sound management of resources, planning and programming to ensure effectiveness, training and technical assistance for building local skills in technical and legal management, autonomy and decision-making power in keeping with local values and practice, and, finally, participation as a means for ensuring local accountability and equity.

Indicators identified by communities are compared and matched with national indicators. By doing so, indigenous communities are better able to communicate local experiences and findings based on the parameters set by the state, which requires the efficient and effective use of resources allocated to the territorial entities. Expected results at the community level, which are comparable to those identified at the national level, include such indicators as the efficiency of the health and education sectors, (i.e. in terms of coverage (accessibility) and sustainability of activity

Box 7.1: Sample indicators used for soil–forestry conservation

(i) Conservation
Protection
○ Native trees established by plot
○ A separate area of forest on the plot
○ Degree of reduction in the burning of fields and felling of trees in the community where the plot was established
○ Volume of water in summer from the source protected by the plot
○ Level of sedimentation of the water source protected by the plot
Biodiversity
○ Species of animals attracted to the plot
○ Plant species established by year on the plot
○ Species of vegetables that regenerate naturally established on the plot
○ Non-harmful species used for control established on the plot

(ii) Respectful use of the land
Soil fertility
○ Amount of organic material increased over time
○ Amount of micro- and macronutrients in the soil
○ Soil texture and structure
○ Cultural practices
○ Plots that select and conserve seeds
○ Plots that plant according to the phases of the moon, by species
○ Plots that produce fertilizers using byproducts of the farm
○ Plots that practise crop rotation

(iii) Spirituality
Perception of the surroundings
○ Degree of satisfaction that the farm gives the farmer
○ Families in the community motivated to set up the plot
○ Attitude towards the surroundings
○ Consultations made by the farmer to the traditional doctor
○ Indigenous rite performed on the plot by a 'medicine man', to bring harmony or heal the land, plants, animals or human beings
○ Farmers who establish a harmonious relationship with the environment

(iv) Sufficiency
Supply
○ Amount of food produced by the farmer and consumed by the farmer's family
○ Amount of surpluses, by product
○ Sustainability
○ Percentage of inputs produced on the farm
○ Percentage of inputs obtained with income generated by the farm

(v) Reciprocity
Attitude of receiving and giving back
o Kilos of organic material incorporated per square metre, per year
o Families in the community trained by the farmer who uses the system
o Amount (in kilos) of plant seed donated by the plot for setting up other plots
o Amount (in kilos) of organic material donated by the plot for setting up other plots
o Amount of fish spawn donated by the plot for setting up other plots

(vi) Harmony
Integrality
o Plots that develop and appropriate all the components of the system
o Plots on which the family and the community participate actively
o Activities that generate interaction among the components of the plot
o Quality of life
o Production by crop
o Animal production
o Phytosanitary tolerance on the plot
o Species consumed by the farmer's family
o Members of the farmer's family who get sick each year
o Families in the community that benefit from the plot

and conservation of natural resources). However, in some instances, communities still select indicators based on their own prioritized objectives, which are locally meaningful and unique to Paez indigenous culture but which may differ from those set by the state – for instance, communities focus on achieving self-sufficiency rather than surplus production.

Local impacts of the PM&E process

The ACIN's M&E process has allowed indigenous communities to take advantage of new opportunities brought about by the recent legal reforms. Communities are playing a greater role in defining their own development process, and reaffirming their own knowledge and culture. At least four main impacts on the community may be highlighted as a result of the PM&E process:

o strengthening community participation
o increasing public accountability
o becoming better decision makers and managers
o changing power relationships and creating horizontal relationships.

Strengthening community participation

This process has encouraged the entire community to become actively involved throughout the development process, from planning, implementation, monitoring and evaluation. Community members, regardless of their formal education backgrounds, take part in decision making and learn how to develop a common vision, reach consensus, analyse information, and work towards achieving their goals. All discussions take place using the local language in order to encourage all members to participate and to capture unique aspects of the local culture. Even those who are non-literate are encouraged to participate by using visual forms of communication (i.e. bar graphs, histograms, maps, models, videos, photographs, etc.). Thus, communities are able to visualize their objectives, check their progress, and verify their achievements, recognize obstacles, and re-adjust goals and expected results accordingly.

Reaching consensus and making collective decisions have been critical outcomes of the PM&E process. However, conflicts have also been generated because the process allows contradictions and differences between individual and group interests to be aired. Therefore, an idea or action rejected by the general assembly often results in harboured grudges and resentments, which, in turn, have caused some to work against the entire process – for instance, in one municipality, a popular mayor was killed by an opposition group. Nevertheless, because much of the M&E work is carried out through the assemblies, it is generally difficult for any one individual or group to dominate or manipulate the process. In some instances, the process had weakened the traditional influence and power of politicians in the assemblies, but many young people are now emerging as important leaders as they take on greater roles in co-ordinating assemblies and overseeing M&E activities.

Increasing public accountability

In promoting increased community participation, the M&E process has also built local accountability into the development process. Communities assess their own institutions who are held liable in terms of fulfilling their commitments and responsibilities. There is also greater local awareness with regard to how local governments (municipalities and *cabildos*) allocate resources and design programmes and projects. Communities now help in formulating investment plans and determining budgets, which, in turn, creates a local sense of responsibility in moving their development plans forward and achieving their objectives.

Becoming better decision makers and managers

The process has also been important because it generates information and improves local understanding regarding the use and management of state resources. Communities are better able to assess their overall performance over time, know where they are and where they are headed in terms of achieving development objectives, and may even compare their achievements with other communities. Hence, they become better decision makers and managers of their own development process. This entails knowing how to formulate plans and projects, allocate resources, and seize other opportunities that would allow them to improve daily life. Developing these local capacities is especially critical, as state resources are increasingly limited and communities are required to demonstrate efficiency and effectiveness.

Changing power relationships and building horizontal linkages in the region

As communities recognize their own potential and exert greater control over their territories, the process is transforming traditional power relationships and establishing horizontal linkages across the region. Communities now see themselves as legitimate stakeholders, especially in the development of their territories – for instance, information generated from the M&E process is being used by communities to negotiate and establish alliances with both the private sector and national government. Indigenous communities have forged partnerships with private businesses, and are discussing how natural resources (i.e. large mine deposits) under indigenous control can be utilized for their mutual benefit. Communities also use the M&E information to negotiate with government at regional and national levels to gain greater access to state resources. Information is further used to advocate more appropriate and practicable policies which favour the interests of indigenous communities. Currently, the ACIN and other indigenous representatives are working to pass laws on indigenous healthcare, education, natural resource management and food security.

8

Monitoring Local Development with Communities: The SISDEL Approach in Ecuador

VICTOR HUGO TORRES D.

Introduction

COMUNIDEC IS AN Ecuadorian non-governmental organization (NGO) that promotes development by designing and using participatory methodologies that help empower local communities and grassroots organizations. It is implementing a local development programme that focuses on building the human capacities of small rural municipalities and community-based organizations, especially located in regions marked by poverty and an indigenous population. Over the past five years, COMUNIDEC has been experimenting with participatory monitoring and evaluation (PM&E) methodologies to strengthen local development planning. It has developed a planning, monitoring and evaluation system based on participatory approaches, known as SISDEL (*Sistema de Desarrollo Local*, or Local Development System), which aims to build alliances within municipalities in order to co-ordinate efforts, share risks, and mobilize resources.

For these objectives, SISDEL is a relatively new methodology, developed and used only over the past two years, with first lessons just beginning to emerge. Essentially, it is a self-evaluation approach designed to encourage participation of various social actors involved in each phase of the development project cycle, integrating planning, monitoring and evaluation: it helps reach consensus on project design; promotes agreement on expected impacts; assists in decision making to improve project implementation through monitoring; and systematically evaluates the impacts to encourage learning. SISDEL builds on another self-evaluation methodology used since 1994 by the Inter-American Foundation (IAF), known as the grassroots development framework (GDF, *Marco de Desarrollo de Base*).[1]

SISDEL may be used by municipal level rural extension and field workers, leaders and promoters of rural organizations, NGOs, and government extension workers, amongst other local development actors. SISDEL is directly being used in five municipalities (and indirectly in another ten); each municipality has experienced more than ten years of systematic development interventions through NGOs, government programmes, development aid agencies, churches, community-based organizations, and, in some cases, the private sector.

The context for developing the SISDEL approach stems from socio-cultural and political changes occurring over the last 30 years in Ecuador. There has been a trend towards greater decentralization of power, with increased emphasis on the development priorities of rural areas rather than towns. This has given rise to what might be called the 'ruralization of local power' (Carrasco, 1993: 22–69) and has shifted local powers to rural parishes (*parroquias*)[2] with predominantly indigenous populations. These changes, in turn, have encouraged municipalities and municipal leaders to seek new forms of concerted action or collaboration (*concertación*) and to engage in decentralized strategic development and planning. In addition, the proliferation of rural organizations and coalitions or 'social capital' has encouraged their more active involvement in supporting local economic activities and natural resource management. These trends have resulted in a greater demand for participatory methodologies to help strengthen local institutional capacity, including local development committees, rural assemblies (*asambleas cantonales*), round tables of regional consultation (*mesas de concertación regional*), indigenous parliaments and other, similar, local institutions.

While there are increased opportunities for a more decentralized, participatory development process, most local institutions or organizations lack sufficient knowledge and skills to address community needs effectively and take on new roles associated with decentralized governance. In order to seize the full potential of innovative municipalities and the strengthening of 'social capital', methodologies are needed that are simple and quick to learn, but that also address capacity building needs of local institutions. It is here that SISDEL aims to make a contribution – as a methodology that continuously evolves and is enriched by the experience of its users. In this chapter we describe how SISDEL is being used towards strengthening local institutions involved in community development, and document our experiences in creating a PM&E system.

'Concertación'[3] *as the basis of participatory planning, monitoring and evaluation*

In applying the SISDEL approach, local communities occupy a central role throughout the project cycle (Kottak, 1995: 529). SISDEL involves training the teams that manage local development projects to co-ordinate resources and opportunities, and promotes the synergies necessary for sustaining impacts in the long term. The SISDEL strategy is based on the following three critical attributes.

○ Existing civil society organizations are the decisive factors that determine whether development projects achieve expected results and impacts. What is essential is their involvement as collective actors. It is less important that they are formal organizations but they must be able to establish linkages across different groups in society and mobilize resources to address local needs. They should be able to reconcile diverse local interests and identify common goals through consultative processes. By involving grassroots organizations, local authorities, NGOs and private enterprise in the development process, their shared commitment can help sustain benefits and achieve long-term impacts.

Hence, if the aim of such partnerships is to enhance collaborative energy, then monitoring and evaluation can support such a process.

o The project must be clearly formulated and should consider PM&E as part of planning and implementation. In Ecuador we have applied the GDF in 30 projects over a three-year period. Our experience in applying the GDF taught us the importance of integrating PM&E within the project cycle (Ramón and Torres, 1995). For a project to become a useful learning experience for those involved in implementation, it is not sufficient merely to carry out participatory reporting of impacts at the end. Consultations should be undertaken throughout the project cycle, first reaching consensus on expected results, then monitoring the implementation of planned activities, and, finally, assessing outcomes against the expectations of all those involved.

o However, the process should build on local capacities and existing forms of collaboration. SISDEL recognizes the importance of local culture and daily practice, thus using methods that are compatible with local customs and conditions. These local forms of participation, co-operation and solidarity should then complement efforts to promote consultation (see Box 8.3 later in the chapter).

The belief underlying this work is that constant feedback amongst local actors is crucial as this provides for valuable collective learning. The project cycle cannot be exclusively driven by development experts and external agents; rather, local control and learning are central throughout the entire process of planning, implementation, monitoring and evaluation. This also means that the implementing–evaluating team should remain closely linked to local organizations and institutions. The cycle represents a continuous process of collecting and systematizing information to solve management problems, linking local leaders and authorities with residents, and technicians, entrepreneurs, and officials with others participating in project activities.

SISDEL is currently being implemented in five local development projects to varying degrees:

o Bolivar-Carchi, where we trained the municipal project management team
o Cotacachi, where an association is being organized to include NGOs, indigenous leaders, and municipal authorities
o Guamote, where a technical team was created, composed of municipal experts and leaders of organizations
o Otavalo, where an indigenous NGO, the Centre for Pluricultural Studies (CEPCU) has a management team that initiates collaborative efforts and is an example of 'civil society' taking the lead role in promoting local development
o Suscal, where an NGO coalition serves as the local management team.

The structure of SISDEL

In practice, SISDEL is a collaborative process of self-reflection between organizations and institutions in one locality. This process is effectively a structured way of sequential planning and learning: by prioritizing problems and identifying proposed solutions, co-operative action is then undertaken and impacts are compared against local expectations of change. An essential step in this process of designing a long-term programme vision is the identification of indicators for the construction of the 'cone' (or GDF). The indicator design is followed by a pragmatic prioritization of activities to be undertaken in the short term in line with the long-term objectives.

Levels and nature of expected impacts

SISDEL focuses on impacts more than activities. It identifies three levels of impacts as a result of local development processes. Each level has a different scope, but each is equally important. The first level considers immediate impacts and direct benefits for individuals and families. The second level involves broader impacts that affect 'social capital' or local organizations, namely in terms of their empowerment and representation. The third level relates to the overall impacts on local society.

At each level, the forms of expected impacts may also vary. Impacts may have material, human and spiritual attributes. These are seen across a continuum of tangible and intangible impacts, including environmental, productive, and physical changes, as well as overall transformations at the individual and community level. Tangible impacts are changes that can be observed directly, and measured and documented quickly. Intangible impacts are more subtle, internal or attitudinal changes that can also be documented but often in a more 'qualitative' manner. Figure 8.1 illustrates the different levels and forms of impacts considered in SISDEL.

Categories, variables and indicators

The conceptual framework of SISDEL is based on the logic of applied research: practical experience is expressed in terms of categories that are defined by variables, which, in turn, are measured by indicators. The combination of three levels and two types of impacts means that there are six main categories that represent local development objectives to guide activities throughout the project cycle. At each level of impacts, two categories are identified in terms of the tangible and intangible:

○ At the individual or family level, tangible impacts relate to changes in the *quality of life*, including people's environment and livelihoods. Intangible impacts refer to *personal capacities*, concerning changes in individual expectations, motivations and actions.
○ At the organizational, or social-capital level, tangible impacts pertain to *local management* (*gestión local*) which reflect the capacity of organizations and municipalities to engage in local development. Intangible impacts refer to *commitment to collaboration* (*vocación colaborativa*) which looks at changes in the development values and practices of local leadership.
○ At the level of the society as a whole, tangible impacts includes creating *civil society opportunities* (*espacios cívicos*) that deal with the institu-

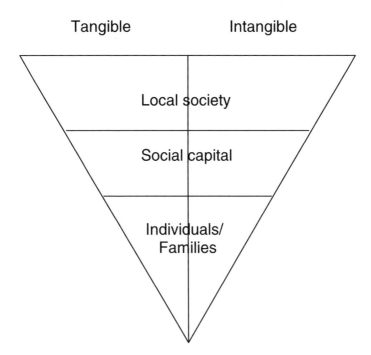

Figure 8.1: *Levels of impact considered by SISDEL*

tionalization of democracy. Intangible impacts measures the basis of citizenship in terms of changes in *culture* of *citizenship* (*cultura ciudadana*), or collective behaviour, towards greater tolerance and respect for social and cultural diversity.

Under each category many variables could be identified by different actors. We have selected 20 that we consider to be the most representative and applicable for our own use of SISDEL in Ecuador (see Box 8.1). Depending on their specific concerns, users may adapt or add to these variables, and may choose to focus on particular thematic issues, such as gender relations, livelihood, the environment or culture.

Each variable is assessed by identifying indicators. Indicators can measure both positive and negative impacts, and can be numbers and opinions to reflect quantitative and qualitative change. Data collection is facilitated by using one-dimensional indicators, which are used to make comparisons over time against baseline information. While it is possible to have many indicators, our experience cautions against allowing the 'tyranny of indicators' to occur and shows that it is better to select only those indicators considered strictly necessary. In our work as COM-UNIDEC, in assessing the impact of certain projects, we limited ourselves to two indicators per variable, having pre-tested them in communities. We chose those indicators that also garnered the widest consensus, after extensive discussions with our colleagues working in similar institutions (see Table 8.1).

113

Box 8.1:   Summary of variables and their definitions

Basic needs: satisfaction of local needs in education, housing and health

Equipment: provision of equipment for recreation, production, education and cultural activities

Employment/income: creation and improvement of jobs, income generation through productive and business activities

Skills: recovering and using local knowledge

Self-esteem: appreciation of the individual condition in order to strengthen local intervention

Cultural identity: sense of belonging to the territory and the group as a condition for human growth

Critical thinking: ability to recognize errors and learn from them

Creativity: willingness to introduce innovative actions in the local context

Decentralization: local capacity for self-government (discharging functions and disposing of resources)

Local planning: formulation of long-term local development strategies

Leadership: facilitating participatory processes in decision-making

Resources: mobilization of human, financial and material resources for local development

Local vision: ability to see beyond the present and to anticipate change

Conflict management: ability to treat conflicts and disagreements in a collaborative manner

Linkages: vertical and horizontal ties to resolve problems and mobilize resources

Consultation: skill in promoting spaces of co-operation among local actors

Regulations: legal provisions at the municipal level relating to local development agenda

Policies: public action intended to solve the problems of the local population

Values: concepts and ideas of equity, justice and solidarity that guide collective action

Practices: widespread dissemination of local alternatives

The difficulty is not in the selection of indicators, but actually in demonstrating their usefulness in terms of providing information on project impacts. Indicators must be able to capture the changing reality of the project, provide sufficient information for making timely decisions during project implementation, and facilitate collective learning based on the management experience. At present, there are extensive indicators available that have been formulated by universities, evaluation teams, consultants, NGOs, and government and development agencies. While many of these indicators are standardized, the question remains: how are they considered useful?

Table 8.1:   List of tangible and intangible indicators

Tangible	Intangible

Civil society opportunities
Laws
  ○ Promulgation, modification or repeals of laws
  ○ Application of legal provisions
Policies
  ○ Influence of local interests over public measures
  ○ Implementation of public policies
	Culture of citizenship
	Values
	  ○ Degree of civic and social responsibility
	  ○ Tolerance of local social and cultural diversity
	Practices
	  ○ Replication of alternatives on the appropriate scale
	  ○ Dissemination of results

Local management
Decentralization
  ○ Autonomy of political decisions
  ○ Expenditure under local responsibility
Planning
  ○ Incorporating local demands into plans
  ○ Degree of flexibility in adjusting plans
Leadership
  ○ Degree of local participation in strategic decisions
  ○ Willingness to facilitate local processes
Resources
  ○ Proportion of resources mobilized
  ○ Degree of self-management
	Commitment to collaborate
	Local vision
	  ○ Identification of opportunities for action
	  ○ Ability to anticipate consequences and modifications in the local context
	Conflict management
	  ○ Ability to recognize incompatibilities
	  ○ Ability to promote agreement
	Linkages
	  ○ Degree of participation in networks and fora
	  ○ Number and type of local problems resolved within networks
	Concertation
	  ○ Degree of recognition and acceptance of plurality of local interests
	  ○ Degree of competence in negotiating techniques

Quality of life
Basic needs
  ○ Satisfaction of housing, educational and health needs
  ○ Changes in the quality of life perceived by the local population
Equipment
  ○ Type of community equipment
  ○ Collective services provided
Employment/income
  ○ Number of jobs created or maintained
  ○ Average annual income
Skills
  ○ Type of local knowledge integrated
  ○ Events into which local knowledge was integrated
	Personal abilities
	Self-esteem
	  ○ Number of persons whose perception of themselves changed
	  ○ Types of new roles assumed by individuals
	Cultural identity
	  ○ Intensity of sense of belonging to the locality
	  ○ Degree of appreciation of local customs and traditions
	Creativity
	  ○ Degree of openness to innovation
	  ○ Application of innovative solutions
	Critical thinking
	  ○ Ability to explain reality
	  ○ Recognition of and learning from errors

The indicators proposed by the SISDEL framework may be used, adapted or replaced, based on local information needs. Each local management team selects its variables and identifies indicators by examining project objectives and intended results. Comparing what is desired and what can be achieved makes it possible to 'zero in' on the indicators. Through an open dialogue between experts, promoters and leaders, agreement is reached on the most appropriate indicators. Indicators may refer to specific activities, to products, or to impacts. They are defined using the same local language, to allow 'us' to keep track of changes and outcomes.

In our experience, local management teams have good ideas about what they hope to achieve, but are not always able to articulate them clearly. Formulating indicators, in some instances, have helped communities better define their project goals. For example, in Bolívar, indicator development led to the realization that many projects were in fact not projects, but were planned actions that required a strategic focus. In Cotacachi, defining indicators made it possible to limit project objectives and consider local capacities. In Guamote, indicators helped in project programming which established sub-projects, each with respective annual operational plans and monitoring systems. Box 8.2 describes how indicators were selected for a community

---

Box 8.2: Guamote: developing indicators for monitoring local reforestation

Indicators were identified to measure the impacts of a community reforestation project in a watershed area in Guamote. Specifically, indicators were used to look at changes in improving soil conditions as a result of community reforestation in the upper watershed areas. The criteria for selecting indicators were the following: (i) that which permits trust in the technical quality of data, and (ii) that which can be easily compiled or collected by local leaders and promoters (*promotores*).

The indicators were initially proposed by the members of the Local Development Committee of Guamote, which implements the reforestation project. Their initial proposals were then discussed with local promoters of indigenous organizations, and indicators were validated by looking at community practices for natural resource conservation.

Indicators selected measured tangible impacts at the level of local society. These were considered as a pilot monitoring experience, which reflects community reforestation practices that can potentially transform or influence municipal policy on local sustainable development. Indicators included:

o volume of water (in litres per second)
o use of water sources
o total suspended matter in the water (in tonnes per hectare per year)
o increase in vegetation in reforested areas (number of trees per hectare per area reforested)
o percentage of deforestation (in cubic metres per hectare).

In this first exercise, no indicators for intangible impacts were established, thus allowing full concentration on community monitoring of tangibles.

---

reforestation project in Guamote. In developing indicators, there should be a balance between the tangible and the intangible: often there are unanticipated outcomes that are intangible but prove to be more important – in terms of understanding project impacts – than anticipated tangible results.

Indicator development should also fit the local context and draw from the individual creativity of local management teams. This helps establish a common information base that can be shared and understood by the local population. The Local Development Committee of Guamote (*Comité de Desarrollo Local de Guamote*), for example, is exploring new forms of disseminating findings by verbally reporting indicators comparable to the traditional way of presenting financial accounts in community assemblies. In this manner, the local population is kept informed about the status of ongoing community projects. The case of CEPCU in Otavalo is different, as indicators were more systematically monitored and used as a technical reference for progress reports submitted to donors. Community members helped construct a small-scale model of their community (its general environment, geography, infrastructure, population, economic and natural resources, social and cultural features, etc.), with removable pieces used as indicators to monitor changes that result from project activities. Such models serve as visual forms for reporting monitored information, by which different groups of the local population and neighbouring settlements or institutions can easily learn from the results and thus improve natural resource management.

Beyond the indicators

SISDEL, then, is not a rigid framework, nor does it consist only of indicators. Rather, it is used flexibly and adapted to focus on whatever level or category is being considered, using different combinations of variables and different indicators. This will vary depending on particular contexts, objectives and characteristics of each project. Our experiences demonstrate that there are various ways of applying SISDEL. For instance, in Guamote, the Local Development Committee sought to focus on civil society opportunities in order to institutionalize the practice of local consultation and collaboration as the basis of a new municipal policy (see Box 8.3). In Bolívar the municipality concentrated on strengthening 'social capital' by creating civic organizations in order to reform community services. Furthermore, many indigenous federations in the highland *sierra* region use the approach to focus on improving leadership; thus, they promote greater commitment to collaboration so as to improve the capacities of their members. Organizations in Quito prioritized impacts at the level of local management that were considered necessary for the improvement of quality of life at the individual or household level, or to promote the strengthening of civil society.

Applying SISDEL in the project cycle: a flexible monitoring and evaluation (M&E) process

SISDEL can be used at each phase of the project cycle. It provides techniques for consultation and self-evaluation during project formulation,

Box 8.3: Participatory monitoring in Guamote

Guamote is one of the poorest *cantónes* (rural municipalities) in Ecuador. Poverty affects 90 per cent of the population, and there is heavy pressure on natural resources. Until 1974, most land holdings were privately owned, but since then most have been converted to common property. As a result of agrarian reform and state interventions over the last 40 years, there is now a dense network of rural organizations that establish linkages between communities and external agents.

The municipality of Guamote initiated a participatory process to take advantage of public policy, which now enables citizens and indigenous communities to become more actively involved in formulating public mandates and reaching consensus. These new spaces for participatory decision making and accountability include such institutions as the Popular and Indigenous Parliament of Guamote (*Parlamento Indígena y Popular de Guamote*) as well as the *cantón* assembly representing all communities.

The agency directly dependent on this Parliament is the Local Development Committee of Guamote, which represents 12 rural federations and the municipality. The Committee is responsible for implementing development projects, in co-ordination with the municipal government, and conducts monitoring and evaluation of the projects. The Committee's technical and local management teams have applied the SISDEL approach for monitoring soil conservation, using data gathering instruments that rural organizations (i.e. water and irrigation canal associations) already use daily. These methods include:

○ '*aforo*', soil loss measure, which is a monthly measurement of soil deposits in the water currents: water is collected to filter out settlements, which are then measured as soil loss. It is a simple technique routinely used for irrigation control, which SISDEL has adopted for measuring impacts of reforestation
○ *river topography*, which is a topographic sampling survey in four critical areas along the riverbed, based on direct knowledge of the farmers; it is in these areas where *aforo* is practised
○ *counting*, i.e. using direct observation of reforested areas and counting the number of tree species planted and protected

The technical team of the Committee is conducting the first training with the rural organizations involved in irrigation and reforestation, and is accompanying them in the first measurements, analysis of samples and report writing. Representatives from these organizations then continue the monitoring work and report information to the Committee, which, in turn, presents a report to the municipality and the Popular and Indigenous Parliament of Guamote. As this monitoring system is becoming refined, and made more efficient, it will be incorporated as a procedure for citizens' control of *cantón* regulations for the ecological management of natural resources.

118

supports negotiations during project design, produces tables and historical diagrams that facilitate monitoring during project implementation, and uses interviews and workshops to evaluate impacts against local expectations.

The whole cycle is linked by the project management system, a set of procedures and instruments to help achieve objectives. Project management includes mechanisms for decision making, actions for directing project activities, and techniques used by the team during implementation to channel energies based on the course of action established by the organizations. In practice, SISDEL assumes a pluralist and eclectic approach, combining different techniques to collect data and to systematize results. The methods used are drawn from different disciplines and range across two extremes. There are techniques that are simple and quick and those that are complex and demanding, as well as other intermediary methods (see Box 8.4).

In selecting techniques, one must strike a balance between addressing different interests while responding to local expectations and communicating results to different local audiences. For instance, with regard to evaluation, the local development team needs to demonstrate tangible impacts to donors, while ensuring that the local population takes ownership over the project; or integrating project monitoring into a more strategic development plan of local government while responding to daily needs of farmers. Choosing the most appropriate method will depend on a number of factors: the capacity of local management teams to apply techniques, the information needs of users or the target audience, and how the findings will be organized and presented. The fundamental question is how to apply methods in order to encourage different audiences or actors to discuss impacts as a basis for learning about project management.

Combining different actors, roles and methods

COMUNIDEC's experience in using the SISDEL methodology in the five municipalities involved building the facilitation skills of local management teams through training. We worked on the principle of learning by doing and trained local project teams, nominated by village authorities, to assume direct responsibility over project planning, implementation, monitoring and evaluation. Members of the project teams varied across different localities, including municipal leaders and authorities, technical experts, representatives of NGO, organizations and institutions.

Trainings begin with project formulation, specific to each provincial context of the collaborators. The key commitments to participation by different actors are established. Project formulation is carried out by holding a three-day workshop on Self-evaluation of Resources and Opportunities (*Taller de Autoevaluación de Recursos y Oportunidades* or TARO). A project profile is drawn up, alternative strategies proposed, and existing resources evaluated. TARO is a forum of local organizations and institutions, open to the general public. Information is collected around the six themes of the cone (see Table 8.1), conducting paired surveys, and semistructured interviews. Proposed solutions are examined in groups until a

---

Box 8.4: A continuum of techniques

Complex, Time-consuming, Qualitative

▲ Prospective design (simulation with geographic information systems)
  Comparison with control groups
  Comparison before-after/with-without project
  Baseline study
  Strategic analysis of actors
  Case study
  Census
  Survey (pre-codified questionnaire)
  Interview with closed questions
  Structured, non-intrusive interview
  Survey with closed questions
  Evaluation and analysis workshop
  Structured interview
  Consensus workshop
  Focused conversation
  Paired surveys
  Open questions
  Transect
  Focus groups
  Documentary revision
  Ethnographic interview
  Semi-structured interview
  Participant observation
  Informal interview
  Counting
  Checklists
▼ Observation

Simple, Quick, Qualitative

---

final agreement between local participants is reached and the baseline information produced. While the training is attended by various local representatives, the local management team and the promoters of farmer organizations ultimately take responsibility for the project activities, but include leaders of the principal farmer organizations in the monitoring and decision making.

In Guamote, for example, the project team headed by the Mayor took charge of the technical process of project implementation, while the leaders of peasant organizations headed project subcommittees for co-ordination and supervision of each project. Together, the project committees, popular leaders and municipal authorities report to the Popular and Indigenous People's Parliament, the most important local organization.

During monitoring, three types of monitoring activities are undertaken by using the agreed indicators:

○ monitoring the achievement of inter-institutional agreements
○ measuring baseline information to determine whether the implemented activities are achieving the expected results
○ producing information to take project management decisions.

Data is collected in several ways. The method of data gathering most commonly used by local management teams is to conduct group observations during visits, along with using maps and interview guides – supplemented, in some cases, by focus group interviews. The information collected is compiled into tables and the findings are organized graphically in the form of histograms, models or drawings based on the selected indicators. Collected information is exhibited publicly, in the project offices (as was the case in CEPCU in Otavalo, for example), or in the municipal office (as in Guamote).

Monitoring activities are undertaken based on the programmed activities of each project, with information reported at specified intervals, usually twice a year. The monitoring process may vary and be made more complex as the project team integrates other methodologies. For example, in the municipality of Suscal, the local management team is establishing the 'Strategic Provincial Plan of the Cantón' and is working with an NGO to develop a simulation through a geographical information system (GIS) programme. The simulation will be based on the monitoring information collected through transects, mapping and interviews. In Otavalo, meanwhile, the indigenous people of the project 'Management of the Lake San Pablo Basin' built small models representing pre-hispanic cultural scales for their baseline, as well as for demonstrating impacts.

During the evaluation phase, it is not considered critical to attribute clear causal linkages between the project and perceived impacts (unless this is obviously the case). Rather, outcomes should be viewed as a shared effort, recognizing the synergy or interactive dynamism between the different actors involved and how their participation contributes to impacts. Methods used include individual interviews with organizations, institutions and key persons using a structured survey questionnaire based on selected indicators. A consensus workshop (*taller de consensos*) is also organized to bring together different groups to interpret the results, using triangulation and statistical analysis. Analysing project findings together with the project team as facilitators helps improve future collaborative processes.

Existing local forms of collective analysis can serve as a basis for carrying out project evaluation. In the five cases examined, project analysis and problem solving took place through community assemblies where public action mandates (*mandatos de acción pública*) are determined. The consensus workshop draws from this cultural practice, but also focuses people's attention on understanding project findings and thereby achieving public recognition of project results. However, the workshop does not function as a community assembly, but rather as a forum for project implementers, local leaders and authorities to discuss project impacts, which may then be reported in a general assembly.

The training of local management teams in the SISDEL methodology has varied in each locality. In Bolívar, where this form of planning is already institutionalized, the SISDEL is being used to combine action-based training (i.e. implementation of projects that integrate health, education and local natural resource management). In Guamote, where there is no formal planning within the municipality and heavy reliance on the leaders' knowledge and expertise predominates, SISDEL aimed to strengthen civic spaces for *concertación* and to improve natural resource management based on joint (municipality and community organisations) agroforestry enterprises.

The compilation and dissemination of results of this participatory monitoring and evaluation process are carried out together by local management teams and COMUNIDEC facilitators. The process seeks to document and, hence, learn from project management experiences, and to disseminate findings amongst local actors. There were two ways of disseminating lessons and findings: publications co-ordinated by the *Grupo Democracia y Desarrollo Local*,[4] and teaching documents used in higher-level continuing education programmes,[5] intended for local leaders, technical experts, and others involved in local development.

Lessons and insights

SISDEL is an ongoing experiment. However, our experiences provide us with three major insights relating to social and political conditions that influence how effectively the SISDEL methodology is applied.

The first major insight recognizes the importance of strengthening collaborative partnerships between local government teams in charge of public policy, and grassroots organizations. While local authorities may recognize the value of a participatory process in community development, few municipalities in Ecuador have as yet the institutional capacity to fully undertake such a process. Where the appropriate knowledge and skills are lacking, SISDEL can help develop the human resources and innovative approaches necessary to sustain local development based on participatory approaches. By training local management teams to become effective community leaders in tracking their own progress, SISDEL can contribute towards the creation and strengthening of local management teams within the context of enhancing good governance of local authorities.

A second insight deals with conflict and conflict resolution in the search for local consensus. In the five projects mentioned, the consultation process sparked conflicts and often divided local actors around varied interests. This brought about confrontation between leaders, authorities, and representatives from rural organizations, who were eventually compelled to decide against authoritarian practices and instead seek to reach common agreements on proposed solutions.

We found that the project cycle inevitably begins in a context of confrontation within which varied expectations are eventually clarified until a consensus is reached, based on the shared interest of local parties involved. Establishing common goals and agreeing on how to work together to achieve these gives rise to transparency, which, in turn, helps facilitate local management of public administrations. Our experiences have taught us that consensus is not a precondition; rather, it is something that has to be dynamically constructed through commitments backed by actions of authorities and local leaders. If appropriately managed, these activities can then contribute to public accountability and the strengthening of local governance.

The third insight acknowledges that establishing a PM&E system such as SISDEL will require that members of the PM&E team have adequate skills to use participatory learning methodologies. Although the clear commitment of leaders, experts, and authorities is also a prerequisite, it is not enough. A PM&E process demands more effective methodologies for managing conflicts, institutional strengthening, social management, and community development planning, amongst others. PM&E is not limited to the mere monitoring of indicators and reporting, but actually aims to establish a continuous learning process through common understanding and the exchange of information and experiences throughout the project cycle.

In conclusion, we feel that no PM&E system can be successful in itself, unless it is integrated within local and regional development plans that are used to guide people's strategic actions. The effectiveness of SISDEL can only be measured in relation to the political changes that its users seek in local and regional contexts.

9

Strengthening Citizen Participation in Evaluating Community Development: The Case of The EZ/EC Learning Initiative in McDowell County, West Virginia

FRANCES PATTON RUTHERFORD[1]

Introduction

ALTHOUGH PARTICIPATORY MONITORING and evaluation (PM&E) is used and promoted in development processes around the world, its use in community-development programmes in the United States is relatively new. And, while many people regard the United States as a highly developed country, in reality, there are within it enormous inequalities between rich and poor people, communities and regions.

This chapter is about the experience of the McDowell County Action Network, located in one of the poorest rural counties in the United States, in using participatory evaluation (PE) as part of its broader effort for community revitalization and development. Located in the heart of the Appalachian Mountains, a rural region known for its sustained poverty, McDowell County, West Virginia is one of 30 communities designated in 1995 to receive support from the Empowerment Zone/Enterprise Community (EZ/EC) programme, established under the Clinton Administration for the revitalization of rural and urban areas.

The challenges we face

McDowell County is the southern-most county in West Virginia, with a population of about 28,000 covering 425 square miles. The county has depended on the coal industry throughout its history, and was, in the 1970s, the largest coal-producing county in the United States. However, the decline in coal industry employment left it with no alternative economic base. Since 1980, the County's population has been rapidly declining, while rates of unemployment have greatly increased. Several major coal companies, including US Steel, owned and operated housing and infrastructure, but stopped maintenance when they no longer needed to support a workforce. When the coal industry pulled out of the region, they left the county without functional physical infrastructures or civic infrastructures to take over leadership and management.

Given the county's historic dependence on coal mining, there are few other economic activities. Three private, absentee land companies still presently own about 85 per cent of the land. Facilities for dealing with sewage are grossly inadequate. The county's distance from any major population or economic centres, its rugged topography and inadequate transportation, and its lack of developable land have hampered McDowell's ability to attract business. As a result, unemployment in the County remains high, and there is heavy out-migration especially of many better-educated and employable citizens and youth. More than 60 per cent of the county's children are living in poverty (the fifth highest of all counties in the USA).

Despite these major challenges, there are also enormous resources on which to build. McDowell County has incredible beauty and rich resources of mountains and forests, a workforce with valuable skills from highly mechanized, unionized underground coal mining, strong grassroots community groups and a dedicated and trained population of professionals in the human services, medical, and educational fields working to improve the quality of life in the communities. McDowell County has a large number of families with diverse ethnic backgrounds – including the largest percentage of African-Americans in the state – who enrich the county's culture. Scattered throughout the county are 78 small communities with strong family ties and mutual support systems.

McCAN and the Enterprise Community Programme

In 1993, the Clinton Administration and the US Congress launched the EZ/EC programme, a national initiative that provided direct grants, tax incentives, and preferential funding towards the revitalization of distressed urban and rural communities. The US Department of Housing and Urban Development (HUD) administers the urban part of the programme, and the US Department of Agriculture (USDA) administers the rural part.

The EZ/EC programme promised to be different from many federal programmes in that it challenged local communities to develop *their own* strategic vision for change, especially focusing on economic opportunity, sustainable community development, and community-based partnerships. In each of these, community participation was to be critical. As the guidelines established by the President's Community Empowerment Board stated:

> 'the road to economic opportunity and community development starts with broad participation by all segments of the community. This may include, among others, the political and governmental leadership, community groups, health and social service groups, environmental groups, religious organizations, the private and non-profit sectors, centres of learning and other community institutions. *The residents themselves, however, are the most important element of revitalization*' (USDA, 1994, emphasis added).

The response was enormous. More than 500 poor communities in rural America entered the competitive process outlined by federal guidelines, and submitted their own strategic plans for community revitalization by June 30, 1994. Designations were made in December 1994, which included three rural empowerment zones and thirty rural enterprise communities, each of which received significant block grants and other economic benefits. McDowell County, West Virginia was one of the enterprise communities.

In McDowell County, the process started in February 1994, when several community leaders (including the author) attended an informational meeting on the EZ/EC programme sponsored by the USDA. We decided to submit an application. We returned to the county, established the McDowell County Action Network (McCAN), began to mobilize the community around a ten-year strategic plan for community revitalization, and were awarded $2.95 million to support the work of McCAN.

The planning process involved hundreds of people, 11 citizen committees, and several months of hard work. Informational meetings were held, with support and assistance provided by the business, political, financial and media sectors. There were high hopes, broad participation and community commitment to work for social and economic growth and development in the county. The strategic plan called for a variety of projects that integrated growth and development in all sectors: the economy, family, community, arts, education, health, infrastructure, and transportation.

McCAN formalized a Board of Directors from people on the EZ/EC steering committee, members of the other planning committees, and emerging leaders throughout the county. The long-range strategic plan was restructured to a strategy to show maximum success with fewer resources in a two-year time span. For the next six months, McCAN held a series of community meetings (18 in total) to ascertain community priorities and establish a process for community-controlled social and economic growth and development in the county. By July 1995, McCAN announced community priorities for support by the EC revitalization project which included a family-advocacy initiative, a training/education/job skills development initiative, an employment/business development initiative, a recreation initiative, and an environmental blight-abatement initiative.

Since 1995, McCAN has developed dozens of projects, addressing a wide array of community concerns. Of particular significance have been a microloan project for the support of new businesses, and the development of a model transitional housing project for victims of domestic violence and homelessness. In addition, McCAN used the EC funding to leverage additional resources, matching the federal funds more than thirty times!

The EZ/EC Learning Initiative

In February 1996, McDowell County also became one of the ten sites selected for a national pilot PM&E project of the rural EZ/EC programme.[2] The pilot Learning Initiative aimed to further support community participation by involving local residents as evaluators of the EC development programme in McDowell County. A Citizen Learning Team (CLT) was to be established in each pilot site to take charge of the PM&E project. The learning initiative had several broad goals including:

○ capacity building through development of skills and leadership of local participants in rural EZ/EC communities
○ continuous improvement of the EC through strengthened citizen participation, feedback and accountability
○ developing research and evaluation skills through local documentation and learning.

Through this process, the learning initiative aimed to strengthen citizen capacity and empowerment, by involving the people for whom the programme was intended in deciding which goals are most important and in assessing how well these goals are achieved. It aimed to build knowledge and skills of communities to do their own evaluation, and therefore strengthen citizen participation and accountability.

This National Learning Initiative was co-ordinated by the Community Partnership Centre (CPC) at the University of Tennessee/Knoxville. Drawing on a range of participatory monitoring approaches, many of which had been developed internationally, the CPC developed an approach to the process and a manual and resource materials for local teams and their co-ordinators. The first training was conducted in March 1996 involving all ten pilot projects. At this training, locally selected co-ordinators, additional team members and researchers from around the country were trained in conducting PM&E research.

Preparing the CLT in McDowell County

In McDowell County 15 members comprised the CLT. The team represented McDowell County's diverse geographic, racial, age, and gender demographics. It included EC implementers, community members, a local co-ordinator and a professional researcher assigned to work with the group. The CLT combined leadership from newly emerging empowerment organizations with staff of established, long-term agencies and organizations within McDowell County. It used technical expertise from the Governor's Office, Rural Development Office of the USDA, and McCAN. From the original group of 15, eight members (seven female and one male) formed the core group that stayed with the entire process and carried out the research. Others participated by attending some sessions, providing information, and collecting data. McCAN, the overall body responsible for the EC programme, endorsed the work and supported the process financially.

The CLT followed the ten steps outlined in the Learning Wheel (see Figure 9.1), which had been developed by the learning initiative. The main activities of the Learning Wheel were undertaken through a series of workshops and included:

○ revisiting EZ/EC goals
○ selecting priority goals to monitor and measure
○ identifying indicators of success
○ determining how to collect the data needed for monitoring and measuring

127

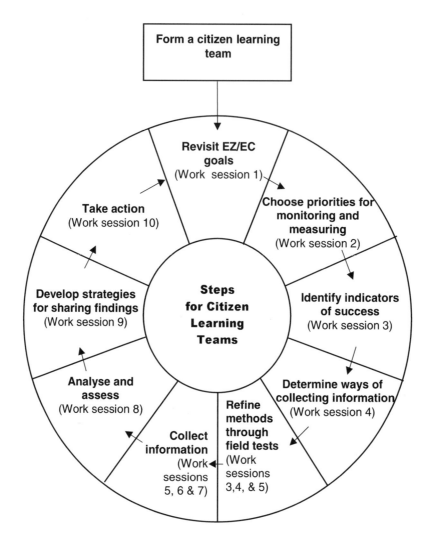

Figure 9.1: *The Learning Wheel*

○ sharing findings and taking action with the EC board, interested stakeholders, and the general public
○ disseminating reports through presentations, newsletters, and public meetings.

Setting priorities for monitoring

Following the initial session to introduce the PM&E project, the team then reviewed the national goals of the EC programme and McCAN's benchmarks. Since it knew it was unable to evaluate everything, the team decided to focus the evaluation process on three of McDowell County's goals:[3]

- Goal 1: Economic opportunity: Job, business and capital creation
- Goal 2: Community partnerships: Community revitalization
- Goal 3: Strategic vision: Inter-agency and intergovernmental collaboration.

In addition, in each of these the CLT sought to assess the following questions:

- How equitably were resources distributed?
- How was the organizational capacity of McCAN and other agencies strengthened?
- What was the nature of communication (formal and informal) between McCAN, project implementers, and the public?[4]
- What kinds of collaboration occurred and with what results?[5]

The learning team divided into three smaller groups, one for each of the three main goals, to become the 'Task Forces' that would be responsible for monitoring and evaluating that particular goal. The groups worked separately, and each developed evaluation plans for its priority goal, but reported to the other members of the learning team. To assess each of these goals, the team also identified existing resources (i.e. available research/evaluation tools, research expertise, etc.) and possible information sources. Through a series of task force meetings and working sessions from April 1996 through December 1996, the team:

- developed indicators and measurement tools
- developed data collection tools
- conducted a wage and labour survey, and a sustainable employment survey
- conducted a social capacity mapping project
- developed social capacity charts
- developed district-specific social capacity summations
- conducted case studies, including board and staff interviews, with McCAN, the McDowell County Economic Development Authority (EDA) and Stop Abusive Family Environments (SAFE)
- participated in reflection interviews of learning team members to summarize findings and make recommendations from the research experience
- reviewed and revised a final report written by the local co-ordinator and supporting researcher, and made dissemination plans for the findings and recommendations.

Choosing indicators and methods

The learning team developed forms that specified indicators, baseline, and methods for measuring each priority goal. Since many projects were just beginning, the learning team concentrated on developing a baseline, measurement standards and tools to allow for ongoing monitoring and

Table 9.1: Indicators for each priority goal

Priority Goal 1: Jobs, business and capital creation indicators	Priority Goal 2: Community revitalization	Priority Goal 3: Inter-agency and intergovernmental collaboration
○ number of sustainable jobs developed ○ number of businesses created ○ number of micro-loans made ○ technical assistance to start-up businesses	○ attitudes of people ○ voting in elections ○ trash collection ○ clean-up of dilapidated structures ○ home ownership	○ level of collaboration within SAFE, EDA and McCAN ○ level of communication, organizational capacity and equitable distribution of resources within SAFE, EDA and McCAN

Table 9.2: Methods for measuring each priority goal

Priority Goal 1: Jobs, business and capital creation	Priority Goal 2: Community revitalization	Priority Goal 3: Inter-agency and intergovernmental collaboration
○ survey of sample of businesses for following data: salary range, health insurance, pensions, new business start-ups, applications for employment, loan applications by geographic distribution, gender, race, age, ethnicity ○ interviews with EDA Board and Director, small businesses, banks, technical assistance providers ○ labour force study by EDA	○ mapping of the numbers and types of community organizations in each community of the county ○ listing of all organizations in each community, using the telephone directory, other service directories and knowledge of local residents ○ mapping of location and service area of each McCAN project and location of major community leaders drawn from Board and committee lists of McCAN and other major development organizations or funded agencies ○ case studies of communities	○ study of McCAN, SAFE, EDA using board minutes, board training manual, status reports, newsletters. Interviews with Directors, staff and Board ○ data analysed for degree of communication, collaboration, organizational capacity and equitable distribution using the following criteria: activities documented in plans, committees for various sectors and communities in county, all segments of community represented

evaluation. The indicators for each priority goal are summarised in Table 9.1 and the methods of data collection used for selected priority goals are summarized in Table 9.2.

The learning team developed its own methods for obtaining specific information needs. To assess the first priority goal, the team carried out a labour survey and a sustainable employment survey. The labour survey was first undertaken, and, while it yielded useful information, the team felt it was not enough for assessing other important aspects of economic development. We therefore decided to conduct a second survey which not only indicated the current level of employment but also measured whether the employment was *sustainable* – that is, whether it would adequately support a sustainable livelihood. We defined sustainable employment in terms of specified income levels together with other benefits, i.e. family health insurance and a basic pension plan.

The task force working on Priority Goal 2 – community partnerships and community revitalisation – was unable to continue its research because several members left the learning team. The CLT had to re-organize and re-evaluate that priority goal. After intensive discussion, the team felt that measuring community revitalization was so important that we decided to take it on as a whole team effort. We wanted to measure equitable distribution and use of EC resources in the county, as people wanted to make sure everybody was getting their fair share. We also wanted to see if the distribution of funds was related to the 'capacity' of the community, or whether the funds were being distributed based on other criteria, such as political cronyism.

The team selected 'social capacity' as a main indicator of revitalization. A list of all organizations in each community was drawn up using various information sources (telephone and other service directories, knowledge of local residents, etc.). These organizations were then classified according to fourteen categories, including arts/culture, civic/social clubs, religious, recreational, co-ops, education, unions, financial institutions, businesses, media, county/state/federal services, and local government. Then, these organizations were classified according to their 'empowerment capacity', based on such criteria as the networks they form, their control over and access to resources, and their development of leaders. To our surprise, we found that of the 78 communities in the county, 42 already had organizations with 'empowerment capacity'. Twenty of them were seen as having larger capacity because they had two or more empowerment organizations.

We initiated a mapping exercise to show the relationship of this capacity to project interventions funded by McCAN and to provide a baseline for measuring community revitalization. Together with the comprehensive list of community organizations, we mapped the location and service area of each McCAN project and the location of major community leaders from the various organizations. In the process, we were amazed to find the breadth of social resources and the untapped potential already existing within our county. We were also able to begin monitoring the growth of community development programmes resulting directly from EC funds and McCAN's efforts, and to examine the basis by which they were allocated.

The group focusing on intergovernmental and inter-agency collaboration (Priority Goal 3) decided to focus on three organizations funded through the EC programme, mainly to assess organizational capacities: EDA, the arm of local government which promotes economic development; SAFE, a transitional housing project for victims of domestic violence and homelessness; and McCAN.

Learning from the learning team

Because the EC programme is in the early stages of implementation, it is too soon to assess its overall outcomes in McDowell County. Because the start-up of projects was slow in the beginning and existing information about the county limited, the CLT concentrated its initial efforts towards establishing a baseline for future monitoring and evaluation.

While the EC projects are still ongoing, in the first year we did prove that a local group can do evaluation. We were not practised in this type of evaluation so the process was sometimes ragged but we learned by doing. The core group of eight people became a very efficient and committed research team. The next section assesses how well we met our goals, highlights some of the major lessons we learned in the process and also points out the challenges we face.

Capacity building through participatory evaluation

Even in the short period of piloting, learning team members developed skills and capacities to analyse their findings and present recommendations concerning EC programme implementation. In the process, members of the learning team learned how their community works and shared this knowledge with others. The learning team participated in several cross-site training workshops with other CLT members from other communities to share lessons about their experiences in the EZ/EC programme and in PM&E. McDowell learning team members also presented their initial findings and recommendations to key EZ/EC administrators and government officials in Washington, DC.

The CLT was thus successful in establishing a PE process that enabled community representatives themselves to monitor and measure progress of their EZ/EC programme as it develops. Members of the learning team learned how to monitor change indicators and to analyse their implications, and shared this knowledge with others in the county. As the team went about data gathering, they engaged in community education and provided a role model for citizen participation. The process provided opportunities to create and expand networks, by helping people get to know one another, become better acquainted with other development activities existing in the county, and build new partnerships for action. Learning team members grew from the experience by developing new skills and increased self-confidence; some have even become involved in other public roles and have pursued leadership positions in the county.

Improvement of the EC through strengthened participation, feedback and accountability

The CLT sustains participation in the EC beyond the planning phase. Local evaluation makes it possible for the team to use the information and to see and understand the impact of their efforts. It provides an accountability mechanism to keep residents informed about EC activities and progress.

Local documentation provided information about ongoing implementation of the EC programme. For instance, the team found that some projects had already made remarkable achievements, i.e. the growth of new businesses and inter-institutional partnerships. However, it also identified other key areas for improvement, including the need to further strengthen and sustain community participation in the EC process after the initial strategic planning process (for further details about findings and recommendations, see Rutherford and Lewis, 1997.) This has helped to establish a process for continuous learning and feedback, and to make midcourse adjustments and enhance impacts, especially in aspects of participation, partnerships, and community empowerment. By providing feedback to McCAN through this process, McCAN was held accountable not only to funders but also to the community and to local stakeholders. Accountability is based on performance, as defined and measured by community representatives, to stimulate action towards improvement.

Collective research and locally generated learning

In addition to developing local capacity and providing feedback for continuous improvement, the CLT helped to provide a method for systematic, locally generated learning and documentation about the implementation of the EC. The ability to do collective research builds on individual growth and provides a vehicle for further community involvement.

The core group members agreed that the CLT and participatory research are valuable methods for evaluation. Although the process was not without its frustrations, team members soon learned how to work effectively and innovate different ways of conducting evaluation. A PM&E process then emerged that was flexible and adaptive and which provided information that was directly useful and relevant.

An important part of the process was taking ownership of the project ourselves. For example, we found that the PM&E manual that had been developed by the University of Tennessee was too specific and awkward for the team to use. Language seemed to be one of the biggest barriers. To our team members, the manual seemed too theoretical. Its language was academic when it needed to be practical. The manual seemed to be more appropriate for people who had experience in evaluation research instead of community people just beginning the process. The steps suggested seemed to be restrictive and inflexible.

So, we soon started developing our own materials. We utilized some of the more important research terms, such as 'monitoring', 'measuring', 'baselines', but we otherwise used everyday language among ourselves and the public when speaking about our research project. We still used the suggested resource materials as a starting point to make sure we addressed the key areas within the pilot PM&E process, but we rearranged timelines and activities and developed our own measuring tools. The members found that it was important to develop a style of working that was comfortable for them, and learned that they worked together best by being less formal and by getting to know each other. For instance, we were most effective when we worked in smaller groups and we communicated more frequently outside regular workshop sessions.

Early in the project, members felt that the process was not very productive, and were unclear about what would come out of it. Learning team members found the early workshops tedious and frustrating as they were eager to begin serious research and documentation. There was discussion as to whom the evaluation was for and what purpose it had. The team decided that *if it was not to strengthen the development process in McDowell County, then it was not worth doing.* The group worried about concentrating on limited goals and not evaluating the total activity of McCAN. These issues and problems were discussed and some of the anxiety relieved as specific plans of action for each task force began to take shape.

If we want evaluation findings utilized, PE is the only way to go. It strengthens the development process. We can judge success better than outsiders can. What others may pass off as not important, we can see and identify as being important and significant. We would not have learned half as much through outside evaluation. One encouraging sign is that some of the EC-funded projects are now planning to incorporate PM&E into their programmes. However, we are also aware that as insiders we might also overlook some things that outsiders would see, and take certain changes for granted. Our desire to look good and appear successful creates a potential bias that requires attention in a PE process.

Sustaining the process

While overall we found the CLT process to be successful in our community, we also learned lessons about how such projects can be sustained, and have the most impact.

Involving the right mix of stakeholders

In the beginning, we deliberately tried to form the citizen learning team to represent a wide variety of stakeholders in the project. In fact, we felt that one of our obligations was to address the issues of as many stakeholders as possible. However, although the task forces collected good data, there was not enough collective analysis of data involving team members and the general public. Future evaluation efforts will need to build alliances and work more closely with other local stakeholders, including the McDowell County Government. This will help ensure that the learning process takes into account different perspectives and interests, and that results and proposed alternatives attain broader-based local support.

Resource requirements and technical support

Another serious constraint faced by team members was the time available to do the research and evaluation. The members were busy people working with agencies that allowed their staff to contribute their time and be part of the evaluation process. However, because of busy schedules and other work commitments, it was difficult to sustain participation of team members throughout the entire process. Although there was a core group working throughout, other members dropped out or were unable to participate regularly.

This raises an important issue of sustaining the monitoring and evaluation process. Getting short bursts is sometimes easy and possible but to maintain it is difficult (although not impossible). PM&E needs a permanent team of committed people who understand how complex and long the process is. However, this would be too much to ask of people with jobs and families, unless there was compensation to their agency or business for time taken off. Fewer formal meetings and more staff support might have helped lighten the task. Continually bringing new people into the evaluation process would also ensure continuity, as the original group already trained in the process could pass on valuable knowledge and skills.

Quality and rigour

We also found that it takes a long time to develop research that is judged by others to be reliable and acceptable as evaluation. PE is often under pressure to undertake high quality research under serious time constraints and by overworked staff. The criticism that PE does not produce high quality information can be met with the answer that it is not funded so to do. PE should be as adequately funded as professional, outside evaluation. With adequate funding, support and professional back-up, a local evaluation team *can* produce high quality research. In our team, the outside professional researcher who worked with us was crucial in providing technical and moral support. The researcher knew the community well, facilitated but did not dictate, and helped the group change course and develop alternative techniques. Otherwise, the team could have fallen apart when the group became frustrated over the manual and the process.

Sharing lessons and celebrating success

We have developed baselines but need to continue to check progress and keep gathering information, as our findings only indicate initial trends and current implementation. Yet, so far, the evaluation findings are mainly in the heads of learning team members. Team members feel that only the learning team really knows what is going on and the implications of their research. More work is needed to ensure better communication within McDowell County about the EZ/EC process. The findings of the evaluation report need to be better publicized and be used to reflect on progress and suggest improvements. We also found it important to take time to celebrate what we had accomplished and to recognize individuals for their hard work and achievements.

Networking

New efforts that promote increased community participation in evaluation – both in the United States and internationally – represent substantive changes in the field of evaluation, with significant implications for development in general. The inception of a PM&E process is increasingly bringing communities to the forefront of development. Not only does this process positively affect the level of community participation and action but it also empowers communities to acknowledge that their ideas, knowledge and experiences are important resources to be used as a basis of action and to affect directly the development they need.

Linking the citizens' learning initiative in the United States with other community-driven PM&E efforts around the world is a significant step towards enriching and sustaining our understanding and experience. We hope to establish a PM&E centre that will create a network of practitioners and advocates nationally and internationally. It will facilitate international exchanges of families and communities from different countries to learn and share their experiences. It will also provide a vehicle for improving participatory approaches and methods, developing training programmes, and documenting impacts of applying PM&E in diverse contexts.

Conclusions

Despite some challenges encountered along the way, what our experience in McDowell County does show is that local communities – and the every-day citizen – can do their own evaluation. Moreover, the benefits of the process were clearly seen by local people. In 1998 when we were preparing plans for a new phase of the project, we had 61 volunteers for the next learning team. The volunteers reflected the diversity of the community – from 10 to 72 years old, from all areas of the county, black and white, male and female, poor and rich, business persons and welfare recipients. This response helps to demonstrate the strength in the project and its potential.

The CLT initiative brings into focus two divergent paradigms that drive development in different areas. The more traditional approach understands development as the arena of a small group of people who are given the task of determining the county's economic future. The participatory model brings citizens directly into the development process. PE provides a vehicle for people ordinarily outside the process to become informed and involved in events taking place in the area.

In so doing, local evaluation adds a component to a development process that outside evaluation does not. It gives results and experiences a greater breadth, depth, and texture in a report which is more likely to be used because findings are locally generated and therefore better understood. There is a sense of ownership in the outcome. Local evaluation makes it possible for the people for whom programmes are intended, to see and understand their impact. McDowell County has always relied on outside people to come in and measure progress, leaving communities with too little capacity to assess their own development. A participatory process develops capacity for people to take more initiative and to exercise control.

Part 3

Changing Institutions

10

Growing from the Grassroots: Building Participatory Planning, Monitoring and Evaluation Methods in PARC

JANET SYMES AND SA'ED JASSER

Introduction

FEW EXPERIENCES DESCRIBE how organizations can support and strengthen participatory development specifically in areas with a long history of political conflict and popular struggle. This chapter looks at the experience of the Palestinian Agricultural Relief Committees (PARC) in developing a participatory planning, monitoring and evaluation (PPM&E)[1] approach for the organization as a whole. First, we discuss the changing political situation in Palestine and its implications for applying participatory methodologies. Second, we examine the ongoing process of building a PPM&E approach at the organizational level, including the steps we have taken to apply this approach and to address the issues that arise.

Using participatory methods in PARC

About PARC

PARC is a Palestinian non-governmental organization (NGO) working in the rural areas of the West Bank and Gaza. It was founded by a group of young farmers and recently-graduated agronomists. These volunteers worked under difficult political conditions to establish extension services and carry out vital grassroots organizing work. PARC targets poor and marginalized farmers – both men and women – and works with them to improve their agricultural livelihoods and to develop a strong Palestinian agriculture sector. The main focus of our work is on food security, development of the agriculture sector, supporting the position of rural women, building civil society and protecting land from confiscation.

The Palestinian context – the people's struggle

Recent Palestinian history has been characterized by the struggle for a homeland. During the 1948 war, Israel forcibly seized large areas of

Palestinian land, and the Six Day War in 1967 led to the Israeli occupation of the West Bank and Gaza. As a result, large numbers of Palestinians have become refugees. Today less than half of all Palestinians live in the West Bank and Gaza, and of those, many are refugees still living in camps. In Gaza over 60 per cent of the people are refugees.

Since 1967 the West Bank and Gaza have remained under Israeli military occupation. The economy has become almost totally dependent on Israel and suffers from a neglected infrastructure, a negative investment climate and restrictions imposed by the military administration. Politically, the Palestinian people are stateless and denied the right to self-determination. During the *intifada* (the popular uprising against the occupation in the late 1980s and early 1990s) curfews were imposed, and movement was prevented for extended periods of time. Mass demonstrations resulted in violent clashes with Israeli armed forces with thousands of deaths and injuries. Indiscriminate mass arrests and torture were commonplace.

Contrary to expectations, the peace process has brought little 'peace dividend'; the daily reality is one of checkpoints, closures and unemployment. The West Bank and Gaza is now a complex patchwork of zones with differing degrees of autonomy – about 70 per cent is still under total military occupation. The Israeli army frequently seals off the main towns in the West Bank where the new Palestinian Authority has control. Since the 1993 Oslo Accords, a closure has been in force that restricts movement. For example, Palestinians need special permits to enter Jerusalem or inside the Green Line,[2] and even these permits are cancelled for extended periods during total closures. Virtually no movement between the West Bank and Gaza is permitted, and restricted access to Jerusalem effectively cuts off the Palestinians living in the north of the West Bank from those in the south and vice versa. The effect has been devastating: in economic terms, UN figures show that per capita GNP for the West Bank and Gaza has declined by 38.8 per cent from 1992 levels, over 100,000 jobs have been lost and unemployment rates have soared. Estimates suggest that up to US$14.7 million in income and US$2.5 million in fiscal revenue per week is lost during the total closures.

Participation under occupation

These circumstances have significant implications for participatory development. On the one hand, the occupation severely limits the control people have over their lives. This environment creates a 'culture of occupation', making it difficult for people to see beyond seemingly insurmountable problems that they feel powerless to change. The power of the gun appears far greater than that of the olive branch when farmers are confronted by the sight of their olive trees being uprooted by Israeli bulldozers. People's sense of powerlessness becomes a barrier to effectively mobilizing and empowering people to promote change through collective action.

On the other hand, the *intifada* saw a huge mobilization of popular power. Men, women and children struggled together to assert their Palestinian identity and to build a Palestinian state that would give them greater control over their own future. During the *intifada*, many of the local Palestinian NGOs were set up to organize people and to provide desperately needed services neglected by the Israeli military authorities. It is within this context that PARC built its close ties with the rural people through day-to-day support during the *intifada* and efforts to counter Israeli policies that aimed to hinder Palestinian agriculture. Initially, PARC's work in the villages was led by volunteers who themselves were often farmers from the villages. Voluntary committees were established in villages and were responsible for local decision making. PARC's work today is rooted in this popular struggle and grassroots organizing.

Looking towards the longer term: the need for PPM&E

During the *intifada*, PARC focused on providing food relief to people in refugee camps or under closure, and organizing rural communities. The extremely unpredictable and volatile situation, the voluntary basis of PARC's work, and the overwhelming need to address immediate concerns made long-term planning difficult. Because the prevailing situation generally required rapid practical action, most of PARC's work concentrated on carrying out short-term objectives. The combination of these factors did little to promote the use of participatory methods, especially in planning, monitoring or evaluation.

The advent of the peace process and more stable situation encouraged a longer-term outlook, shifting PARC's focus away from emergency relief towards rehabilitation and development. PARC began to prioritize programmes and projects with longer term goals, to re-emphasize extension work and to concentrate on building a sustainable and viable agricultural sector. Parallel to this re-orientation, PARC relied less on voluntary work and expanded its employment of professional field workers. The voluntary committees were separated from PARC's organizational structure and became the basis for establishing an independent farmers' union. Although this was seen as essential, both to allow PARC to move forward and for farmers to have an independent voice, this meant that PARC's decision-making process was now less directly linked with the rural communities. Consequently, PARC needed to develop new ways of working and became increasingly interested in measuring and understanding the impact of its work. PARC wanted to learn from its experiences and ensure that it maintained its relevance to the community, but also to respond to increasing interest by PARC's donors to assess the impact of its work.

Building an organizational commitment to PPM&E

The characteristics of PPM&E in PARC

In PARC we recognize the importance of linking PPM&E into a system that operates for the organization as a whole. By participation, we mean the full involvement of both the community[3] and the different levels of PARC's staff in all aspects of the work – from activity implementation to decision making. What is intrinsic in our PPM&E approach is that the concept of participation is applied not just at the project level but also within the organization itself, for example, in strategic planning. The PPM&E work aims to provide a flexible framework through which PARC can learn from its experience. In this regard, linking monitoring and evaluation (M&E) with planning plays a crucial part in our PPM&E approach. Moreover, the PPM&E work aims to give a greater role to the people we work with in defining PARC's direction and their own development process.

The building blocks of our PPM&E approach

The steps we have taken in developing a PPM&E approach are conceptualized in terms of building blocks (see Figure 10.1). Each 'block' should be viewed as part of a continuous process rather than as a distinct step. The blocks can be identified as follows:

○ developing an understanding of participation
○ developing appropriate methods, skills and team work
○ strengthening the elements of planning, monitoring and evaluation
○ linking planning, monitoring and evaluation, and linking levels within the organization
○ creating an appropriate framework and identifying needs and gaps.

Developing an understanding of participation

Despite PARC's grassroots origins there was still a need to develop an organizational understanding of participation. Although rural people have been very much involved in PARC's work and community representatives consulted in decision making and planning, many of the methods used by

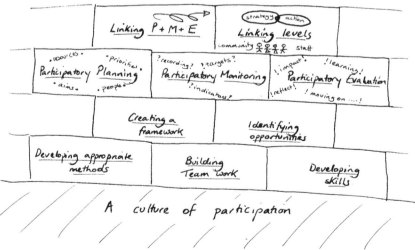

Figure 10.1: *The building blocks of a PPM&E system*

140

PARC limited local participation to consultation. The community was often regarded as an information source rather than as key actors capable of playing a central role in the decision-making processes of the organization.

In order to carry out PPM&E effectively, PARC recognized that it is not sufficient simply to use participatory techniques. There must be a real commitment to the philosophy of participation at all levels within the organization, and a full understanding of what participation means and how to apply participatory techniques in an appropriate manner that would ensure full local involvement.

PARC has invested considerable attention in fully developing such a perspective within the organization. However, we face constraints to promoting participation. These include opposing the 'culture of occupation' and working towards overcoming people's sense of powerlessness. PARC also operates in a social environment that is traditionally somewhat hierarchical. This means that those in positions of community leadership do not necessarily recognize the value of participation nor do they encourage collective action. This perspective is also reflected within hierarchical organizational structures that often preclude the involvement of all levels of staff in, for example, policy formulation or organizational decision making. All these factors have been barriers to developing an organizational commitment to participation, and hence require that institutionalizing participation be viewed as a long-term process. We are approaching this gradually, beginning with several different areas such as training staff in participatory concepts, developing more participatory methods, and providing practical experience in the use of participatory techniques.

To ensure that this commitment to participation is not confined to project implementation, but is carried through to organizational decision making, it is essential for the senior management to be fully involved. By strengthening the understanding of a participatory approach at this level, we have been able to encourage the greater involvement of all levels of staff and the community in carrying out PPM&E work. This has not always been a straightforward matter: there can be some resistance, particularly when involvement affects major decisions within the organization. Broad-based participation can initially be threatening for some, as it can change organizational dynamics and shift the focus of control. We have found that it is important to acknowledge these potential fears and slowly build confidence among key people in using a participatory approach. Through the thoughtful application of participatory techniques, there has been a gradual but enthusiastic shift within PARC towards wider acceptance of a participatory approach (see Box 10.1).

Developing appropriate participatory methods

The second building block of PARC's PPM&E process includes developing appropriate methods, skills and team work. To do this we have been working in several key areas: (i) introducing interactive methods, (ii) building team work, and (iii) developing the skills of our staff.

141

> **Box 10.1   Overcoming fears – building confidence in a participatory approach to evaluation**
>
> **The situation**
> During an organizational evaluation two years ago, despite a willingness to involve the community, there was an initial reluctance from PARC to involve all levels of staff in the evaluation process. It was felt that it was not necessary for field staff to be involved and that their perspectives could be adequately represented by their managers. In an attempt to build confidence in a participatory approach, we encouraged all levels of staff to work in groups according to their common positions in the organization. Management, support staff and female and male field staff groups carried out SWOT (Strengths, Weaknesses, Opportunities and Threats) analyses, defined their priorities and outlined their vision for the future of the organization. Each group presented and explained their responses in a plenary session. From the ensuing discussions, the different groups came to recognize the validity of each other's perspectives and to understand their value to the evaluation and to improving future work in general.
>
> **The outcome**
> Demonstrating the validity of the different perspectives helped to build confidence within PARC in applying a participatory evaluation approach, to recognize the importance of different interest groups and to highlight the value of wider participation in decision making. Many ideas developed during these workshops are now forming a key part of PARC's strategic planning.

Interactive methods.   Recognizing the need for a more effective communication process between our staff and the community, PARC has taken initial steps to develop more interactive methods of working. New techniques have been introduced which draw on our long experience and close links with the villages. These methods include community or interest group workshops which we found particularly useful in our context because they give people the opportunity to discuss and formulate ideas, as well as encouraging more in-depth analysis. The workshops are individually tailored to particular requirements and the techniques used are specifically designed to facilitate reflection and analysis. For instance, we design group activities using a range of tools such as key points on cards, prioritization and variants of SWOT analysis. In this way, a workshop that is part of, for example, a project evaluation process, could start by looking at the perceived achievements and problems, the strengths, weaknesses, opportunities and threats; then move on to discuss the prioritization of issues and their implications for the project and the community; and, finally, identify future steps, thereby linking evaluation with the planning process.

In several situations we have used these interactive workshops in order for women to gain an equal voice in community discussions and decision making. Due to the relatively conservative nature of rural areas in Palestine and the difficulty of involving women in general discussions, workshops have always been held separately for men and women. In this way, women could meet together and have the opportunity to present their own perspectives. One experience describes how workshops involving women enabled them to better assert their views and define their priorities (Box 10.2). We hope to develop these interactive methods further and to introduce more participatory techniques for M&E.

Box 10.2:   Using participatory methods to give women control

The situation
In an integrated village development programme, the planning process involved leading members of the community but overlooked the women. The men defined the activities for women: training courses in sewing and knitting.

The outcome
As a result of working closely together with PARC's Women's Unit, the women set up a separate association to manage their own programme. They met regularly as a group and re-prioritized their activities to include growing and marketing herbs, and setting up a kindergarten.

During an evaluation of the village programme, the men realized how women defined and achieved their own objectives and concluded that it had been the women who accomplished the most: they had been innovative and successful in getting their ideas off the ground. The men expressed appreciation of women's involvement and even began discussing the possibilities of including women in the all-male village co-ordinating committee.

This experience demonstrated how workshops can be instrumental in overcoming some of the social constraints limiting women's participation in village level decision making and in helping promote the position of women in the village.

Team work: sharing experience is sharing learning.   A major feature of our PPM&E approach is team work. For instance, when evaluating specific programmes and projects, a team is set up to lead the process which usually comprises a member of PARC's PPM&E staff, programme and field staff, and members of the community. Promoting team work helps us consider the different priorities of the different groups involved. The importance of community involvement and representing diverse interests in PPM&E is illustrated in an evaluation undertaken with the Palestinian Farmers' Union (PFU) (see Box 10.3).

Box 10.3: Resolving differences by working as a team – the example of the Palestinian Farmers' Union (PFU)

The situation
The PFU emerged from the voluntary committees set up originally by PARC. While close relations remain between PARC and the PFU, each organization represents different interests. PARC invited the PFU to join them in an evaluation of their working relationship. However, once the PFU was involved it became clear that their aims for the evaluation were very different from those of PARC. On the one hand, PARC was interested in evaluating how the creation of an independent farmers' union has affected PARC's work in the community and how it should build its relationship with the new organization. On the other hand, the PFU was interested in conducting a situation analysis for the union in order to define its mandate and future direction.

The outcome
By running a joint workshop it was possible to redefine objectives and satisfy both interests. PARC recognized that they would still benefit by integrating the interests of the PFU in the evaluation. The evaluation process gave the union a greater sense of independence by encouraging them to conduct their own planning process. Moreover, the evaluation established greater opportunities for mutually beneficial work between PARC and the PFU. This experience illustrated the need first to clarify objectives of the evaluation, taking into account differing interests of participants and establishing a co-operative process.

From number-crunchers to listeners: developing the skills of our staff
Using participatory techniques requires that staff possess specific skills such as facilitation, listening and giving marginalized groups a voice. In PARC most staff have technical backgrounds as agricultural engineers and still need to strengthen these skills. For example, monitoring was initially understood by staff as a process of collecting quantitative data on projects, such as how many trees were planted, field visits made, animals treated. The methods used tended to encourage this approach and reinforce the idea that 'scientifically' calculated data were the only valid information. In order to develop the skills of our staff, PARC has provided specific training sessions in participatory principles and methods. We have also encouraged learning from experience through self-monitoring and evaluation. Programme staff and community members are directly involved in designing and conducting their own M&E process. Their involvement enables them to take on responsibility for the PPM&E work, to see it as an essential part of the project process, and to recognize the benefits of participation. As a result, many of the staff are now taking the initiative in applying PPM&E themselves. For example, the Women's Unit in Gaza decided to evaluate their work in more detail. They conducted a self-evaluation to reflect on

the extent to which they were achieving their aims. In the process, they also involved the women participating in their projects in developing plans for their future work.

Strengthening the elements of planning, monitoring and evaluation within PARC

As explained earlier, PPM&E was relatively undeveloped in PARC until recently, and so strengthening the different elements of planning, monitoring and evaluation has been an important part of institutionalizing a PPM&E approach within the organization.

We began by strengthening evaluation work and introducing participatory techniques (see the earlier section on 'Developing appropriate participatory methods'). We chose to focus on evaluation initially because of donor interests to show the impact of our work, but also because of a desire within the organization to learn from our experience. This led us to move towards strengthening participatory planning as a means of moving the evaluation work forward and integrating evaluation findings into the planning process. Previously, planning was seen very much as a separate organizational task to be carried out by senior management (albeit including consultations with staff and the community). Our experience in participatory evaluation helped to demonstrate the desirability of also applying more participatory methods in planning. For instance, PARC developed its strategic plan by using participatory techniques and drawing from previous evaluation findings.

Unlike planning and evaluation, institutionalizing participatory monitoring has been a more problematic issue for us, and we are working gradually to build confidence in applying the concept. One reason for this is that, in Arabic, the word most commonly used for monitoring conveys a meaning related to 'controlling'. This has contributed to a general perception that monitoring is a negative process, designed to 'check on whether we're working by the rules'. By introducing participatory methods and fully involving the programme and field staff in monitoring, staff have started to see the benefits of alternative monitoring approaches in terms of continuously learning from experience and improving programmes.

Our next step is to establish community monitoring as an integral part of our PPM&E approach. We want to develop methods that can help us integrate the informal monitoring that is already undertaken by the community (e.g. their own everyday observations), and develop indicators and tools that the community themselves can use in recording their monitoring information. Our experience shows that we can establish a PPM&E process more easily in programmes that incorporate some degree of individual focus. For example, in the case of a women's programme that incorporates leadership and administrative training for women setting up new businesses with small-scale credit, women have the incentive to develop their own monitoring and evaluation. But in village- or group-wide projects this has been a more difficult process to develop. It would appear that motivation for PPM&E may be increased when people see that they can derive greater or more direct personal benefits from their involvement.

Moving forward – linking planning, monitoring, and evaluation

We are trying to set up a PPM&E system that will help us ensure that planning, monitoring and evaluation are intrinsically linked and are part of a process that operates at all levels within the organization.

PPM&E in the project cycle

The project cycle is usually presented as a circle that links planning, monitoring and evaluation – with planning as the starting point, followed by monitoring and evaluation to assess how a plan has been implemented. This can often lead to the unfortunate image of projects going round in circles! The vital step of learning from experience, moving the development process forward and taking action is often overlooked.

The 'learning loop'

Linking planning, monitoring and evaluation is important, but the *way* they are linked is even more crucial. In our experience, we find that simply building recommendations into evaluation work is not sufficient. It leaves a gap between evaluation and planning future work since no mechanism is in place that integrates learning from experience into the PPM&E process. The nature of the linkages between planning, monitoring and evaluation becomes vital: the learning in PPM&E must be a continuous process of reflection with constant feedback between planning, monitoring and evaluation. This 'learning loop' should include discussion about how to move forward throughout the entire PPM&E process and clearly identify roles and responsibilities of each group involved. If people become enthusiastic about their involvement in (for example) evaluation, there must be a continuation of this process that enables them to follow through with their initial findings to develop future plans; otherwise, expectations may be raised but not met. This important insight is reflected in our experience: we have found the strongest push for linking evaluation to plans and outlining future work comes from the community themselves. They are rarely content to look at impacts without considering what should happen next.

The implications for development in terms of the way planning, monitoring and evaluation are linked is considerable. A process-oriented rather than a project-based approach becomes more essential. In a project-based approach, planning, monitoring and evaluation are treated separately for each project; consequently, it is more difficult to create continuity. In a process-oriented approach, planning, monitoring and evaluation become part of an ongoing process that allows continuous learning. The trajectory may shift, but the momentum will be forward. By using a participatory approach, the community becomes the engine driving this momentum, and they can control its direction.

We characterize this process-oriented approach as the 'PPM&E *serviis*' (shared taxi) (see Figure 10.2). If planning, monitoring and evaluation are treated separately the *serviis* cannot move because it has no proper wheels;

Figure 10.2: *The PPM&E serviis*

if the process is not participatory there is no engine; but if a PPM&E approach is used, then the *serviis* and the people riding in it can move forward.

Creating an appropriate framework

One of the difficulties we face in developing our PPM&E approach is building a suitable methodological framework. Much of the work on planning, monitoring and evaluation systems has been developed by donor agencies and designed with their own reporting and monitoring requirements in mind. Similarly, in PARC an important incentive for developing PPM&E stems from our own administrative needs. Consequently, although PARC now recognizes participation as important, the frameworks used for M&E are based more on an approach that satisfies administrative needs, and in reality does little to help promote participatory or learning approaches. This is partly a result of the logical framework's predominance as a tool for linking planning, monitoring and evaluation (see Box 10.4).

PARC is aiming to develop a more flexible framework for PPM&E that is sensitive to the issues and requirements of all major stakeholders (project staff and communities). By offering people the appropriate tools and encouraging their understanding of the concepts involved, the stakeholders themselves can build their own PPM&E framework. Creating a suitable framework should take into account several considerations:

o identifying the planning, monitoring and evaluation needs of people (including donors)
o ensuring that these needs are met and that the system is both relevant and practical
o encouraging a participatory approach that cultivates the community's ability to control the development process.

Where do we go from here?

We recognize that we still have a long way to go before we can be confident that the community is playing the central role in our PPM&E process and

Box 10.4:   Breaking free of the illogical framework

We have frequently encountered visiting consultants who view the logical framework as a 'magic' tool. They use the logical framework (or logframe) to set out an 'action plan' for their recommendations and as an attempt to find solutions to identified problems. The logical framework is a widely used managerial tool for planning and monitoring: it sets goals, from which objectives, inputs and outputs are deduced, and then identifies quantifiable or verifiable indicators to assess the goals. Although the logical framework may be useful in some situations – and, certainly, having clear objectives and a mechanism for reviewing activities are important – we have found that it is less useful especially when attempting to build participation into the development process. The following points discuss some of reasons why we are breaking free from the logical framework and looking at alternative frameworks in carrying out PPM&E:

○ In most practical applications we have come across, people find the logical framework far from 'logical'. For example, the goals, objectives, inputs and outputs are often difficult to define because the logframe requires a way of looking at the development process that is often alien to the community. As a result, the logical framework is often prepared by managers while the field staff and programme participants are alienated from the planning. Hence, control over the M&E process is concentrated in the hands of the 'logical framework analysis expert', which, in turn, discourages participation in – and community ownership over – the process.

○ The logical framework falls into the trap of promoting M&E as a mechanism for checking planning rather than as a process of learning from experience. People tend to focus on whether each step of the plan has been fully implemented. Flexibility is discouraged and the need for changing or adapting the programme to be more responsive to arising circumstances is considered as a negative, rather than a positive, outcome. The overall goal of the work becomes fulfilling planned activities and not promoting a development process.

○ The logical framework assumes a rational environment where it is possible to deduce activities from clear goals. However, in practice, a plan is rarely implemented without a need for changes – no matter how carefully the plan was conceived. We have often found that in situations where projects are allegedly implemented exactly as planned, this has had more to do with a *lack* of monitoring than it being an exceptional plan responsive to changing local circumstances and needs. This inherent assumption of the logical framework has significant implications for the Palestinian situation, which is generally unpredictable and where people have little control over outcomes. In such circumstances, programme planning requires a degree of fluidity and adaptability which the logical framework cannot offer.

that they are defining the direction of our work. We need to strengthen and widen the scope of the participatory methods we use, to continue to develop an organizational commitment to participation, and to create a planning, monitoring and evaluation framework that encourages learning and greater local control over the development process.

The following points summarize our experience in developing and using PPM&E:

- The transition from working in emergency relief during a conflict situation to focusing on building civil society and the development process has provided a stimulus for PARC to develop its PPM&E approach.
- Political conflict has affected local participation in two contradictory ways: the popular struggle has encouraged community mobilization and participation in the development process, while the 'culture of occupation' has hindered people from having a sense of control over their own future, discouraging long-term planning and collective action.
- Despite its grassroots orientation and history of working with rural people as part of a popular struggle, PARC recognized that it was still important to develop a participatory approach within the organization. The process of institutionalizing PPM&E requires establishing new ways of working to ensure participation at all levels – management, field staff and the community.
- Monitoring and evaluation cannot be separated from planning since they are all an intrinsic part of the development process. The linkages are crucial to establishing a learning process that enables people to move the development process forward.
- Creating a flexible and responsive methodological framework is also important. The framework and methods used must be able to encourage full local participation and to give communities greater control over the development process.

11

Getting the Right End of the Stick: Participatory Monitoring and Evaluation in an Organizational Context

PENELOPE WARD

Introduction

CARE INTERNATIONAL IS a non-sectarian, non-profit development and relief organization. It operates on four continents and in over 50 countries. CARE began operations in Zambia in January 1992 upon the invitation of the Zambian Government. Their activities initially included those related to responding to the severe drought of the early 1990s, and interventions to mitigate the effects of escalating inflation and extreme poverty in urban areas.

By 1994, it became clear that conventional development approaches, such as food for work (FFW) activities, created dependency. Project participants were abandoning marginal income-earning activities for the perceived security of FFW. As a consequence, CARE Zambia decided to reorientate its development strategy. The household livelihood security (HLS) approach was adopted, which provided a more holistic perspective on factors that affect people's livelihoods (Drinkwater, 1994). Fundamental to this reorientation process was a shift from physical development projects towards a more human development emphasis, aimed at building individual and organizational capacities.

Using the HLS approach as a framework, CARE Zambia then began to encourage a more learning-oriented approach within the organization. Becoming a learning organization was perceived as a critical step towards better understanding of HLS, changes experienced by households over time, the impact of project activities, and areas for future intervention. Organizational learning entails learning *along with* local communities and ensuring that villagers are 'getting the right end of the stick'. It is a long process that aims not only towards organizational learning within CARE Zambia, but also towards building local capacities to improve programme planning and intervention.

In this chapter we outline the process that CARE Zambia underwent to achieve the shift towards a more learning-oriented and participatory approach to livelihood development. The Livingstone Food Security Project (LFSP) is used here as a case study to illustrate the steps and strategies CARE has undertaken to improve institutional learning and become more responsive to people's needs and priorities. Our experiences in CARE Zambia reveal the following lessons (which are considered in more detail at the end of the chapter):

- participation is a process, not just an activity
- learning from the project context does not happen automatically; it needs to be integrated as part of project activities
- really 'handing over the right end of the stick' involves more than having villagers collect information for the project
- ownership of the learning process is a vital component of capacity building, which occurs at two levels:
  - the project organizational level
  - the community or village level.

Building a learning organization within CARE Zambia

The HLS approach was promoted within CARE Zambia in order to (Drinkwater, 1997):

- improve CARE's ability to target poor and vulnerable households in its programmes
- monitor and develop a deeper understanding of trends in the improvement or decline of HLS in communities over time
- ensure that project activities address livelihood and food security concerns of households
- create synergistic relationships between projects with the same geographical coverage, so that activities of different projects complement each other and help to address the overall needs of vulnerable households
- create coherent country office information and monitoring systems that are able to measure project impact at different levels within a community/project area.

One significant development in adopting the HLS approach within CARE Zambia has been the need to establish information feedback and review systems. CARE Zambia wanted to monitor trends and changes in HLS, in order to use this information directly to improve its programming and interventions. This then required developing a more learning-oriented approach within the organization that would encourage project staff and local partners to learn from their experiences and to respond more effectively to changing needs and priorities. The following sections briefly describe the HLS framework and the concept of a 'learning organization'.

What is HLS?

Chambers and Conway (1992: 6) define livelihoods as:

'the capabilities, assets (stores, resources, claims and access) and activities required for a means of living. A "sustainable livelihood" is one which can cope with and recover from shocks (e.g. one-off events such as a death, illness or retrenchment) or stress (e.g. long-term events such as prolonged drought, continued unemployment or illness of a breadwinner); maintain and enhance its capabilities and assets, and provide

151

sustainable livelihood opportunities for the next generation; and which contributes net benefits to other livelihoods at the local and global levels over the long and short term.'

Figure 11.1 describes the HLS framework. It illustrates the relationships between capabilities, assets and economic activities. Assets include the capabilities and skills of household members, their physical assets and resources, their access to information and influential people, and their ability to claim from relatives, the state or other agents in times of stress. Using these assets, a livelihood is able to undertake various production (e.g. agriculture, fishing), processing and exchange activities (e.g. trading, manufacturing). These collectively contribute to the household's consumption of food and other commodities and services (health, education, recreation), and, ideally, to investment in strengthening the asset base of the household.

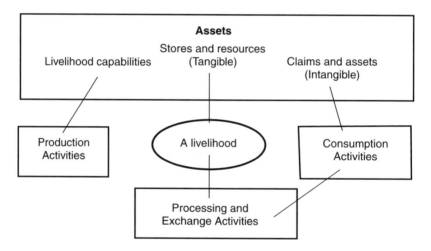

Figure 11.1: *The household livelihood model*
Adapted from: Swift (1989); Drinkwater (1994); and Chambers and Conway (1992)

The 'learning organization' as a concept

Adopting the HLS framework within CARE Zambia has emphasized the importance of building a learning-oriented organization in order to improve its livelihood development activities. The 'learning organization' as a concept is increasingly recognized as a valuable tool for strengthening people's capacities, establishing effective feedback mechanisms, and improving performance (see Box 11.1).

The key features of a learning organization include:

○ adapting to the environments in which it operates
○ continually enhancing its capability to change and adapt

○ developing collective as well as individual learning
○ using the results of learning to achieve better results.

Four levels of learning

The process of becoming a learning organization involves different levels of learning. Hamel and Prahaled (1994) have developed a model that defines four levels of learning to show how organizations evolve and develop new knowledge and skills (see Box 11.2).

According to this model, learning processes at Levels 1 and 2 can be accomplished relatively quickly and easily within an organization. The most critical challenges to higher learning begin when organizations

Box 11.2: Four levels of learning

Level 1
○ Learning facts, knowledge, processes and procedures
○ Applies knowledge to familiar situations where changes are minor

Level 2
○ Learning new job skills that are transferable to other situations
○ Applies knowledge to new situations where existing responses need to be changed
○ Bringing in outside expertise as a useful learning strategy

Level 3
○ Learning to adapt
○ Applies knowledge to more dynamic situations where the solutions need to be developed
○ Experimentation and deriving lessons from success and failure

Level 4
○ Being innovative and creative – designing the future rather than merely adapting to it
○ Assumptions are challenged and knowledge is reframed.

develop from Level 2 to Level 3. At this stage of learning, staff must learn how to adapt their new skills to different situations in the field. This requires creativity and adaptive thinking. Institutionalizing this adaptive behaviour requires time, experience and skilled facilitation. Organizations that have attempted to progress beyond Level 2 often need to develop a number of strategies to encourage creativity and innovation amongst staff. Some of the strategies that CARE Zambia has undertaken to promote institutional learning are described in the following sections.

Institutionalizing learning within CARE Zambia

Seven strategies were adopted by CARE to encourage and institutionalize learning, particularly amongst staff at all levels within the organization (see Box 11.3). Providing staff with training and relevant skills was an important step in this process. These strategies or 'building blocks' may be considered benchmarks in helping CARE staff become more learning oriented.

CARE staff soon found that building a learning organization was not so straightforward and clear cut as they had anticipated. Most of the time, we were unsure of what we were doing and what skills we were learning. We all started out at different levels of understanding and learning, and many of us were completely new in the field. We would try out different approaches simultaneously, and many times we failed miserably. But one important element of CARE's transition was the learning environment it created: staff freely shared their ideas and experiences amongst each other, and were encouraged by higher-level staff. Institutional learning did not always take place formally (i.e. through trainings); more often, staff exchanged ideas during their day-to-day activities, i.e. in corridors, over coffee, during meetings, etc. Hence, learning became part of a larger, more fluid process.

Adaptive and creative learning in the community

Developing community-based monitoring systems

The LFSP is used here to show how CARE Zambia staff attempted to apply a learning-oriented approach to programme implementation at the community level. The case study illustrates the process through which CARE staff learned how to apply new knowledge and skills by using participatory approaches and methodologies. It further describes how CARE staff involved villagers in establishing a community-based monitoring system, not only to improve programming of activities but also to strengthen local institutions in sustaining livelihoods and household food security. Box 11.4 provides a general overview of the LFSP, describing project objectives, activities, and partners involved.

Establishing a community monitoring system

The LFSP staff designed a monitoring system centred around the use of the HLS model. The model was used to structure interviews with individual village households. This information was later supplemented with a wealth-

Box 11.3: Strategies to build a learning organization within CARE Zambia

1 Thriving on change
   o Senior staff and external consultants help to introduce the concept of household livelihood security and participatory learning and action (PLA) techniques into mission programming
   o Existing projects encouraged to make the shift from conventional service delivery activities to a more holistic livelihood approach to development
   o Experienced senior staff able to provide guidance, support and vision on an ongoing basis
2 Facilitating learning from the surrounding environment
   o New participatory methods are developed and applied in the field – resulting in more solid community ownership of project activities
   o Projects are redesigned so that beneficiaries participate more in design and implementation
   o Staff establish and train community-based teams responsible for monitoring and planning project activities
3 Facilitating learning from staff
   o Long-range strategic planning sessions held during which core values and three-year strategic thrusts are drafted for the mission
   o All projects encouraged to produce logframes, monitoring frameworks and annual work plans through team work and discussions
   o Through team work staff are able to demonstrate an understanding of the larger participatory programming framework within which their individual roles lie
4 Encouraging experimentation
   o Appropriate and experienced external consultants employed to design and conduct training and fieldwork to expose staff to new methods; project staff benefit from continuous contact and follow-up by experienced senior staff and consultants. This provides staff with access to necessary skills and resources to practise participatory learning in their work
   o Staff and project participants begin to develop an effective array of their own participatory tools, e.g. household livelihood monitoring systems
5 Communicating successes and failures
   o Projects develop methods to document case studies and share experiences in the field, such as newsletters, inter-project discussions and staff sharing
   o Staff and participants learn to monitor progress, analyse results and to use this information to modify activities

ranking exercise conducted together with participating villagers, who specified their own categories of wealth and identified sustainable livelihood
indicators for future monitoring (Box 11.5). By using the HLS model to
structure household interviews and then applying the wealth-ranking exercise, CARE Zambia project staff and participants gained a better understanding of people's livelihoods status, their coping strategies in times of
stress and shock, and their needs. This initial assessment provided the basis
for developing a monitoring framework.

Because of the large project area and relatively few staff, it became
imperative that the implementation of the monitoring system be conducted
mainly by the villagers or groups within each community. A pilot community self-monitoring system (CSM) was introduced in 45 villages. Participants included members from village management committees (VMCs),
who are elected by villages and who were initially mobilized by CARE
Zambia to manage food relief activities. CARE staff provided training to
build the capacity of these local institutions, including training selected
members in monitoring, collecting and evaluating information.[1] CARE
staff then held follow-up meetings and workshops to help VMC members
analyse information, especially in drawing out trends across the project
area and by comparing data collected by the various VMCs.

Data collected by the VMCs covered HLS trends during the first two
agricultural seasons of the project, 1994–5 and 1995–6. (Between 1996 and
1997 data for the last season was still being collected and had not yet been
completed in most pilot villages.) By repeating interviews with the same
households each season,[2] the HLS framework was used to monitor trends
and changes in livelihoods over the seasons. Distinct trends have begun to
emerge from the CSM data, and it has been possible to see marked improvements in peoples' livelihoods over these two seasons. One of the most
striking trends noticed was the increase in food availability across the
different household wealth categories. CARE staff and villagers related
this trend partly to the amount and types of crops that have been culti-
vated, the project's seed distribution activities, and the promotion efforts

Box 11.4:   The Livingstone Food Security Project (LFSP)

Project objectives
o To develop a community-based seed multiplication and distribution system
o To build the capacity of community institutions to plan, manage
   and maintain activities crucial to drought mitigation and ensuring
   household food security
o To develop sustainable farming systems
o To improve water harvesting methods
o To raise incomes by developing market linkages and improving
   income-earning opportunities

Project area
o Southern Province in Zambia
o 9,600 participating farmers

Project activities
o In the first two growing seasons (1994–5 and 1995–6), the main
   agricultural activity was the introduction of drought-tolerant crops
   through a community-based seed distribution and bulking-up
   scheme. Information on crop and soil agronomy, seed handling
   and post-harvest storage was provided
o In the first season of operation (1994–5) a pilot seed scheme
   involved 330 farmers on an individual basis. During the 1995–6
   season, the scheme was institutionalized. VMCs were
   established. These registered a number of seed groups, each
   consisting of four to seven households. 180 VMCs were
   established with over 6,800 participating farmers
o In 1996–7 the project area expanded and the number of participating farmers increased to 9,600

Project partners
The community participatory planning process involved three sets of
actors:
o project field staff
o district and field staff from the Ministry of Agriculture and Forestry
   (MAF)
o the villagers living in Southern Province

led by the VMCs and village seed groups. Reasons given by villagers to
explain low agricultural productivity especially in poorer households –
namely inappropriate choice of crop, soil type, poor farming practices, pest
attacks – provided important lessons on how to improve household food
security and suggested new or revised project strategies.

CARE staff, who were now quite familiar with using participatory
methods in the field, grew more confident and began applying the different
tools more consistently throughout the project cycle. More importantly,

Box 11.5: Wealth ranking with communities

'Wealth' or 'well-being' ranking is a common tool used to establish and define local terms and definitions of wealth status. It is useful for obtaining a quick, general understanding of the nature of wealth differences in a project area, and for determining the approximate wealth status of participants.

Three types of livelihoods were identified by communities together with LFSP staff:

1 Rich households[3]
   o Can maintain household livelihood security on a continuous basis
   o Able to withstand shocks (a one-off event, such as the death of a breadwinner or a season of drought) and prolonged stress (a long-term event, such as continued drought, illness or unemployment)
2 Moderate households
   o Suffer shocks and stress, but have the resources to be able to recover relatively quickly
3 Poor households
   o Become increasingly vulnerable as a result of shocks and prolonged stress

CARE project staff found that identifying people's criteria of well-being and livelihood categories were critical elements in establishing baseline information for subsequent monitoring activities. The wealth-ranking exercises enabled staff to:

   o develop a deeper understanding of vulnerable households within their project area
   o identify criteria for monitoring the improvement or decline of household livelihood security over time, particularly in poorer households
   o review and target project activities more specifically at households' livelihood and food security needs.

they soon developed a better understanding of the principles of participation and adapting what they had learned in training to actual field situations. However, developing a CSM system still posed a challenge to CARE staff and revealed areas of their work that needed further improvement. For instance, monitoring workshops were still initiated and designed mainly by LSFP staff, who played a greater role than the local community in identifying indicators for monitoring project impact. Little input was sought from the community regarding their data needs and expectations, and their main role was limited to that of data collectors. As a result, villagers still perceived the CSM largely as a CARE-driven process. Villagers have not been sufficiently involved in analysing information and using data to regard the monitoring process as fully their own.[4]

Institutionalizing learning at the community level: experiences of the LFSP

A major thrust of the LFSP has been to strengthen the capacities of local institutions to better plan, manage, and maintain livelihood activities. Monitoring the project's progress towards this objective is crucial to ensuring the continuity of project benefits beyond the lifetime of the project itself. In developing a CSM system, project staff have moved through four levels of learning – although learning, as noted earlier, was a much more dynamic, backwards and forwards process.

Learning facts and knowledge

Initially LFSP staff had limited or no experience in applying the HLS framework and using participatory techniques. As part of their training in participatory rural appraisal (PRA), project staff conducted a series of participatory appraisal activities (including wealth ranking) in three different farming system zones within the project area. CARE staff gained hands-on experience, working jointly with communities to establish baseline information, analyse farmer livelihoods, and learn about key issues affecting livelihoods and people's priorities (Mitti, Drinkwater and Kalonge, 1997).

At this stage, staff were simply acquiring new skills and knowledge and still absorbing new ideas and applying their training. Many had little experience of using participatory methods in the field and had yet to grasp the full implications of applying participatory approaches throughout the project-cycle. Their previous work experience with conventional projects (i.e. hand-out type activities) still strongly influenced their behaviours and attitudes in the field and in programming livelihood activities. Hence, external consultants and senior project staff needed to provide continuous support and advice. Regular reinforcement of team learning and self-assessments was critical in preventing project staff from returning to conventional, top-down planning.

Learning new job skills transferable to other situations

In March 1996 a project baseline exercise was conducted by LFSP field staff in 20 villages within the project area. Various PRA tools, including wealth ranking, were used to collect this data over a two-day period spent in each village. LFSP staff learned how to apply their new skills in participatory appraisal methodologies towards developing a baseline. The baseline was designed to provide a general impression of the current local context as well as a foundation for future monitoring exercises.

However, senior CARE staff were still needed to provide guidance in determining how collected information should be used. There still appeared to be a tendency amongst project staff to gather information without having a clear strategy for its use or for conducting follow-up activities. This then tended to make the process of obtaining baseline information extractive. Village participants functioned more as providers of information, rather than as active partners in analysing and using the information collected. In the future, follow-up activities and action planning will be needed if the project intends to use collected information towards refining its existing strategies and involving communities in project design and implementation.

Learning to adapt

Initially CARE staff used the HLS framework mainly to conduct a needs assessment for determining interventions and establishing baseline information. As project staff grew more confident working with villagers and gained a better understanding of local situations, project staff then carefully re-oriented their strategy to emphasize the strengthening of community institutions. Project staff sought to build local capacities by establishing a CSM system through VMCs. Project staff worked together with VMCs to analyse and compare information across the project area, and to discuss how this information could be used to improve project interventions.

Being innovative and creative

The project is currently reviewing the initial CSM system and looking at different ways to improve and make the process more participatory and locally inclusive. Our experiences so far show that the level of community involvement in recording information and participating in the monitoring process has not been consistent. Some VMCs have been more conscientious in their data gathering than others, while several villages have not completed data collection. This is partly attributed to limited community ownership of the monitoring and evaluation process itself. There is limited, or lack of, local involvement in data analysis and in directly using information. There remains a tendency for staff to control the process and to conduct data analysis themselves, at the expense of community and local institutional learning. Emphasis is still on individual learning amongst project staff: generally, one or two staff members conduct data analysis in isolation. As a result, key lessons and insights are not widely shared, limiting new ideas and innovations from taking shape.

In the future, staff will need to provide greater support to VMCs by encouraging them to identify more locally-meaningful indicators and to use collected information directly for their own purposes. By encouraging villagers to find innovative ways of using information, it is hoped that they will begin to monitor their progress and teach or assist other villages in the project area. This would be an essential step towards creating strong and capable community institutions that will continue work on securing household livelihoods even after the project itself has been completed.

Lessons learned

Several of CARE Zambia's programmes have already implemented an HLS community-monitoring system to keep track of household livelihood trends and to monitor the impact of project activities. Our experience in establishing such a system has been mixed.

Lessons from this experience can be summarized as follows:

○ *Participation is a process, not just an activity.* CARE staff have been trained and have had to apply participatory methodologies in the field within a relatively short period of time. Adequate time must be given to the process of internalizing and applying these new attitudes and behaviours if they are to be sustained. Adequate training, follow-up and mentoring (especially from top-level management) are all critical components of this process.

○ *Learning from the project context does not happen automatically, it needs to be an integral part of project activities.* One problem that staff encountered is developing the ability to analyse and document the lessons that they are learning in the field. Staff have stronger interactive than recording skills; consequently, key insights are communicated mainly through anecdotes and remain undocumented. This then limits the potential for institutional learning. Hence, more effort and resources need to be invested in monitoring and evaluation, which should be considered an integral part of project activities.

○ *Really 'handing over the right end of the stick' involves more than villagers collecting information for the project.* Although VMCs have participated in the CSM process enthusiastically, they did not play a significant role in designing the self-monitoring surveys or analysing and using the information afterwards. Little thought was given to how communities might use the data themselves. As a result, villagers see monitored information as belonging primarily to project staff and being for CARE's use.

○ *Ownership of a process is a vital component of capacity-building.* Field staff need to follow up with VMCs more regularly to sustain progress, and provide support in dealing with problems that arise. Progress has been slow in some villages due to sporadic follow-up and lack of VMCs' sense of ownership of gathered information. In order to strengthen local capacities and to sustain community monitoring, villagers will need to play a greater role throughout the entire monitoring process, and not simply act as data gatherers.

The most important challenge is trying to overcome the tendency to extract information, and to empower participants through proactive self-monitoring and learning. Many of the tools used have great potential for encouraging participation at the grassroots and for genuinely involving project beneficiaries in the analysis and use of information. However, there is a danger of the process becoming extractive if insufficient dialogue is sustained with communities, and if they are only used as information-gatherers. When this occurs, information – and hence learning – will flow one way: out of communities and simply into project management. Joint analysis and discussion help communities and staff learn from each other and identify ways to improve programme planning and to build local and organizational capacities. A learning-oriented, monitoring process helps in motivating and empowering communities to take action themselves, which, in turn, strengthens local capacities and promotes self-reliance.

12

Participatory Monitoring and Evaluation: Lessons and Experiences from the National Poverty Alleviation Programme (NPAP) in Mongolia

DAVAA GOBISAIKHAN AND ALEXANDER MENAMKART

An overview of the NPAP

SINCE THE COLLAPSE of the socialist system and the initiation of transition to a market economy in 1990, Mongolia has been experiencing severe economic and social hardship. This has been triggered by the sudden loss of its traditional sources of assistance and trading partners, as well as by the austerity measures introduced to stabilize the economy. As a result, the incidence of poverty and unemployment has increased considerably. The education and the health-delivery systems have also deteriorated. As of 1996, the State Statistical Office estimated that over 452,000 or 18.8 per cent of 2.4 million people in Mongolia lived in poverty. Those especially affected include the unemployed, elderly, female-headed households, children, pensioners and small herders.

To address the urgent needs of the poor, the Government of Mongolia introduced a comprehensive, six-year, multi-sectoral NPAP in June 1994. The NPAP was formulated through a consultative process involving central and local government, non-governmental organizations (NGOs), and donors (including the World Bank, the Asian Development Bank (ADB), the United Nations Development Programme (UNDP), the Swedish International Development Agency (SIDA), Save the Children Fund UK, and bilateral sources).

Objectives of the NPAP

The NPAP aims to promote the ability of the poor to take part in economic and social activities, to alleviate human deprivation and human capital erosion, and to substantially reduce the level of poverty by the year 2000. Therefore, it focuses not only on alleviating economic poverty, but also on preventing poverty and promoting the overall development and well-being of people. The NPAP aims to achieve these objectives by supporting basic education, skills training, rural healthcare, women's advancement, care for the disabled, and emergency assistance to the very poor and vulnerable segments of society.

Operating principles

The NPAP operates on the basis of two main principles:

o decentralization, which makes local and provincial administrators responsible for undertaking all aspects of project work – namely appraisal, selection, implementation, monitoring and evaluation
o community participation, which aims for full community involvement in project formulation and operation.

These principles allow the beneficiaries and local governing bodies to become the principal decision makers on matters that are directly related to their livelihood and welfare. Past experience has shown that a more decentralized, participatory approach can be more effective than a top-down management approach to poverty alleviation.

Programme components

The NPAP essentially represents a plan of action to achieve its stated objectives. It has six components:

o *Poverty alleviation through economic growth and employment promotion.* This promotes employment and income generation opportunities in order to contribute to equitable economic development.
o *Protection of human capital.* This aims to strengthen human capital formation through improved delivery of education and health services.
o *Alleviation of women's poverty.* Special attention is given to ensure women's advancement as full partners in all aspects of human life through their participation in the poverty alleviation process.
o *Strengthening the social safety net.* Human deprivation is mitigated by establishing a social safety net targeted at the poor who are unable to benefit from new employment opportunities.
o *Alleviating rural poverty.* This ensures the improvement of living standards among the rural poor, especially herders.
o *NPAP policy management and institutional strengthening.* This establishes suitable institutional structures responsible for poverty alleviation. In particular structures are required to organize, implement, and administer programme activities.

The Poverty Alleviation Fund (PAF) mechanism

The PAF was designed as an integral part of the NPAP to facilitate the implementation of the various components in the programme. The PAF mechanism allows governments and donors to channel funds towards specific poverty alleviation activities according to their priorities and preferences. The PAF is divided into four independent but complementary subfunds, each with a specific focus and target group to finance small-scale projects at the local level:

o a Local Development Fund (LDF): comprised of
  • loans for vulnerable group organizations (VGOs) for income generation

- grants for public works, basic education, rural health services, pre-school education and support for the disabled
- a Women's Development Fund (WDF): loans and grants to provide employment opportunities for women and capacity building of local NGOs to facilitate women's full participation in the poverty alleviation process
- a Targeted Assistance Fund (TAF): transfers in cash and in kind to help the most vulnerable among the poor to meet their basic needs (food, fuel, clothes, and educational assistance)
- an Income Generation Fund (IGF): implemented together with the income-generating components of LDF and WDF.

Institutional framework

The institutional framework refers to the management structures established at the central and local levels to organize the implementation of the NPAP, and is closely linked to the administrative divisions of the country. The country is divided into *aimags* (provinces), *aimags* into *sums* (provincial districts) and *sums* into *bags* (provincial sub-districts). Ulaanbaatar, the capital city, is divided into *duuregs* (city districts) and *duuregs* into *khooros* (city sub-districts).

The composition and responsibilities of the management units at the central and local levels are as follows:

- the National Poverty Alleviation Committee (NPAC), which is headed by the Prime Minister and is represented by line ministries and NGOs. The NPAC is responsible for co-ordination and consensus building at the policy level, as well as for the overall implementation of the NPAP
- the Poverty Alleviation Programme Office (PAPO). The PAPO functions as a secretariat to the NPAC. It is an autonomous body responsible for resource mobilization and for the operative management of the implementation of the NPAP and PAF mechanism
- *Aimag*, Ulaanbaatar and *Duureg* Poverty Alleviation Councils (APAC, UPAC, DPAC). These are representatives of local administration, NGOs, employers and co-operatives. They are responsible for the appraisal and selection of projects that have been screened and endorsed by *sums* and *khoroos*, as well as for the disbursements of funds to the projects. Project management and quarterly monitoring at the provincial level also fall under their responsibility.
- *sum/khoroo* Poverty Alleviation Councils (SPACs/KPACs). These bodies can be considered as the *sum/khoroo* branches of APACs/DPACs and are similarly constituted. They are responsible for facilitating the identification, formulation, implementation and monthly monitoring of projects as well as promoting community participation.

Implementation

After a period of preparation and piloting, the NPAP was launched nationwide in March 1996. A new round of projects is selected every three to four

164

months for implementation. As of early 1998, four rounds of project selection have been completed, with the period for implementation varying for each project. Total costs of projects have amounted to about US$1.5 million. A total of 1,018 VGO income-generating projects, 84 rural health projects, 60 basic-education projects and 138 public works projects have been implemented, with 78 per cent of the projects consisting of income-generation activities.

The projects are implemented in *khoroos*, *sums* and *bags*. Previously, VGO loans were allocated to project groups for a period of four years, 20 per cent of which have to be repaid in the second year, 30 per cent in the third year and the remaining 50 per cent in the fourth year – with interest charges equivalent to the rate of inflation. As of early 1998, loans are now given only for a maximum period of one year, with an interest charge of 1 per cent per month. Loans used to range from US$500 to US$2500 depending on the number of beneficiaries in a group, but at present loan sizes have been reduced to a maximum of US$1200 per project.

Projects cover a wide range of activities such as clothes making, bakery, vegetable growing, boot making, knitting, carpentry, pig breeding, poultry farming, etc. The public works, rural health and basic education projects are formulated by the APAC and UPAC based on local needs assessments.

Monitoring and evaluation (M&E) as part of the operational management of the NPAP

M&E has been incorporated as part of programme implementation from the beginning. The NPAP aims to implement a more participatory M&E process by requiring that provincial and local stakeholders (APAC/UPAC/DPAC/KPAC) carry out monitoring and evaluating on a quarterly and semi-annual basis. Staff from the PAPO central office also makes random visits to *aimags* and *duuregs*.

The rationale behind promoting a participatory M&E approach within the programme is that:

o it complements the operating principles of the NPAP (namely that of decentralization and community participation)
o it helps local administrators and beneficiaries develop their capacity for management and problem solving.

Introducing a revised system for participatory monitoring and evaluation (PM&E)

Reasons for developing a revised PM&E system

The M&E experience during the first three rounds of project selection and implementation revealed that the M&E system in place had several shortcomings. Because no training on M&E had been given to the local poverty alleviation council members or their secretaries, there was much confusion over the real meaning and interpretation of the term 'monitoring' at the provincial and local levels. In the Mongolian language, there is no equivalent word that adequately translates the concept of monitoring. It is often confused with 'supervision', 'surveillance', 'control' or 'checking'. Hence, there was a need to convey a clear understanding of what is meant by 'monitoring' and 'evaluation'. Because of the lack of proper guidance and training support, local councils did not monitor projects in a structured and systematic manner once funds were disbursed and projects got under way.

The initial M&E system was developed by the PAPO management staff. Forms and reporting formats were primarily geared to meet donor information needs; therefore, much of the information obtained remained highly quantitative. This included recording the date and amount of funds disbursed from PAPO to *aimags* and *duuregs*, funds received by the project groups, the number of beneficiaries, the number of male and female project group members, the number of items produced and sold, the salaries of project members, the average monthly project incomes, etc. They included little qualitative information, such as the sustainability of projects, group efficiency and dynamics, participatory decision making, transparency, gender equality, etc. An understanding of local bodies and their involvement in M&E was almost non-existent.

In order to remedy these pitfalls, the PAPO felt the need to review and revise the system and a decision was taken to collaborate with a local consultancy group, the Centre for Social Development (CSD). These efforts also obtained support from the ADB and Save the Children UK.

Process of developing the revised PM&E system

In early 1997, a revision process was initiated to develop a new PM&E system, headed by a team of four specialists (two representatives from PAPO and two from CSD). The team visited a representative sample of *sums* and *khoroos* in different *aimags* and *duuregs*, where various types of projects were being implemented. They interviewed members of the local poverty alleviation councils (APAC/DPAC/KPAC/SPAC) and project groups for their views and experience. They also visited the project sites to see how the projects were implemented or how they were functioning.

The review process resulted in a number of changes. The English words 'monitoring' and 'evaluation' were kept but adapted for local usage to avoid further misconceptions. Drawing from the PM&E literature available from international organizations and based on their own experiences, the team of specialists defined participatory monitoring as 'an ongoing collaborative process in which the beneficiaries and others stakeholders at different levels work together to assess a project and take any corrective action required'. Although monitoring and evaluation were seen as two different activities, they were regarded as complementary parts of an integrated system.

Given the information needs of donors, management and project participants, as well as the inadequacies of the M&E system in place, the team of specialists first devised a preliminary three-tier system outlining the objectives, indicators, methods and the persons responsible for monitoring at the different administrative levels. The basic premise of the new system was to

166

enable the stakeholders at the various levels to assess progress and to ensure project sustainability, while obtaining vital information for management needs.

The proposed system was reviewed by the SPAC and KPAC members of selected *aimags* and *duuregs*, where it was also field tested. At the project level, beneficiaries (particularly the VGO groups) welcomed the new system. At the *sum/khoroo* level, the council members proposed inclusion of additional indicators, such as psychological factors and skills acquired. As the new system allowed adaptation and flexibility, the local councils could actually improve and add to the PM&E framework. In the light of these grassroots level consultations and field experience, the proposal for a revised system was re-examined and modified in joint review sessions of the PAPO and CSD.[1]

A comprehensive manual of the newly revised PM&E system was produced with clear explanations of the purpose and procedures. It explains the monitoring objectives, criteria and methods and identifies the stakeholders involved in carrying out M&E at the different administrative levels. It contains guidelines, questionnaires and forms for collecting, analysing and reporting information.

Finally, a four-day training workshop was organized with the assistance of CSD in Ulaanbaatar in September 1997 to introduce the system and to train the PAPO management staff, the poverty alleviation council secretaries from the *aimags* and *duuregs* and community activists. This initial workshop trained 21 *aimags* and nine *duuregs*. It was followed by another four-day training workshop to train the local trainers including NGOs and *aimag* and *duureg* representatives, who in turn were supposed to train SPAC and KPAC members. Community activists, NGO partners, and *sum/khoroo* council members were then given charge of training VGO members in self-monitoring, which is now ongoing.

Main features of the revised PM&E system

Overall objectives

The overall objectives of the PM&E system are:

o to enable PAPO to assess the progress and sustainability of projects towards alleviating local poverty and to take timely corrective action if need be
o to build and maintain a reliable M&E database on the status of project implementation in PAPO's management information system (MIS)
o to produce reports containing M&E information for the government, donors and the public
o to build the capacity of the local poverty alleviation councils, particularly in *sums* and *khoroos*
o to support the development of the project
o to build the capacity of the project groups in problem solving, analysis and management and to achieve active participation of all members, and enhance transparency within projects.

167

Scope of PM&E

The system is designed to assess projects in three areas:

○ project input monitoring assesses the effective and efficient use of project inputs
○ project process monitoring concentrates on the activities of the project, looking at what is being done, and how and by whom it is being done
○ project impact monitoring and evaluation examines the changes that have occurred to the beneficiaries and their lifestyles as a result of the project. It is an assessment or an evaluation of project impacts.

Stakeholders' responsibility for carrying out monitoring and evaluation

Stakeholders include all those who have an interest in, or are in some way affected by, the project. At the project level, they are the VGO members, beneficiaries, service users, etc. At the *sum/khoroo* level, stakeholders are the members of SPACs/KPACs, community activists and participating NGOs. At the *aimag* and *duureg* level, they are the members of APACs/DPACs and their secretaries.

Implementing PM&E at different levels

Monitoring is done at three levels according to identified monitoring objectives, performance indicators and methods of verifying indicators by relevant stakeholders (see Figure 12.1). Evaluation in the formal sense is carried out semi-annually. The objectives and indicators used are the same at all levels, but the methods and the stakeholders carrying out M&E are different at the different levels. Table 12.1 shows an example of the monitoring system for VGO projects at the *sum/khoroo* level. It describes some (not all) of the monitoring objectives, indicators, and the data gathering methods, and identifies who obtains the information and when. Box 12.1 lists some examples of guide questions used at the *sum/khoroo* level to assess project monitoring objectives for VGO projects.

M&E at the project level

VGO members (the direct beneficiaries) are expected to have their own self-monitoring system. They can design their own system according to their own priorities to assess project status, whether people are actually benefiting from their being involved, if there are problems, and how they can be corrected. Some VGOs hold monthly group meetings to assess project performance and to evaluate their members' economic well-being and living conditions. The information generated at this level is useful for VGO members, but is also shared with SPAC/KAPC during their monthly visits and quarterly meetings and with the APAC/DPAC during their field visits.

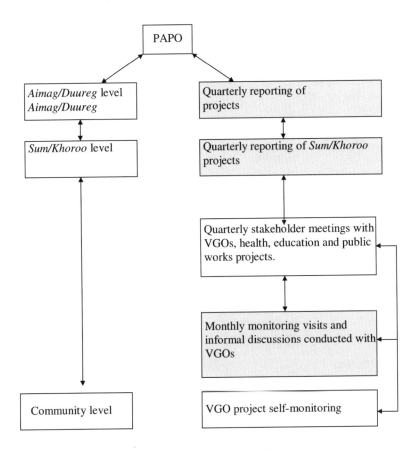

Figure 12.1: *Different levels of the PM&E system for poverty alleviation projects*

However, in March 1998 an evaluation of the PM&E training revealed that many VGOs did not actually receive adequate training and support. Hence, many did not properly understand the process of carrying out PM&E. To address this need, much of the ongoing training is now more focused on VGO self-monitoring.

M&E at the sum/khoroo *level*

The SPAC/KPACs, assisted by community activists or NGOs, monitor VGO projects on a *monthly* basis. They use a monthly monitoring sheet provided for this purpose and keep it in a separate file. The public works projects and community projects are monitored during implementation and on a quarterly basis thereafter. The SPAC/KPACs hold quarterly meetings with project members and other beneficiaries to discuss their findings and to provide feedback to the VGOs. They send a quarterly report to the APAC/DPAC which summarizes the findings and analyses the information for identifying trends, problems and progress.

Table 12.1: Monitoring system for VGO projects at *sum/khoroo* level

Monitoring objective	Indicators	Method of verifying indicators	Who and when
1. *Project input monitoring* To assess the means used in the operation of the project	○ cost of fixed capital ○ operating cost for the month	○ receipts, interviews	KPAC/SPAC: monthly
2. *Project process monitoring* To assess group dynamics, equality and transparency within the group	○ members' knowledge of finances ○ decisions made and by whom ○ problems encountered ○ problems resolved ○ regularity and attendance at group meeting ○ role of group rules/norms	○ group meeting and interviews	KPAC/SPAC and Bag Governor: monthly
3. *Project impact monitoring* To assess improvement in income and livelihood of project members	○ average salary of members: of men, of women ○ range of salaries ○ other: bonuses/ benefits (in cash and in kind) ○ current number of households that moved above the poverty line	○ records and interviews	KPAC/SPAC and Bag Governor: monthly and quarterly

M&E at the aimag/duureg *level*

APAC/DPAC members monitor VGO and SPAC/KPAC performance through the SPAC/KPAC reports and supervision visits to *sums, khoroos* and VGOs. Monitoring at this level is conducted on a *quarterly* basis. There is a quarterly APAC/DPAC meeting to review reports, their own findings and the overall implementation of projects. The outcome of this meeting, along with a summary of the quarterly reports prepared by *sums/khoroos*, serves as a basis for giving feedback to SPAC/KPACs on their performance and the performance of the VGOs. A quarterly M&E report of the APAC/DPAC is prepared which is sent to PAPO in Ulaanbaatar for analysis and feedback. PAPO will then analyse, summarize and report on these findings to the government, donors and the public.

Box 12.1: Guide questions for *sums/khoroos* to assess monitoring objectives for VGO projects

Project input monitoring: To assess the means used in the operation of the project

○ Has the project fund been delivered on time? If there was a delay, at what level and why?
○ Are the project operating costs reasonable in comparison with the number of items produced or customers served?
○ If they are very high, how can they be reduced?
○ Have materials been purchased at the lowest price?
○ What percentage of the operating costs is spent on salaries?

Project process monitoring: To assess level of members participation in project activities

○ Are all the group members actively involved in the project?
○ If not, why not? (Note whether they are men, women, disabled.) How should this be dealt with?
○ If some have left the group (dropped out) why did they do so? Who decided they should – the group, individuals or the leader?
○ If some have joined, how were they identified and based on whose decision (e.g. *sum/khoroo* governor, group leader, group)? Are the new members poor?

Project impact monitoring: To assess improvement in income and livelihood of project members

○ Does every member receive a monthly salary? Are the salaries adequate and above the minimum wage level (as specified in the VGO project impact monitoring)? If not, how can they be increased?
○ Are there any differences between men and women, people with different roles, such as leader and accountant, people doing different activities, etc.? How are these differences agreed and justified? Are they fair?
○ Are the salaries fair in comparison to the amount of work done?
○ What other benefits or bonuses have been given to members, e.g. food, clothes, lunch at the workplace, etc.? How are these shared and is this fair?
○ Have the per capita incomes of members' households changed?
○ Have any households moved off the poverty list? If so, it should be monitored whether this movement is permanent, temporary, fluctuating according to season, etc.
○ How do the average salaries of this group compare with other local VGOs? If there are significant differences, what are the reasons for this?

171

The focal point of the system is at the *sum/khoroo* level, where project implementation really takes place. Information is gathered and analysed each month and feedback is given to the beneficiaries at the VGO level and to the APAC/DPAC at the *aimag/duureg* level. Feedback at the project VGO level often takes place informally through discussions between VGOs and *sum/khoroo* council members, who also conduct regular field visits. *Sums/khoroos* feed information back to *aimags/duuregs* generally through quarterly reports. Quarterly reports, which are compiled by the PAPO, are then disseminated to respective APACs/DPACs and SPACs/KPACs.

The problems identified at the VGO and *sum/khoroo* levels help the VGOs improve their work-plan, production, and sales income. They also help the SPAC/KPAC and APAC/DPAC in targeting and selecting projects. The PM&E findings have helped the PAPO in identifying several policy changes within the NPAP programme. For instance, the NPAP has since introduced family loans, focused on smaller cohesive groups, emphasized business trainings, and reduced loan periods from four years to a maximum of one year.[2]

Reflecting on our PM&E experience

The new PM&E system was introduced in September 1997 and so has only recently been operational. *Aimags* have already submitted the quarterly M&E reports to PAPO and a review of the M&E implementation has been carried out by an external consultant in March 1998. The experience of the new system thus far may be summarized as follows:

○ In some *aimags* and *duuregs*, the VGOs and prospective grass-roots groups have not yet received adequate training on the new M&E system. VGO self-monitoring has therefore not been properly understood or implemented, which, in effect, has limited community participation in carrying out M&E work. In some cases, even the *sum* and *khoroo* officials have only limited familiarity with the new system. Hence, future training on PM&E and follow-up, especially at VGO and *sum/khoroo* levels, will be critical.

○ The initial PM&E work does show that poverty alleviation councils and secretaries are capable of collecting and documenting information. However, it also points out the need to further improve people's skills in analysing and reporting the information.

○ Not all APACs/DPACs and SPACs/KPACs give a high priority to poverty issues and supporting community initiatives, and therefore seem to show little interest in promoting the PM&E system. This is evidenced by tardy and incomplete reports. While heavy workloads are often cited to explain delayed reporting, lack of incentive for officials also partly reflects common attitudes that time and money are better invested elsewhere, i.e. supporting infrastructure development or working with the more educated rather than prioritizing poverty alleviation.

○ However, in areas where the *sum* and *khoroo* governors or deputy governors are active, dynamic and committed, the VGO self-monitoring and

172

SPAC/KPAC monitoring work is being carried out more effectively (i.e. through more continuous and open feedback mechanisms). This highlights the importance of gaining the support of higher-level institutions and actors, in order to better establish and sustain PM&E efforts.

Lessons and insights

From experience, we have realized that to ensure viability and sustainability of income-generating projects, problems have to be identified and corrected in a timely fashion based on informed decision making. Building the capacity and responsibility of local stakeholders to monitor and evaluate their projects themselves is considered by project beneficiaries and administrators as a more effective method than allowing external actors to control the M&E process. Outside experts are accustomed to obtaining information that mainly satisfies management and financial needs rather than identifies and responds to the changing needs of the project. Our initial experiences have highlighted the following constraints to the PM&E process but have also helped us identify alternative solutions.

o There is a lack of qualified and trained workers, who in turn could train local administrators and the beneficiaries in M&E. At present, trainings are being conducted with *aimag/duureg* secretaries, community and NGO activists. These trained local M&E 'experts', can then train other local activists. As of June 1998, community activists will be working more closely and directly with *aimags* and *duureg* councils in order to provide continuous PM&E training and support.
o The lack of monetary incentives make it difficult for local activists to undertake and continue M&E work indefinitely, as they often work on a voluntary basis. In most cases, local individuals are engaged in other activities, and therefore find it difficult to carry out M&E activities simultaneously. We attempted to address this problem by providing local M&E activists with a daily allowance when they conduct trainings.
o We found the NPAP's institutional network and linkaging to be the main enabling factor for conducting PM&E. The PAPO has set up poverty alleviation councils at all the administrative levels and thus are able to maintain communications with remote villages and settlements to help them with project formulation, selection, implementation, supervision, monitoring and evaluation. As pointed out earlier, PACs at the *sum*, *khoroo*, *aimag*, and *duureg* levels have in-built, specific M&E functions and feedback mechanisms.

Overall, the PM&E system has succeeded in revealing the strengths and weaknesses of the programme activities. This has helped policy makers to replicate and build on successes of the NPAP and modify policies to improve programme implementation (i.e. identifying the need for training in business practices and marketing and the shortening of the loan period). It is worth noting that results from the PM&E system were expected to form an important input into a joint evaluation of the NPAP to be conducted by the UNDP, the World Bank, and the Government of Mongolia in September 1999.[3]

In conclusion, the objectives and importance of the PM&E system are increasingly gaining stakeholder recognition and acceptance at all levels. However, the sustained operationalization of the PM&E system depends on further capacity building and training of local administrators, VGO members and prospective project participants.

13

Giving Evaluation Away: Challenges in a Learning-based Approach to Institutional Assessment[1]

FRED CARDEN[2]

Introduction

'While institutional capacity development is strongly assumed to be beneficial, there has been relatively little systematic analysis of institutional capacity and its growth subsequent to intervention.'

(Lusthaus *et al.*, 1995: 2)

THE ADOPTION OF a learning-based approach to evaluation presents special challenges to a research funding agency with a mandate to strengthen research and research capacity with partners in less industrial countries, or in the South. While the general practice has been to evaluate funded projects, there is increased recognition that the project may be the wrong unit of analysis. Projects are a way of organizing work, but they are not the end in development. They do not, in themselves, serve the purpose of building institutional capacity, and their implementation and evaluation may in some cases be detrimental to the strengthening of an institution. The adoption of a learning-based approach to evaluation within a funding agency leads to the realization that there is also a need to apply this evaluation approach within recipient organizations and potential benefit from so doing. This highlights a significant change in perspective on the use of evaluation for both the donor and the recipient. Such an approach presents significant challenges and opportunities to increase participation in the evaluation process. Giving evaluation away to those most directly affected calls for new approaches to evaluation, which both recognize the need for accountability and quality control and build the internal capacity of organizations for using evaluation for their own organizational planning and management purposes.

In 1995, the International Development Research Centre (IDRC) published a framework for institutional assessment for research organizations (Lusthaus *et. al.*, 1995) which was originally commissioned to meet the needs of the centre in assessing the organizations it funds. It was quickly recognized that this framework had considerable potential as a participatory self-assessment tool and as a mechanism to assist organizations in building evaluation into their planning and management systems. Trials were carried out in several organizations in West Africa and South Asia.

In this chapter we explore the background to the development of a model for institutional assessment at IDRC, to support our interest in strengthening capacity with our partner institutions. We focus on perspectives from a funding agency because that is where our experience lies, but also because funding agencies have driven a significant part of the evaluation agenda in development work for the past 20 years.

IDRC is a public corporation funded mainly by the Government of Canada. IDRC was established in 1970 and funds research and research capacity building in developing countries, with a view to supporting local capacity building for scientific research in support of development. While in the early years of IDRC the primary focus was on building individual research capacity, there has been increasing emphasis on building strong research systems, organizations and institutions.

Background

The field of international development has a particular relationship with evaluation. Evaluation has been used primarily by donors to assess the utility of their projects in countries they are assisting. In this context, donor agencies generally set the evaluation measures and establish criteria based on donor agency programmes. This approach to evaluation remains an important dimension of accountability for any donor agency, whether in the public sector or a non-governmental organization (NGO). From the point of view of recipient organizations, evaluation has thus been viewed largely as a policing mechanism, and in donor agencies its implementation has largely been on a compliance basis. What is assumed in this approach, is that good projects were selected to begin with and that these projects will lead to an overall beneficial effect. Evaluation of projects often serves as a proxy to assess executing agencies: if 'good' projects are happening, then the executing agency is considered good (and vice versa).

Frustration with this donor control of the evaluation agenda, together with an early recognition by community groups and community voices that there was an essential role for the community in evaluation, has led to the development of a number of approaches to evaluation based in the community, such as participatory rural appraisal, among others. While the donor community has been slow to deal with this issue, it is increasingly recognized that the current approach to project evaluation has not yielded the most beneficial results, either for the donors themselves or for their recipients. It has not been particularly helpful to donors because the focus has been primarily on individual projects, without recognizing overall contributions to development. As we are pushed increasingly to demonstrate results, there is an emerging realization that the results are not evident solely in the projects, but also in the environments where the projects are implemented. Because results are generally translated into short-term measurable impacts of projects, the very nature of research for development to build capacity for the future is at risk.

Project evaluation is also less useful to recipients because this approach remains focused on donor funding agendas, without taking into account the local context in which projects are implemented. As Bajaj (1997) noted, donors and recipients want very different things out of an evaluation. Recipients want to learn about how their objectives are being supported by this work, and what they can learn about their progress in evaluating a given project. Donors want to learn about the project itself, and then relate it back to their programming objectives. As the same study noted, the lack of involvement of recipients in the design stage of evaluation studies, or even the data gathering stage, means that the needs and interests of the donor dominate the evaluation agenda. Recipients only tend to be brought into the evaluation to help with the logistics and to hear the results. If they have not been actively involved in the design of the evaluation process itself, it is hardly surprising that most evaluation results are irrelevant to the recipient organizations.

In summary, the project may be the wrong unit of analysis. Rather, the analysis should be more specifically focused on the results we are trying to achieve, whether to strengthen a field of research or to contribute to a domain (such as health, employment, food security) in national development. In other words, instead of regarding projects as the end, they should be viewed more as the vehicles to achieving larger development objectives. That is certainly the intention in funding the work in the first place; however, the evaluation process does not reflect that reality. If we move in this direction, results are then measured in terms of progress towards the objective, not only in terms of the (project) vehicle's successful performance.

That projects should be regarded as a means rather than the end is not a novel concept. It is in the implementation that projects have become the focus and for many purposes, the end point. As Najam (1995) notes in a review of the literature on project and policy implementation, only when the actors are viewed as the unit of analysis and implementation is seen as a political process do we begin to build an understanding of the enabling and constraining factors in any initiative. In contexts where there are many actors, both individual and institutional, the process is even more complex; hence, a project-focused evaluation approach will take one further away from a clearer understanding of the interactions and interests driving the success or failure of an initiative. Both the problem area and the project context are critical in the evaluation process, as are the roles and functions of implementing agents and those affected by the activity or project.

Viewing evaluation from this perspective has major implications for the evaluation programmes of donor agencies and granting councils, where learning has been largely based within the funding agency and where the project has been the basic unit of analysis. With the focus on performance measurement and results-based management, a project should be assessed in the context of how it is contributing to the larger goal of development. This means that there has to be learning both for the funding agency and the recipient organization. The unit of analysis changes and – perhaps more importantly – it means that performance is measured against progress in a development context, not solely against achievement of the project.

From project evaluation to institutional assessment

The growing awareness within the donor community of the importance of institutional[3] capacity building as a critical part of development work in the

South is part of moving away from a project model of development to a more systemic model. It is recognized that institutions and organizations play vital roles in how a community evolves and what opportunities it acquires. Institutional capacity building takes a variety of forms: some argue that organizational structures need to be created and reinforced; others argue that alternate forms of support such as networks of support among researchers in different countries are a more effective mode than building organizations. But in all cases, there is recognized need for a support structure so that strong and capable individuals do not operate in isolation (Bernard, 1996; Lusthaus *et al.*, 1995). There is a need to create a space for consultation, a space for bringing along junior researchers and a space for action and influence on the policy-making process that extends beyond the individual reach of any one person.

The establishment of strong and capable local institutions – and not only strong projects – is necessary to make decisions effectively and to implement programmes. This need is part of the recognition that development agencies don't deliver 'development' but rather deliver pieces of the development puzzle which countries, organizations, networks or individuals can choose to use or not. Many different types of programmes have been designed around this issue, both on the research side and on the development side. They include organizational support grants for research centres, the creation and strengthening of research networks, support to government agency capacity building, support to NGOs, and so on; they include specialized research area grants, core grants, and training programmes. An issue that emerges is how to evaluate progress in this area. What constitutes institutional capacity strengthening? How does it differ from individual capacity building? And what criteria should be used and who should be involved in the assessment process?

In many countries where IDRC is working, individual research capacity has grown significantly over the 25 years that the centre has been operating. We find that we are working with an increasingly sophisticated research community (Salewicz and Dwivedi, 1996). While many efforts are under way to expand research capacity both within the traditional university-related research community and outside, an increasing emphasis is on the institutional structures within which individual researchers operate. Strong researchers need institutional support structures to conduct their work and mechanisms through which to influence the policy process. This may mean the building of traditional research structures – university departments, research institutes – but it may also mean building other forms of institutional support, such as research networks. Whatever the strategy, there is a need to explore the most effective patterns for institutional support and to build a capacity to assess the organizations and institutions that are created or strengthened. As the centre moved towards this direction, several requests were directed to the Evaluation Unit at IDRC to identify some appropriate tools for assessing institutional development, to complement the existing abilities in assessing individual research capacity.

The Evaluation Unit of IDRC undertook to develop a framework for the assessment of institutional capacity with a particular focus on research institutions. This framework was developed with the Universalia Management

Group (Lusthaus *et al.*, 1995) and was the basis for development of an approach to diagnose organizational strengths and weaknesses and provide a basis on which to identify and determine potential areas for support. What is unique about this framework is that it explicitly addresses several dimensions of institutional strengthening. While most institutional assessment work focuses primarily on capacity within the organization as the critical dimension, this framework looks equally at four dimensions of an organization:

○ *capacity* (leadership, management, human resources) remains important, but balanced with
○ *motivation* (history, mission, culture, incentives) and
○ *environment* (legal, social, technical, etc.). These three key elements are situated in a
○ *performance* framework, based on effectiveness, efficiency, relevance and financial viability.

The approach is based on the premise that performance demonstrates the results of the organization's work – in efficiency, effectiveness, relevance and financial viability. Performance is then the synthesis and result of the way in which the organization uses its capacities, builds motivation, and deals with its environment. In order to assess these areas of performance, the three areas of capacity, motivation and environment are assessed.

Since each institution or organization is unique – with different capacities, environments and mission – this framework for institutional assessment is not prescriptive. Rather, this framework provides a set of

Figure 13.1: *Institutional assessment framework*

guidelines around the key areas that need to be addressed. These factors are interrelated, as illustrated in Figure 13.1.

The framework can be used for external or internal review. It can be used for a comprehensive review of an organization, or to address a specific issue or problem. It was developed in the first instance as a tool for a funding agency to assess its partnerships. However, because of the factors noted above (i.e. the importance of ownership in the use of results, and the relevance of assessment as part of the capacity of an organization), we tested the framework as a self-assessment approach. Several case studies based on use of this model were presented at the Canadian Evaluation Society meetings in Ottawa in May 1997. At that point, the work was just coming to a close in most of the organizations that adopted the self-assessment framework. Since then, we have had the final reports which give us further insights into the areas covered, the problems encountered and the potential for this work.

What we will do here is to elaborate on the findings of testing this framework and explore their implications for applying the model and for strengthening future work in the area of participation in institutional assessment. Based on our experience, this model is not restricted to research organizations but is also useful for other types of organizations. While the cases presented here are all research oriented, they nonetheless provide useful insights more generally in the area of participatory institutional assessment. What emerges from these experiences is that a participatory monitoring and evaluation approach should form a key part of any organizational assessment, as organizations are the platform from which actions and initiatives spring.

Experiences in institutional self-assessment

We present experiences here as a synthesis of the self-assessment work undertaken in several research institutions in West Africa and South Asia,

---

Box 13.1: The research institutions featured in this chapter

The self-assessments involved four organizations supported by IDRC: the Council for the Development of Social Science Research in Africa (CODESRIA); the *Centre d'Études, de Documentation et de Recherche Économique et Sociales* (CEDRES) in Burkina Faso; the *Centre Ivoirien de Recherche Économique et Sociale* (CIRES) in Ivory Coast; and the Center for Integrated Rural Development for Asia and the Pacific (CIRDAP) in Bangladesh.

In three of the four research centres, the exercise was successfully completed, beginning in 1995 and ending in 1997. CIRES did not complete the self-assessment cycle. In CEDRES and CODESRIA the cycle took much longer (18 months) than anticipated. In the cases where the cycle was completed with some delays, it is too early to conclude whether the results would make an impact on institutional policy. In CIRDAP, where the project was completed in the time allocated, some follow-up strategic planning activity is already evident.

---

rather than highlighting any one case (see Box 13.1).[4] First, we outline what we thought would happen; then we summarise what actually happened. We then explore some of the lessons that emerge and the potential we see for ourselves, other funding agencies, and the recipients gaining more control of the evaluation process. Finally, we will raise some issues for future research.

The plan

The institutions involved in self-assessment were approached on the basis of recommendations and suggestions from IDRC programme officers. The concept was that this would be a joint assessment, involving both IDRC and the recipient, as both had learning needs about capacity of the organizations. The process was to be facilitated by Universalia Management Group, who would assist in the identification of terms of reference with each institution, identification of tools, support for methodology for data collection and analysis, and commentary on the final report. IDRC would remain involved to some degree with the participating institutions in the expectation that the reviews could be of value to IDRC and could obviate the necessity for external review in some cases. It was also expected that IDRC would learn more about the potential of the assessment as a tool in building organizational capacity. Time frames were individually established; however, it was intended that there be considerable overlap in timing amongst the three institutions in West Africa – in part to save on travel costs for the facilitators, and in part so that there would be some opportunity for comparisons and joint work by the organizations.

In South Asia the process was slightly different, integrating a strategic planning process into the self-assessment. This entailed a workshop following the assessment in which the members of the organization met for a week to discuss how the diagnosis influenced their strategic plan.

In both settings, an initial visit by IDRC to propose the institutional self-assessment was followed by a consultation with the Universalia team to discuss 'readiness'[5] and to begin the definition of terms of reference and a work plan; to establish a process in each organization; and to consider the resources (internal and external) that would be needed to conduct the assessment. Finally, the consultants were asked to provide a comment to IDRC on the external review, not so much in terms of the conclusions of the team, but rather in terms of the quality and reliability of the data on which the conclusions were based: did they ensure full data collection? did they ensure access to reliable data? did they identify all relevant sources? and so on. The purpose of this comment was to provide back-up to IDRC on the legitimacy and quality of the assessment so that it had the potential to be used for IDRC purposes as well.

In West Africa, IDRC has a regional evaluation officer based in Dakar. She worked closely with Universalia to provide back-up for the institutions participating in the process. Her role was to keep the process moving, either by providing assistance herself, or involving a programme officer, the consultants or the evaluation unit as needed. She was involved from the beginning of the assessments and maintained a watching brief, assisting where appropriate.

It was anticipated that the assessment would result in a report that could be used not only by the organization in its own planning but also by IDRC as part of its accountability requirements.

What happened

These case studies were all within organizations that have received funding from IDRC, in West Africa and South Asia. They are all research/development organizations, but of somewhat different types – from regional institutions, to research institutes within a university. All engage in development research and all seek to influence development policy at the national and regional levels. All are engaged in work that is intended to create an 'indigenous body of knowledge' in their respective fields of endeavour (economics, social sciences, rural development) – that is, all are seeking to create or adapt models of research for local conditions.

There was initial scepticism in most of the organizations. This was based on previous experiences with evaluation and organizational assessment (where it had been used in other contexts to down-size, reduce funding, etc.), on concerns about the links between the assessment and ongoing IDRC support, and on the perceived commitment of resources to a process advocated from outside. Not surprisingly, scepticism was least pronounced where there was no direct link between the assessment and any projects, both in terms of timing and programme officer involvement. In the process of implementation, scepticism was slowly overcome in all but one case, and the assessments proceeded effectively. Overcoming the scepticism was an incremental process; it happened as the participants perceived the relevance of the process to their own needs. In one case, scepticism persisted and is, in our view, the primary reason that the assessment has not been completed to this date. Start-up was slower where scepticism was higher.

The work was carried out by providing facilitation support to design an institutional self-assessment process around the framework. The actual development of terms of reference, data collection and analysis were carried out by the organizations themselves, with some involvement of the facilitators and some external expertise commissioned in some cases. In West Africa, the self-assessment process emerged as a result of a joint design workshop involving all three research institutes with IDRC and the facilitators. The workshop was called to outline the nature of the self-assessment, develop terms of reference for each study and begin to design data collection instruments. It was both helpful and a distraction to have the three organizations working together. To some extent they were able to learn from each other and to strengthen the development of terms of reference and data collection. At the same time they each needed a very different process and needed to address different issues. On reflection, perhaps a one-day workshop together, followed by individual organizational workshops would have been more productive. Data gathering by each organization was structured differently and teams to manage the self-assessments were set up according to the prevailing norms in the organizations. In one case, the executive director created a self-assessment team composed of several young professionals led by the head of training. The team was responsible for all aspects of the process, and their work was reviewed by the executive director. This case illustrates how both senior-level support and staff commitment were critical in successfully conducting the entire process (see Box 13.2).

In another organization, the process was led by a team of two very senior managers who subcontracted external consultants to carry out specific aspects of the process such as data collection and analysis of some issues. The team then integrated these external reports into their own synthesis outputs. In a third organization, the senior management operated as a steering committee responsible for the strategic aspects of the self-assessment and mandated various individuals inside the organization to conduct parts of the process.[6]

Different mechanisms were employed in the organizations, from placing the bulk of the work in the hands of relatively junior professionals, to actively involving senior managers throughout the process. The organizations themselves determined which mechanisms to apply. For instance, in one organization the executive director's role was intentionally minimal during the process of the self-assessment; however, his role was crucial in ensuring that important stakeholders would provide needed data. He is influential and respected in his region and he personally called stakeholders both within and outside the organization and encouraged them to respond to the questionnaire that the operational team was sending. The response rate increased significantly with his intervention. In another case, the organization involved a former executive director (the founder of the centre) as part of the evaluation team, and he was able to provide the historical perspective on many of the issues discussed. The individual became the 'wise' adviser and his role was invaluable.

In all cases where the assessment has been completed, there has been strong support from management for the initiation of this process, and there have been human and financial resources dedicated to completion of the work. In the one case where the process is not yet complete, there has not been strong support from the management of the centre: in the midst of discussions it became clear that the director would be leaving his post and from that point on he had no incentive to engage in the process. A new director may or may not make a difference to the process. Discussions have to be undertaken with the new director to determine whether or not the process could usefully proceed at this stage. What will need further clarification is how much the new director will see this as an opportunity to assess the structure and functions of the research centre, or whether he or she will see it as a compliance mechanism. To some extent, the new director's own views on his or her own mandate will be a determining factor, as will be the role and position of IDRC in the process (as is discussed further below).

A joint workshop involving the leadership of all three centres in West Africa was held to introduce the framework, discuss the nature of the process, and the intent of the assessment. However, given the different starting points of each organization, it was not possible to maintain the

Box 13.2 Assessing institutional performance from within: The experience of CIRDAP

CIRDAP is a regional organization based in Dhaka, Bangladesh. It was established by the Food and Agriculture Organisation (FAO) in 1979 with the support of other United Nations' bodies. The organization was set up to support rural development in its member countries (11 in Asia and the Pacific), and to promote regional co-operation amongst rural development agencies. It functions as a servicing institution for member states by providing them with technical support for integrated rural development work.

The organization embarked on a self-assessment process, which was strongly supported by the executive director. A core team was appointed with members from each of CIRDAP's programme divisions. Mid-way through the self-assessment there was a change in executive director; however, it is important to note that the incoming director was also supportive of the process. The assessment was facilitated by Universalia, the group involved in the design of the framework.

In addition to testing the institutional self-assessment framework, CIRDAP was also looking at the linkage between assessment (diagnosis) of the organization and strategic planning for the future (prescription). A strategic planning process was integrated into the assessment, with the assistance of the Asian Institute of Management (AIM), based in the Philippines. At the beginning of the exercise, the core team outlined the schedule for the design of the evaluation instruments, data collection, analysis, and recommendations. This schedule was followed, often through long hours put in by the staff involved. The core team did most of the data collection, through document reviews, interviews, and focus group discussions with other staff members. The team maintained good records of its work and communicated regularly with all staff on progress of the assessment.

Because of sustained institutional support and staff commitment, the self-assessment in CIRDAP moved successfully beyond the diagnosis phase towards strategic planning as the final activity. The final assessment report served as the core document for the strategic planning workshop.

---

same time frame on each process. This meant a slightly more expensive process and a slightly more significant time commitment by all parties concerned. It also complicated the start-up of the exercise: as the parties were at different points and held different views, a collective exercise was difficult to use effectively. The experience of the joint workshop revealed the importance of recognizing the different perspectives and interests of each institution as key to securing their commitment to the process (Box 13.3).

Box 13.3: Building trust to move the self-assessment forward

The research centres in West Africa – CODESRIA, CEDRES and CIRES – participated in a joint workshop to initiate the self-assessment. It was felt that a joint workshop would help reduce overall costs: only one visit by the facilitation team would be necessary to serve all three centres, and it also provided an opportunity to design a common methodology that would allow the organizations to compare their experiences.

However, the joint workshop also created some unanticipated tensions in the process. Each centre faced different issues and concerns. Hence, it was much harder for each organization to become readily open to and involved in such a collective exercise. By creating some individual space for action and by focusing on each centre's specific issues, the facilitators were able to gain their trust, which was key to designing the self-assessment. Once the institutions obtained a clearer understanding of the objectives of the self-assessment and how these addressed their specific needs and concerns, they were able to move the process forward successfully to the next step.

The role of the funding agency (in most cases, only IDRC) in the self-assessment process varied. In some cases, programme officers from the donor agency were actively involved, and in others, assessments were undertaken without the involvement of the programme officers (other than awareness that the process was underway). The case work shows quite clearly that it is possible for the granting agency to be involved in supporting this process, but that there must be some clear boundaries. Where a programme of funding is coming to closure (whether a project or an institutional support grant), there are risks that partial information may be used against the organization. This happened with one of the participating centres. In the course of the self-assessment, a number of discussion documents were prepared and circulated within the research centre. These documents were part of tentative ideas raised by different staff members – some of which were generally agreed to, while others were new issues coming up for the first time. Because IDRC was involved in working with the group on its self-assessment, the documents were also given to IDRC. In one instance, an IDRC staff person noted some issues in the report, and used the occasion to challenge what was being done in the research centre. This created concern about the use of information and a fear that openness could be penalized. It can be extremely difficult to draw the line between open engagement in discussions and raising issues from outside before the internal conclusions have been reached.

As has been noted in relation to other points above, the assessments generally took longer than anticipated (one is not yet complete). No one realized in advance the implications of a self-assessment process in terms of involvement of staff, members and other constituents. Overcoming some of the barriers outlined above had to be achieved with all the different constituencies. For example, in one case, a member of a self-assessment team had had a difficult experience in the past with an external consultant who was involved in conducting a self-assessment exercise; as a result, this team member raised a lot of initial resistance to the process. The consultant facilitating the self-assessment had to acknowledge and deal with the resistance before the process could actually move forward. This was achieved primarily through dialogue, negotiation and persistence. In another example, a self-assessment was undertaken officially and everyone in the organization was informed. In practice, however, the staff members responsible for the self-assessment did not have enough time to simultaneously conduct the assessment and continue their normal professional activities. Ultimately, the team brought the issue to management to resolve, and the staff member was allocated more time for this task.

In all cases, the self-assessment resulted in focusing on issues pertaining to the mission and direction of the organization – as Bajaj noted in her study (1997) it is the organization itself, not the project, that is of most interest to those being evaluated. What emerged in all cases, was that there were fundamental changes that should be considered in the mission or structure of the organization. For instance, one centre realized that in its efforts to be well-funded and become a strong organization, it had started to compete with its members for donor-funded projects. The board and management realized that they had to change the nature of the projects supported, in such a way that they would complement and support their members' efforts, rather than take projects away from them. Instead of obtaining funding solely for project implementation, management identified a need to obtain support to provide training for their members, to explore new research areas their members could work in, and in general to find ways to enhance their members' capacities so that they could carry out the work in their own countries.

This outcome of the self-assessment process that leads to a greater organizational focus is not surprising in the sense that as the environment changes, the discordance between any organization's structure and mission with the environment increases. The institutional assessment work creates a timely mechanism for addressing this issue. Since the extent of the potential for change was not appreciated at the beginning of most of the assessments, this meant that not enough time was allocated to consider these issues: it was generally assumed that the assessment would lead to fine-tuning more than anything else. However, it usually resulted in revealing the potential for much more fundamental change, for which time requirements are more long term.

What we learned

Each organization we dealt with in the process was unique. They were all at different stages in development and all had different issues as a starting point. This highlighted the individual nature of the process and confirmed for us that there is no single approach that can be advocated. Each assessment needs to be defined in the context of the specific setting, and each design has to be sufficiently flexible to adapt as the layers of the organization are peeled back. The experiences to date have suggested several important lessons, both as to the design and to the process of self-assessment. The main insights are highlighted below.

Those inside are not necessarily easier on themselves than an external reviewer would be

In the cases conducted, the leadership has addressed, and in some cases adopted, recommendations that fundamentally challenge the governance structures of the organizations. Because the investigation, analysis and recommendations were drawn from inside the organization, the potential for application is much stronger. The following examples show how results from the self-assessment have been utilized directly by those involved.

○ One organization learned that it needed a much stronger capacity to provide training and technical support to its members. As a result of the recommendations of the self-assessment, they have since strengthened the training unit and given it much more prominence in the work they carry out.
○ Another organization continued the self-assessment process with a three-day strategic planning exercise, during which the self-assessment data was used as a basis for the development of strategies.
○ One organization used its self-assessment report to develop a special Board session at their annual meeting.

However, one particular case illustrates that ownership over results may not always be achieved in the process. In this case, the organization never fully completed the exercise due to various changes in leadership. The director left just as the process was to begin. A new director was not in place for some time. There has been no follow-up, and the draft report is likely to be shelved.

There is always the possibility in a self-assessment that the self-interest of those involved will lead them to paint a rosy picture of the situation, either to maintain a view that things are going well or to present a picture to the outside that will lead to further funding. We did not find this to be the case. Difficult issues were raised and addressed in the course of the self-assessment in all the institutions. Challenges to their missions were made and recommendations have included some quite fundamental changes. There are several reasons for this:

○ The nature of the self-assessment process involved a range of actors, not only one 'level' of actor in the organization. This means that there are opportunities to raise different perspectives and issues. No organization consists of only one perspective; by involving different actors in the self-assessment, these different perspectives and concerns are brought out.
○ In addition, all of those involved have at one point experienced external reviews in which they had to deal with someone who failed to unravel the layers of complexity in their organization, and who therefore was unable to present relevant recommendations. Those involved in the self-assessment appreciated the opportunity to deal with the issues in depth with a group of participants aware of the complexities within the organization.

o In the end, it is the staff and membership of the organization who have to live with its successes and failures, not the external reviewers. They, therefore, have a stake in taking the opportunity presented to do everything they can to improve the organization.

The self-assessment process is most effective when it is de-linked from the project cycle

One of the first challenges in the self-assessment process was scepticism about motives: was this simply an alternative way for the funding agency to get inside the organization to decide about future funding? This concern was exacerbated in those organizations closest to the end of their current funding cycle. Since most evaluation is conducted as part of determining whether or not to continue funding of a project or an organization, this remained a problematic factor in the self-assessment cycle. Thus, while the concept of self-assessment should make it part of institutional strengthening, there was a natural tendency to consider how the assessment will affect the project cycle. In instances where project funding was coming to a close, there was a strong tendency to expect the outcome of the assessment to lead into the next (potential) project.

In the one case where the process was de-linked most explicitly from the funding cycle, implementation was much smoother. In this case, the donor agency programme officer was not actively involved with the self-assessment exercise. There was an open discussion of this issue between the donor agency programme officer and the staff of the recipient organization in the beginning of the assessment; it was clearly agreed then that the assessment would not be linked to the project, and that the programme officer from the donor agency would not be directly involved in conducting the assessment. This agreement was fully upheld during the implementation. The programme officer was kept informed of events over the course of the assessment, as well as of the outcomes of the assessment; but he was not necessarily kept informed about the details of the assessment as it took place. While it is possible to develop a collaborative approach to institutional self-assessment, and that assessment can be useful for both the organization and the funding agency, the parameters of that collaboration must be clearly spelled out at the beginning. The principles which would seem to apply are that:

o the terms of reference should be developed collaboratively
o the process documents should be shared judiciously and their receipt by the recipient organization should be treated as a demonstration of trust and collegiality; the contents should not be used against the organization nor should there be a perception of use in that way
o the purpose of the self-assessment needs to be kept clearly in focus. For the organization, it contributes specific change recommendations. For the funding agency, it is not so much the specific outputs that are at issue, but rather the identification of capacity building through effective assessment, followed by implementation of the recommendations.

Self-assessment and external review fulfil different purposes

Both external review and self-assessment are legitimate review processes. External review is often needed for accountability of funds received and also for quality control. But, without some parallel review processes internal to the organization, external review does not necessarily contribute to institutional strengthening and capacity building. Self-assessment fulfils that need, by providing the mechanism for an organization to look at its own progress and determine what changes should be made. It strengthens an institution's capacity for reflection, a key component of any learning organization and helps organizations deal on a more equal footing with external stakeholders (i.e. funding agencies). This means more capacity to negotiate with donors on the design of evaluations, resulting in a stronger focus on the progress of the organization as a whole rather than the success of the individual project.

Lessons from the process

Aside from these key areas of learning, there are a number of elements of the self-assessment process that proceeded differently in each organization. The successes and problems encountered suggest some adaptations to the process that should be considered by both implementing organizations and facilitators:

○ The self-assessment needs a 'champion', but the champion needs to put a system in place to ensure full participation and continuity if the process is going to proceed clearly and smoothly.
○ The self-assessment needs the support of the relevant interest groups, both within the organization (staff and members) and in the surrounding environment (those affected, government departments, other funding sources, and so on).
○ The organization should be prepared to have discussions on both the mission and structure of the organization. While there was not an intent in most cases to move the assessment to this level, this is what happened in all cases.
○ The process often leads to an ongoing interest in evaluation as a mechanism for learning and organization building. In that context, the establishment of an ongoing monitoring and evaluation process (or a modification of an existing evaluation role) is sometimes an outcome. The concept of a learning approach to evaluation has major implications within the organization in terms of human resources and time investment in evaluation.
○ While the self-assessment process may have been a more time-consuming process than external review, the recommendations are readily understood when they are presented, and do not require the sort of review and internalizing that is required when recommendations come from an external review. Time lag from recommendation to implementation, therefore, is greatly reduced. While we have not tested this idea, it would appear, if we look at time requirements (starting from the

beginning of assessment to the implementation of recommendations) that self-assessment is no more time consuming than external review – and may actually be less so.

○ There is a need to determine the optimum relationship in a collaborative self-assessment when external actors are involved. While we still don't know what best defines such a relationship, an open exploration of the issues and potential conflicts would certainly be an essential ingredient in the design of a collaborative self-assessment.

The research agenda and next steps

Giving evaluation away to those most affected remains a strong research agenda in building capacity for participatory evaluation within our organization and in work with our partners. The potential for learning from evaluation is much stronger in such a context, and the relevance of evaluation is more clearly demonstrated. The ongoing frustration on the part of evaluators as to whether or not anyone actually uses their results is mitigated when the conclusions are reached by those most affected. As these cases demonstrate, when it is within their power to do something, the members and stakeholders in an organization will conduct an assessment that addresses questions fundamental to the organization and their future work. Several critical questions remain unanswered.

○ We don't know how sustainable the interventions for institutional self-assessment will be. Hence, follow-up with the participating organizations over the next several years will be critical.

○ We are only beginning to work with these and other partners on the question of the design of relevant internal monitoring and evaluation systems that will assist them in such processes on an ongoing basis.

○ We don't know if and how the process could be repeated in an organization: would there be reluctance to get so deeply into mission and structure again? Or is there potential for follow-up on a more *ad hoc* basis, dealing only with a few issues?

○ While we hypothesize that self-assessment will be seen as relevant to the donors, we don't yet know how true that is: will it help the organizations reduce the amount of external review to which they are subjected? Will the donor community begin to see this as a relevant demonstration of built capacity?

○ To date we have not distinguished clearly between institutions and organizations. One distinction may be to describe institutions as policy-making entities and organizations as the structures to implement the rules and policies. Thus, can the same conditions apply in institutions as in organizations? While it is complicated to assess an organization in a participatory manner, moving to the level of an institution (such as the educational system) significantly increases the complexity of applying a participatory-assessment approach: it will have to take into account a larger range of actors, a number of issues, and the different organizations involved.

These are some of the outstanding questions in operationalizing a participatory approach that we will be exploring over the next few years. Other remaining issues deal with methodological considerations, such as issues related to concepts of 'validity', 'rigour', and 'objectivity', which need to be addressed if participatory monitoring and evaluation is ever to be seen as legitimate and relevant, and if its results are going to be applied seriously beyond the boundaries of the community using the approaches.

We became involved in this kind of process because of our own experience in IDRC in terms of its limited use of evaluation and the centre's philosophy of collaborating with Southern partners rather than simply providing expertise that they do not have. For that collaboration to be effective, our partners need to drive their own decision making and development, and our role is to engage with them in that capacity building. In the case of evaluation, it is very much a joint search for new approaches as we are only at the beginning of understanding a more effective role for evaluation in our own setting. Our partners, who have more often than not been the subject of evaluation, bring strong direct experience to those issues that could strengthen our own use of evaluation as well as their control of the evaluation process in their own settings.

14

Conceptual Tools for Tracking Change: Emerging Issues and Challenges

DINDO M. CAMPILAN

Conceptualizing participatory monitoring and evaluation (PM&E)

THE DEVELOPMENT OF clear concepts is indispensable for building and communicating knowledge about PM&E. In general, concepts are used to analyse social phenomena, classify the objects of the observed world, impart meaning through explanation of these phenomena, and formulate higher-level propositions on the basis of these observations (Marshall, 1994). In the field of PM&E, concepts are essential because they allow us to compare and share varied experiences by developing common understanding about its practice. In other words, concepts serve as building blocks for learning.

Over the years, the growing popularity of PM&E has generated a diverse range of concepts used to describe and explain its processes, structures and relationships. While this may be one indication that PM&E is entering the mainstream of monitoring and evaluation as a field of study, it also points to the need for practitioners to further build and clarify understanding about PM&E.

In general, the central goal of development interventions is to change a situation, from one that is considered problematic to one that is desired. Tracking this change is thus a key concern for such interventions and the underlying reason for monitoring and evaluation (M&E).

To the extent that the main focus is placed on measuring change, *participatory* M&E is not so different from other more conventional M&E approaches. One way of distinguishing PM&E from other M&E approaches is its conceptualization of *how* to measure change, *who* is involved, and *for what* purposes. In this chapter, these conceptual dimensions of PM&E are explored and discussed, together with other related issues raised at the Philippines Workshop.

Appreciating diversity in PM&E practice: Workshop highlights

Workshop participants pointed to two emerging trends in the conceptual development of PM&E. One trend reveals that there is an increasing diversity in PM&E concepts that is a reflection of the range of reported field experiences. Table 14.1 presents a comparative view of the conceptual

Table 14.1: Overview of key concepts used in the PM&E cases

Case Experience	PM&E Approach	Associated Concepts	Key Features
Hamilton *et al.*	Self-monitoring and evaluation	Internal learning, institutional analysis	'. . . to provide a forum that allows forest users to express their views and needs, and to negotiate a set of common objectives or goals for their institution'
Blauert and Quintanar	Participatory stakeholder evaluation	Institutional learning, social audit, use of local indicators	'. . . assesses the social impact and ethical behaviour of an organization or project in relation to its aims and those of its stakeholders'
Lawrence *et al.*	Participatory development of indicators	Stakeholder analysis, technology evaluation, use of local indicators	'. . . focuses particularly on indicator development and the merits of using matrix scoring as a method for evaluating the impacts of new farming technology.'
Sidersky and Guijt	Participatory monitoring	Impact monitoring by stakeholder groups including trade representatives, farmer experimentation groups, an NGO and community associations	'To allow the collection and processing of more useful information . . . for farmers to know whether they are to continue with their efforts . . . to change practices and strategies . . . and influence for broader policy changes (at municipal and state levels) by using the local "data" . . .'
Abes	Participatory impact evaluation	Longitudinal impact evaluation, learning and sharing	'. . . [A] positive factor was the participation of leader researchers in the evaluation process, because they have a grounded grasp of realities . . .'
Espinosa	Community monitoring and evaluation	Community-driven M&E	'. . . proposals and decisions put forward in the (PM&E) process by the community are used as the basis for formulating local government programmes . . .'
Rutherford	Community monitoring	Participatory evaluation research through citizens' learning teams	'We proved that a local group can do evaluation. We were not practised in this type of evaluation so the process was sometimes ragged but we learned by doing.'
Ward	Participatory monitoring and evaluation	Institutional learning and community control	'Organizational learning includes learning along with local communities and ensuring the villagers are "getting the right end of the stick".'
Symes and Jasser	Participatory planning, monitoring and evaluation	Strategic planning through learning loops	'. . . concept of participation is applied not just at the project level but also within the organization itself, for example, in strategic planning.'

Case Experience	PM&E Approach	Associated Concepts	Key Features
Torres	Monitoring local development	Self-reflection through *sistema de desarollo* (local development system)	'. . . experimenting with participatory monitoring and evaluation methodologies to strengthen local development planning . . . to co-ordinate efforts, share risks and mobilize resources.'
Gobisaikhan and Menamkart	Participatory monitoring and evaluation	Stakeholders' self-monitoring	'. . . an ongoing collaborative process in which the beneficiaries and other stakeholders at different levels work together to assess a project and take any corrective action required.'
Carden	Institutional self-assessment	Learning-based approach, institutional capacity building	'. . . to develop a framework for the assessment of institutional capacity with a particular focus on research institutions.'

approaches used in the case studies included in this volume. Establishing inventories such as this can serve as a starting point for systematizing PM&E concepts.

Despite the variety of approaches, workshop participants agreed that one way of distinguishing between the different 'types' of PM&E is by defining the different purposes or functions in undertaking PM&E. PM&E may be applied within the context of a community development project, as an integral part of institutional/organizational development and learning, and/or as a means for influencing policy and ensuring greater public accountability. This process may be internally or community driven or may build on a broader stakeholder approach (see further discussion below).

The second trend is that the diversity of understanding surrounding PM&E has also contributed to a great deal of confusion and conflicting interpretations. During the workshop, sessions usually started with participants exploring and clarifying their various definitions of concepts, before they moved on to the actual points for discussion. In the process, workshop participants learned that constructive discussions can be maximized by identifying and building on their shared understanding(s) of PM&E, while at the same time accepting possible differences. This helped provide a more positive environment for mutual discussion than imposing participants' conceptual frameworks on each other would have done.

Other insights shared by participants during the workshop included the following:

○ Any exercise to develop an inventory of PM&E concepts needs to take place in an atmosphere of open-mindedness and mutual respect for divergent opinions. There are usually different levels and stages towards reaching consensus. A good starting point is to identify those areas of general agreement; subsequent discussions may eventually open up other areas of consensus.

○ One challenge is being able to share a common language to describe PM&E. While some suggested more operational definitions, there were also those who put forward metaphors (e.g. bean counting), abstractions (e.g. humanizing the PM&E process) and culture-specific terminologies (e.g. using symbols associated with characters in the Chinese language).

○ Given the multiple meanings associated with these concepts, one key task is to monitor the 'language' being used, in order to communicate more effectively what the terms 'P', 'M' and 'E' represent (see Table 1.1, in Chapter 1). This is important for developing a general lexicon for PM&E – one made specific enough to be practicable but also general enough to accommodate a variety of applications.

Participants in PM&E

Despite growing recognition of PM&E as being distinct from conventional M&E, it is sometimes not easy to distinguish between a monitoring and evaluation process that is participatory and one that is not. Nonetheless, it is important to differentiate between participatory M&E and other M&E approaches that merely use participatory methods. In PM&E, participation becomes a central feature of the entire process, from defining objectives and information needs to analysing and using results. For instance, this includes efforts that involve local stakeholders in developing the PM&E system itself (see Chapters 5 and 9). PM&E is distinguished from other M&E approaches that may make use of participatory methods (e.g. in data collection) but that are still mainly controlled and determined by outsiders or selected individuals and groups. In reality, however, there is no clear-cut dichotomy – they are but extreme points of a continuum in which lie various combinations of more and less participatory approaches.

A process that is said to be participatory requires participants. Hence, identifying who participates is a crucial preliminary step towards undertaking participatory M&E. However, identifying and selecting participants often becomes problematic. Power relations among key actors can determine who eventually is able to participate and under what particular circumstances (see Chapter 17). This is partly because the role of monitor and evaluator allows individuals or groups to wield power over others in determining how to interpret change. Allowing or disallowing certain parties to participate depends on who has perceived ownership over the PM&E process. As a consequence, interested parties may not always freely come forward to participate in M&E. Either they strategize to establish their position in the PM&E arena, or they have that opportunity bestowed upon them by other more powerful actors. Such difficulties point to the need to examine how we conceptualize who 'participants' are in the PM&E process.

The cases in this volume view PM&E as a process either involving:

○ the local people/community primarily
○ a partnership between project beneficiaries and the usual external M&E specialists/experts
○ a wider group of stakeholders who are directly and indirectly involved in or affected by development interventions.

In general, there is a trend towards the inclusion of a wider group of stakeholders as participants in PM&E. There is also shared recognition that some form of involvement by *local* people is an essential feature of PM&E. However, this raises important questions about who 'local' people are, and what their specific roles and functions are throughout the PM&E process.

The 'external–internal' dichotomy is often used to distinguish one group of PM&E participants from another. For instance, external actors or outside 'experts' with no previous involvement in a particular initiative may be brought in to establish and/or facilitate a PM&E process. This is contrasted with other PM&E approaches that are carried out mainly by 'insiders' or those who are directly involved in a development intervention. Insiders may include field-based project staff, community-based groups, villagers or community residents.

Another perspective seeks to combine internal and external approaches to M&E. So-called 'joint' or collaborative M&E takes place when participants comprise both insiders and outsiders. Joint M&E is intended to provide a more balanced, multiple perspective in measuring and interpreting change. Several case studies in this volume are examples that draw on the relative strengths of combining internal and external stakeholder groups in PM&E (see Chapters 2, 3, 4, 5 and 12).

The search for 'cornerstones' of PM&E

Given the diversity in PM&E thinking and practice, workshop participants nevertheless agreed that a useful starting point for exploring conceptual issues in PM&E is to identify 'cornerstones' that can serve as 'non-negotiable' principles to anchor any PM&E practice. This perhaps represents one of the major challenges for PM&E practitioners. Formulating 'cornerstones' would have to take into account the following: why PM&E is being undertaken and for whom, what the role of participation is in PM&E, and when participation takes place in PM&E. Attempts to define 'cornerstones' would also have to consider the strategic choices often made in the case of M&E approaches that are initially less participatory. We will now look at each of these issues in turn.

Why is PM&E being undertaken and for whom?

As discussed earlier, participatory M&E is not so different from conventional M&E inasmuch as both approaches are concerned with measuring and judging performance (results and outcomes) in order to decide on future action. However, PM&E aims to go beyond simply judging and making decisions, and also seeks to create an enabling environment for stakeholder groups – including those directly involved and affected by a particular intervention – to learn how to define and interpret changes for themselves, and hence to take greater control over their own development. For example, self-monitoring and evaluation by forest user groups can be an instrument for gaining leverage over policies that govern natural resource use (see Chapter 2).

As illustrated in the case studies, PM&E generally carries a multiplicity of goals, reflecting the diverse interests and concerns brought forward by those participating in the process (see Table 14.1). Whichever goals are pursued, what is important is to ensure that:

o first, the agenda for PM&E should be made explicit to all parties or stakeholders involved. Admittedly, this is not easily achieved, because in many cases stakeholders may not be clear about their goals and objectives in doing PM&E until they actually 'do' it and participate in the process
o second, deciding on which PM&E goals to pursue should also be made participatory. The process will need to recognize that there are multiple concerns for undertaking PM&E and that this necessarily involves negotiations, consensus building, trade-offs or compromises.

Clarifying goals and objectives points to the question: for whom is PM&E being carried out? Unlike conventional M&E approaches that are often driven by the information needs of outsiders (e.g. donors, central management and other external interest groups), PM&E aims to cater to the information needs and concerns of a much wider range of actors who have a direct or indirect stake in development changes and outcomes.

What is the role of participation in PM&E?

There are a number of reasons that can justify why participation in M&E is important (see Chapter 1). However, those who advocate stakeholder participation in M&E often do not make explicit whether they regard participation as a means or as an end – or both. For some, participation in PM&E is a means to achieve other development objectives (e.g. greater efficiency, improved delivery of services). For others, participation is regarded as an end result (e.g. empowerment). In one case study in Colombia, for example, empowering local assemblies through community monitoring and evaluation means transforming what are supposed to be the 'end-beneficiaries' into 'proponents' and 'planners' of development interventions (see Chapter 7).

Despite the rationale for promoting participation, there is a lack of hard evidence to demonstrate what difference participation actually makes to the monitoring and evaluation process. For instance, one case demonstrated how citizen learning teams monitored citizen participation in the M&E process, and assessed the impact of their work on local development policy and decision making as well as on personal development and community capacity (see Chapter 9).

However, there are few studies that critically examine the role and nature of participation in M&E, the impact of participation in such a process, and the (enabling and disabling) conditions for its practice. Establishing methods and standards for systematically assessing the supposed added-value of 'participation' would make the concept more empirically grounded and tested. This is critical in deepening our understanding of what participation in PM&E actually means and how this can be successfully translated into practice.

197

When does participation take place in PM&E?

Most practitioners of PM&E recognize that participation does not take place uniformly throughout the entire M&E process but, rather, varies across temporal and spatial contexts. Hence, it is possible to distinguish between different levels and types of participation by stakeholders at particular events or stages of M&E.

First, participation in M&E may change over a project cycle, or from one M&E event to the next. A participatory approach to M&E may be adopted right from the beginning (i.e. from project planning) and continued throughout, or it may only be undertaken during selected events (i.e. towards the end of the project). Second, PM&E may not have the same level of participation by all stakeholders at each point of the process. Often, the degree of involvement by various stakeholder groups varies from one event to the next. For instance, PM&E may start with a selected group of stakeholders, which could later expand or contract in size as some join or drop out in the process.

What is important to point out, however, is that PM&E does not become participatory simply on the basis of the numbers of stakeholder groups involved. The bottom line is to make sure that stakeholders are involved in deciding and planning who should participate, and how, at each stage of the PM&E process.

Conclusions

Given the range of experiences and innovations in PM&E, it would be difficult and even questionable to seek universally accepted definitions of concepts and to define strict typologies to categorize its practice. There are at least four underpinning issues and challenges in the conceptual development of PM&E, as described below.

First, M&E as a formal field of study is new when compared with the classical scientific disciplines, which are already anchored upon a dominant body of theory, methods and standards. This is even more true for PM&E as a specialized area within the M&E field. Refining concepts, labels, or definitions are an inevitable part in the early stages of building the theoretical base of any professional field.

Second, PM&E – and M&E in general – is an inter-disciplinary field that draws on concepts and tools from various disciplines, including the social and biophysical sciences. It is more appropriately considered a 'transdiscipline' (Scriven, 1993), with its diverse disciplinary roots and branches (Horton, 1998). While this feature underscores the wide applicability of PM&E across disciplines and subject areas, this also makes it more difficult to locate PM&E within the global body of professional knowledge. A major challenge is helping the multi-disciplinary community of PM&E practitioners (and theorists) communicate through a shared understanding of PM&E, which includes recognizing its inherent conceptual diversity.

Third, the rapid expansion of PM&E practice has not been accompanied by a similar development towards building its theoretical foundation. This is largely because of PM&E's wide appeal as a highly pragmatic and user-

Box 14.1   Moving toward a new mainstream
by Gelia T. Castillo

If you truly believe in the merits of participatory monitoring and evaluation, you must aim for a new mainstream, not just a narrow alternative path, even if participatory. Do not settle for the comfort of being on a micro pedestal shooting gently at the macro blue chips entrenched in the traditional mainstream. Be the blue chips in a new mainstream.

What makes me think that PM&E should aspire for a new mainstream? New 'spaces' in governments, bureaucracies and international organizations have created opportunities for advocating participatory approaches. It is now the 'in' thing to do even for the World Bank. The world is entering into an era of participation culture. Many countries are democratizing and decentralizing which is opening up spaces for communities, civil society, and ordinary citizens to participate in the development process.

It has been said that PM&E is an enabling and empowering process. But it still lacks institutionalization into the field of development. At the moment, the body of knowledge about PM&E is young, fragile, and vulnerable to 'attack' from critics and sceptics. Without champions in the right places, it could fade away as another passing fad in development.

A number of questions and observations come to mind in thinking about the journey towards mainstreaming. Firstly, how do we harness our collective wealth of knowledge, skills, experiences, energies, and commitment to PM&E? PM&E is energy- and time-intensive. It is often portrayed as a process, but what are the products from this process? What is the value added to PM&E, given that it requires considerable investment of human resources? Secondly, when you say participation as a core principle is non-negotiable, what does this mean? For participation to be truly participatory, it must allow the freedom (choice) not to participate. Finally, PM&E and external evaluations are often caricatured in contrasts, such as: internal/external; participatory/conventional; subjective/rigorous; qualitative/quantitative; formal/informal, etc. This caricature *is* a caricature. The reality is often not about these two extremes. How can PM&E be useful for external evaluation, and vice versa? Quantification and participation need not be adversaries: qualitative documentation requires as much rigour as quantification, if it is to be credible and meaningful.

There are a number of issues that should be considered en route to the mainstream and the professionalism of PM&E:

○ developing a body of knowledge, including concepts and an articulated philosophy for PM&E
○ documenting experiences that describe the characteristics and the value added in doing PM&E

driven process. Practitioners turn to PM&E for its direct and practical applications in concrete field situations. For many, theorizing about PM&E practice is not a primary concern. However, it is important to realize that formalizing PM&E knowledge is far from simply being an academic pursuit – the knowledge base that is established can serve as a platform for improved learning and sharing of what constitutes 'best practices' in PM&E.

Fourth, efforts to document and consolidate diverse PM&E experiences into an updated and comprehensive 'state of the art' still remain limited. Documentation is critical for building a more coherent body of knowledge in PM&E. However, for most practitioners, there is generally little time (and few resources) available for systematic, long-term documentation. Effective documentation often requires additional skills, e.g. meta-level analysis and report writing, which many PM&E practitioners may not be fully equipped to, nor capable of, carrying out.

Working towards the conceptual development of PM&E will mean accepting diversity but also clarifying our understanding. Establishing 'cornerstones' or 'core principles' of PM&E has been regarded as critical for building our knowledge base of PM&E. However, this raises the question of whether or not it is important – or even necessary – to strive towards conceptual convergence and to develop a 'common language' for PM&E. Another related question is whether or not there is a need to professionalize and mainstream PM&E as a field of study and practice (see Box 14.1). While these remain challenging questions, what seems clear is that PM&E advocates and practitioners recognize the importance of achieving wider understanding and expanding learning about PM&E.

15

Methodological Issues in Participatory Monitoring and Evaluation

IRENE GUIJT

AFTER HIS FIRST experience in designing a monitoring and evaluation (M&E) system, a farmer in Brazil said: 'This stuff is worse than *tiririca!*' *Tiririca* is a local weed that sprouts many new shoots when cut. For every question the group had just answered in designing the first stage of their participatory monitoring and evaluation (PM&E) process, several new questions had emerged. When would the questions stop, he wondered?

Core principles such as participation, learning, flexibility and negotiation (see Chapter 1), radically affect the design and implementation of M&E – adding layers of complexity, as that Brazilian farmer quickly noticed. This chapter discusses methodological questions that arise when such new principles shape monitoring and evaluation efforts, namely: who needs what information, in what form, at what point, and for what. The issues extend far beyond simply which methods works best, as these are but a small part of the extensive communication processes that lie at the heart of M&E.

This chapter is divided into two parts: the first discusses three key practical aspects of PM&E – core steps, indicators, and methods; the second highlights five dilemmas and challenges that require better understanding and practice if participatory M&E is to grow in scope and quality. The material in this chapter is derived mainly from the case studies in this book, with additional material from the Philippines Workshop proceedings (IIRR, 1998) and other relevant experiences.

Practical aspects

Core steps

Participatory M&E occurs in many diverse forms. Some are small initiatives, restricted to a local organization in a limited geographic area, while others focus on inter-organizational learning and cover entire regions or countries. Each has been developed with its own combination of objectives in mind (see Chapters 1 and 14) and have involved different groups of stakeholders in unique ways – some assuming more community homogeneity, others recognizing and working with internal differences. Yet amidst this diversity, discussions at the Philippines Workshop revealed some core steps (see Box 15.1) that most PM&E approaches seem to follow (see also Figure 1.1 in Chapter 1).

Box 15.1:   Core steps in developing PM&E

1 Identify who should, and wants to, be involved.
2 Clarify participants' expectations of the process (what are their information needs), and in what way each person or group wants to contribute.
3 Define the priorities for monitoring and evaluating (on which goals/objectives/activities to focus).
4 Identify indicators that will provide the information needed.
5 Agree on the methods, responsibilities and timing of information collection.
6 Collect the information.
7 Adapt the data collection methodology, as needed.
8 Analyse the information.
9 Agree on how the findings are to be used and by whom.
10 Clarify if the PM&E process needs to be sustained, and if so, how. Adjust the methodology accordingly.

Although these steps look like a simple cycle of answering questions and implementing them, the sequence varies and there are small internal cycles of repeated steps. For example, Step 9 is fundamental to the process and should be discussed continually, right from the start. But the quality and type of information that finally emerges will require revision to the original ideas about who the end-users are, hence its appearance later on – after Step 8. Also, indicator and method selection are intertwined. An ideal indicator may be selected, but if no feasible method exists to assess it, then the indicator must be adjusted. The discussions at the Philippines Workshop also recognized that these core steps are embedded in a set of design principles, such as 'rigorous identification and inclusion of all groups[1] within a community throughout the steps' (while recognizing the limits of 'total participation') and 'immediate analysis of data and quick feedback to participants' (IIRR, 1998).

As raised in the 'conceptual issues' section, what makes these steps different from conventional M&E is the answer to the question 'who participates?', or, as Estrella and Gaventa (1998) write, 'Who counts reality?'. In PM&E processes, people who are normally not involved in deciding what is assessed, or in deciding how this is carried out, take a more active role. The 'excluded' are often community members, so-called 'primary stakeholders', but can also be junior staff in a project. From data collectors, they become process designers, process critics, data analysts, and information users.

Two types of variations occur in relation to these core steps. First, different steps are sometimes included, such as 'data validation by local communities' which Abes mentions. Espinosa includes 'training of community leaders or representatives' in monitoring and evaluation as being important in his work with indigenous communities in Colombia. Second, variations also occur in the degree of involvement of different stakeholders. Hamilton *et al.* describe how, in Nepal, programme staff developed four types of

PM&E that varied in terms of who was involved in which ways, thus leading to alternative core steps for each of type of M&E. For example, the forest users group (FUG) Health Check was created by the staff, without forest user identification of indicators (Step 4). Nevertheless, their active participation in analysis (Step 8) still made the Health Check useful for the FUGs. Differences in steps also emerge when end-users are not 'communities'. They may be graduates from a leadership school (Chapter 6) or institutions (Chapters 12 and 13), thus requiring other steps in order to accommodate different audiences and/or scales of operation (see 'Levels of analysis' later in this chapter).

The quality of the PM&E process depends greatly on who is involved, and *how* they are involved, at each step. Therefore, careful identification of stakeholders is crucial, and involves more than simply listing important groups. Who should be involved will depend on what is being monitored and for what purpose. Blauert and Quinantar explain how they carefully identified ten stakeholder groups at the onset of their work in Mexico, with more groups emerging over time and being included. In Brazil, on the other hand, an explicit choice was made to limit participation to three stakeholder groups, and to expand slowly as and when this became feasible – and desired – by those involved (Chapter 5). The question of who participates in PM&E is discussed in greater detail in the conceptual issues section (Chapter 14). Suffice it here to stress that PM&E is not exclusively used with communities or sub-groups in communities, but touches a range of audiences and varying degrees of involvement – all of which have methodological implications in terms of issues, methods, process and results.

The significance of the core steps lies not in their strict, uniform application but in stimulating a more reflective planning process for the M&E work. This helped Espinosa, at least, to achieve 'the creation of a system for the M&E of development plans that allows communities to remain actively involved in the efforts . . ., and in their oversight and control'.

Negotiating indicators and non-indicator alternatives

Indicators grab the attention and occupy much of the time of M&E initiatives.[2] This is perhaps not surprising, since they are approximations of complex processes, events or trends. However, they do not have to be perfect – only sufficiently relevant and accurate for those who are going to interpret the information to be able to do so.

Ideally, indicators reveal changes related to a specific phenomenon that, in itself, represents a bigger question or problem. For example, 'ownership feeling of forest' is an approximation for people's sense of responsibility to maintain it well (Chapter 2), or 'whether colleagues know each other's work' is an expression of access to information and the overall democratic style within the organization (Chapter 3). A second function of indicators lies in the negotiation process itself, which acts as a 'leveller'. By bringing different stakeholders together to identify which information is critical, it helps clarify goals and views on change, information needs, and people's values (see Chapter 8). A third, related, function is that of 'empowerment'. Many consider primary stakeholder participation in indicator identification to be empowering, as it allows local views to dictate what constitutes success or change. For example, Lawrence *et al.* describe how some farmers are now designing their own evaluations after learning the role of systematic indicator tracking. Also, Blauert and Quinantar conclude in their work that 'the search for indicators . . . led . . . to reflection and even negotiation of differences over concerns about accountability and democratic organizational rules and procedures'. However, for indicator development to be empowering is an impressive feat and one that few M&E efforts can correctly claim to have achieved.

Indicators can be quantitative or qualitative. The choice of quantitative and/or qualitative indicators depends entirely on the objectives of the PM&E process and the information needed. In Laos, research on the impact of aquaculture focused on quantitative indicators, but distinguished between 'indirect' effects (or indicators) and 'direct effects (Chapter 4), some of which reflect complex changes, such as 'improved family diet', and others more simple ones, such as 'rice production'. By comparison, Abes' work focuses on assessing leadership skills, therefore indicators related to 'democratic processes' and 'management skills' were more important. Torres, Espinosa, and Blauert and Quinantar all include highly qualitative indicators, such as 'degree of recognition and acceptance of plurality of local interests' and 'tolerance of local social and cultural diversity'. Torres, in particular, stresses the importance of balancing tangible and intangible indicators: 'Often there are unanticipated outcomes that are intangible but prove to be more important in terms of understanding project impacts than anticipated tangible results'.

A common debate regarding which of the two indicator types is better is not an issue for many of the contributors to this book, who urge the importance of both. And, indeed, they show how many so-called 'intangible' qualitative impacts can be measured with quantitative indicators, or vice versa. Rutherford offers an interesting example from the USA, where one citizen learning team chose to assess changes in 'community revitalization', by counting the numbers and types of community organizations in each community.

Selecting indicators is one of the most difficult steps in setting up a PM&E approach, even if those involved accept that good – rather than perfect – indicators are adequate. This stage highlights, more than any other, the different information needs and expectations that the different stakeholders have of the monitoring work. The question that guides the indicator selection is crucial. In Espinosa's experience, indigenous groups in Colombia asked themselves what 'fruits' they expected to see from their efforts. Sidersky and Guijt asked trade union members to focus on what 'information' would best tell them whether they had reached the objectives. The debates that followed revealed that what one group considered 'trustworthy' information did not necessarily hold for the others. Abes recounts yet another approach without questions, in which stories and discussions were converted to core indicators by non-governmental organization (NGO) staff and village leaders.

Indicator identification can be pursued in different ways and with varying degrees of analytic depth. Blauert and Quinantar describe their elaborate approach to find suitable indicators, structured around indicator areas that are based on the 'cone' (Ritchey-Vance, 1998; see Chapter 8). Each stakeholder group gave its own set of indicators, which were clustered by the external research team (including farmers), with the objective of each of these sets being presented back to the community and adopted. By contrast, Lawrence *et al.* were tackling a simpler topic and used only one method – matrix scoring – to identify indicators, based on open-ended discussions with farmers about their expectations. For Sidersky and Guijt, who were seeking consensus between different stakeholders, mixed groups discussed indicators for each objective until they agreed on the best fit – and then revised them when necessary during the actual M&E work.

Despite such variations, in each of these experiences indicators were identified by primary stakeholders, often local people who live with the changes being tracked. Involving more groups usually requires a shift from pre-defined and 'objective' indicators, to 'negotiated' and context-specific indicators. The negotiation process becomes critical, as different views and priorities need to be reduced to a limited number of indicators. Decision makers at every level and scale, from an individual within the household to national and international policy makers, will find very different kinds of indicators relevant to their decisions. Therefore, reaching consensus about objectives and indicators will be less straightforward when more 'layers', and therefore groups, are involved.

Such negotiations can reinforce a shared vision of development (see Chapter 8; see also Ricafort, 1996) particularly when working with groups that differ strongly, within and between communities as well as other external groups. However, as development visions or policies change and information needs shift, indicators and trustworthiness norms will need to be renegotiated continually, so flexibility and communication become crucial. Sometimes different perspectives will not merge smoothly or may not be reconciled. As Macgillivray and Zadek (1995) write: 'This is not merely a question of which indicators are best for describing a particular process or set of events. It is more a matter of who is empowered or disempowered in the process of selection, development and application'. A good example of the link between ownership of indicators and empowerment is provided by Hamilton *et al.* They describe how the FUGs use parallel sets of indicators, some of which were identified by programme staff and others that were negotiated. One set of indicators were identified by local women, who now, as a result, have a stronger role in decision making and are more vocal in the FUGs.

Not only is indicator selection itself more dynamic with more participants, but when applied in participatory projects or programmes, further flexibility is required. Such projects commonly start tentatively with small interventions based on participatory appraisals or with capacity building activities. Only after discussions have created consensus about development activities will more substantial and focused activities be formulated. During the course of such projects, new partners often join, new insights are generated and new development goals emerge. With each change, comes the need to review existing indicators. Several authors discuss the changing nature of indicators – it is not an isolated phenomenon. Lawrence *et al.* note how farmers shifted from negative criteria, which reflected their apprehension of the new technology, to positive ones once beneficial effects of the technology emerged. Sidersky and Guijt found that some indicators became obsolete once new insights had been gained, goals had been adjusted, and field activities adapted. Hamilton *et al.* note that where understanding was weak, such as 'institutional analysis or timber yield regulation, indicators are also weak'. As understanding grows, indicators can become more precise. Thus, some indicators used in participatory initiatives may be continually modified, making it difficult to establish clear trends over longer time periods.

Given the complexity of indicator selection and adaptation, an emerging question in PM&E is that of alternatives to indicators. Two interesting options offer food for thought, both of which are based on general statements or events rather than specific indicators. First is an approach developed by the Christian Commission for Development in Bangladesh and Rick Davies, that records 'significant changes', whatever they might be, related to key objectives rather than pre-determined indicators (see Box 15.2). A second option is based on verifying assumptions (Harnmeijer, 1999). The evaluation team identified project assumptions about changes they were expecting to see on the ground in a community-based irrigation initiative in Zimbabwe, such as 'women, and notably poor women, are the main beneficiaries of the project's efforts'. They then set about finding evidence to support, refine or reject the assumptions. While their focus was 'evaluation', the basic idea can easily be adapted for monitoring and be made more participatory.

The magic of methods

Besides indicators, participatory methods are another popular topic within M&E as that is where many people – incorrectly – think the differences lie between more and less participatory processes. Some newcomers to PM&E may expect to find many exciting and novel methods in use.

Box 15.2   Monitoring without indicators?

A particularly innovative example has been developed by the Christian Commission for Development in Bangladesh (CCDB). Each credit group funded by CCDB reports, on a monthly basis, the single most significant change that occurred amongst the group members related to people's well-being, sustainability of people's institutions, people's participation, and one other open-ended change, if they wish. The report asks for the 'facts' (what, when, where, with whom) and an explanation of why that change is the most significant one of all the changes that have occurred. This last aspect ensures a process of reflection and learning by the group members, an aspect that is missing from most M&E systems that seek numeric data without any interpretation of the numbers. So, instead of pre-determined questions, CCDB's monitoring aims to find significant examples related to its long-term development objectives.

(Davies, 1998)

However, it is more common to find only a limited number of known methods being used. Symes and Jasser essentially focused on workshops, while Lawrence *et al.* restricted themselves mainly to matrix scoring, and Gobisaikhan and Menamkart mention group discussions and forms.

Methods serve various purposes in a PM&E process. They help to identify indicators, reach consensus, collect information, collate and make sense of the data, and facilitate feedback of the findings to others. With such a range of uses, it is clear that methods have diverse outputs and benefits as shown in Table 15.1. This table also highlights that much innovation *can* occur when principles such as participation and usefulness drive the choice of methods, rather than fixed ideas about what others (notably scientists and policy makers) would consider acceptable.

Table 15.1: List of methods used in the case studies and their benefits

Method	Benefits and outputs	Chapter(s)
Visualized forms that give a score or rank	Provoke reflection and discussion; inclusive of non-literate; simple	2
Semi-structured interviews	Provided more in-depth information through confidentiality	3
Impact flow diagrams	Appraising team internal dynamics and visioning for their organizational future; unanticipated impacts (particularly for outsiders)	3
Matrix ranking	Identify criteria to assess performance and for villager assessment of extensionist performance	3, 4
Wealth ranking/social mapping	Provides baseline information for assessing poverty changes; helps to construct a useful sample	11
The grassroots development framework or the 'cone'	Identifying indicators; provides an analytical framework for the data	3, 7, 8
Household livelihood strategies	Provides baseline information	11
Bio-resource flows	Identifying local indicators of change, learn about farmers' priorities	4
Story-telling	Helps researcher and participants to switch roles; is a familiar tradition of information exchange	6
Mapping	Collects data, facilitates sharing, stimulates discussion	4, 5
Key Judges	To synthesise findings from open-ended discussions	6
Questionnaires	Data collection	5, 7

The need to ensure rigour and participation (see 'Rigour or participation?' below), as well as to consider different information needs, makes it inevitable that a combination of methods (and methodologies) is used in many PM&E experiences: qualitative and quantitative, local and externally created, logframe-based and open-ended, oral and visual. In Mexico, for example, Blauert and Quinantar combined interviews to ensure confidentiality and to gain deeper understanding, with participatory rural appraisal (PRA) methods in indicator development. Lawrence *et al.* used a broad situational analysis to zoom in on matrix scoring. Torres' work in Bolivia uses over 20 methods that range from the simple and quick to the complex and demanding. To make an appropriate selection, discussion about which methods are effective and viable is clearly important.

The first question that comes to mind with PM&E and methods is the extent to which they are, in fact, 'participatory'. There is no doubt that many diagram-based methods commonly associated with participatory appraisals have been used very effectively for data collection and joint analysis in M&E. However, it cannot be assumed that visual methods are always the most participatory of methods. Questionnaires can be very participatory, as Espinosa describes, while monitoring with group-based maps or matrices can become extractive and unanalytical. Learning to see the essence of methods rather than the mechanics takes time. Ward writes: '[Project staff] learned to apply the principles of participation and learning in different situations, rather than merely being tool-driven or simply replicating training exercises'. The potential contribution of methods to successful PM&E derives from an interactive and analytical process, which requires skilled facilitation (see 'Roles and responsibilities' below).

For methods to be socially inclusive, they must be clear for the users – and by developing them together, clarity emerges. If a participatory method is to be interactive, it has to be locally adjusted. Just as questionnaires should be field-tested, so should the more innovative methods that have the added advantage of being more adjustable than fixed conventional methods. Joint involvement in method creation or adaptation helps ensure local appropriateness. Many authors in this volume stress the importance of understanding local conditions and communication forms when selecting/adapting methods. Abes discusses how Filipino psychology as an approach helped refine the process within which methods were applied. Lawrence *et al.* note the marked difference between Bolivians' and Laotians' use of matrix scoring that tied in closely to social and organizational cultures (see 'Documentation and sharing' below).

If a participatory method is to be analytical, then two other issues require consideration. The first involves reflecting on how the nature of analysis changes depending on an individual or group-based application. Many people equate participatory methods with group discussions under trees. But experiences such as Rutherford and Abes describe show that one-to-one interviews or documentation can be powerful tools for reflection by the people and social groups involved. For Lawrence *et al.*, understanding variability of individual perspectives and experiences was important but group discussion tended to culminate in consensus views. To ensure more analysis, they developed indicators based on group consensus but then asked each individual to evaluate their own experiments independently. The second issue is to see whether the 'germ' of debate can be built into methods. In Nepal, Hamilton *et al.* discovered that shifting from three-tiered to four-tiered scoring – a seemingly small adjustment – made an easy middle compromise impossible and encouraged more discussion. In Brazil, initial work shows that indicator-based monitoring is less inherently analytical than the 'significant change' method (see Table 15.1) which stimulates intense debates.

Many newcomers to participatory development, including PM&E, look to methods as something magical that delivers the promised goods. However, methods need skills (see Chapters 10 and 11). The magic only works if the 'magician' understands the tricks – which makes facilitation of method development and adaptation fundamental to success (see 'Roles and responsibilities' below).

Dilemmas and challenges

Rigour or participation?

Critics of PM&E often attack one aspect of it in particular – its supposed lack of 'rigour'. This stems, they say, from the lack of scientific standards in methods, indicators, data collection, and interpretation. By opening up the process to 'unskilled' participants, the quality and credibility of information is assumed to decline. Often, other issues are at stake. For those worried about the shift towards more local involvement and less scientific direction, there is resistance to unfamiliar and unconventional methods, discomfort with data collection carried out by non-scientists, and unwillingness to let go of professional standards, irrespective of whether these are relevant or not. In some cases, when findings from participatory M&E are politically uncomfortable or contentious, critics try to discredit the findings on the grounds that the methodology 'lacks rigour'.

Meanwhile, supporters of PM&E say that the findings are more meaningful and credible to the users than those that unnecessarily fulfil external scientific standards and that are often a waste of time and resources. They speak of 'real' criteria of change and empowerment. To be locally relevant, M&E must be participatory and action-oriented. To be locally viable in the long term, it must be simple – not scientifically complex – and also adapted continually. Yet sometimes quality has been compromised by these views.

The issue of rigour within a participatory process is raised particularly when there are many and diverse expectations of partners. This begs the key question of which partner defines what 'rigour' is? The perceived 'trustworthiness' of information is intimately related to the source of the information. For example, farmers and NGO staff in Brazil felt that other farmers would not be motivated to take up contour planting on the basis of evidence such as the 'increased percentage of soil moisture' (Guijt and Sidersky, 1996). Yet statements such as '18 of the 24 farmers noted a significant increase in soil moisture in critical periods' would motivate them into action. Hearing testimony from respected peers, be they farmers or scientists, is perhaps the most important factor in accepting data as 'trustworthy'. In a participatory process, this calls for more negotiation about what each stakeholder group considers 'rigour' to be (see Estrella and Gaventa, 1998) and greater acceptance of different information sources and methods.

The question of ensuring both local participation and external validity also depends on the level at which monitoring information is needed and by whom it is used. One Australian research scientist explained: 'Community monitoring does not . . . have to stand up in court . . . What the community needs are methods which give direction . . . at the small subcatchment or property level' (Rob Tanner, cited in Alexandra *et al.*, 1996). Yet when local data is needed at levels beyond the catchment or community, it will be increasingly important to consider conventional standards of validity and rigour. There are several options for dealing with the unresolved 'rigour or participation?' debate. One approach is to view it as a sequential process of skilling (Abbot and Guijt, 1998). Gubbels (cited in Rugh, 1995) suggests that initially the participatory aspect can be emphasized. As those involved become more skilled in undertaking a participation process, they can then gradually work to ensure that results are considered externally valid. Ward (Chapter 11) describes how CARE Zambia is learning to implement new M&E skills where 'rigour' was initially the focus to the detriment of group learning and participatory behaviour. But this is slowly being adjusted as skills grow.

A second option is of interest in situations where comparability between different project sites or communities is important (for example, see Chapters 2 and 12). This option entails some standardization via a minimum set of indicators for all areas, with data that will not be collected through participatory processes, but which sits *alongside* context-specific and locally-driven M&E. Minimizing differences helps comparison, but, as Hamilton *et al.* state, analysing how communities chose to assess changes also allows insights into different perspectives to emerge. Not surprisingly, methodological complementarity is common to most, if not all, PM&E work. PRA methods become a means for validation, with open-ended methods used to seek out unexpected impacts alongside logframe-based indicator monitoring. Other efforts to standardize participatory methods are underway (NRI and University of Reading, 1998) to ensure some level of statistical validity that might help with the rigour/participation tug-of-war.

A third option requires a deeper paradigmatic shift, as it depends on developing new standards of rigour and credibility (Estrella and Gaventa, 1998). In Nepal, FUGs need clear trends and impacts to make decisions, yet farmers and staff are busy and facilitators inexperienced. This is a reality for most, if not all, experiences mentioned in this book. This begs the questions of whether the information is good enough to move forward or whether it is perfect, and whose norms count – thus calling for a reappraisal of conventional standards of external and internal validity, rigour, and replicability (Lincoln and Guba, 1985).

In practice, the balance between scientific rigour and local participation will depend greatly on the objectives of the monitoring process itself and its audience. This tension is likely to be more significant when the PM&E process focuses on local social groups than when working with other groups and levels of participation, such as graduate leaders (Chapter 6), provincial credit groups (Chapter 12), or institutions (Chapter 13). If monitoring is less about providing proof to others, and more about improving learning and planning, then participation of primary stakeholders can be prioritized. If local proof of impact is needed, then local indicators of change and local norms for 'trustworthiness' can be adopted. Yet if proof is needed for scientific and/or policy audiences, then externally acceptable approaches might be needed, to demonstrate changes in ways that are compatible with these groups.

The debate on rigour is closely linked to issues regarding PM&E and the logical framework in the project cycle. The main tension here lies between the straitjacket of the cycle and framework, and the need for flexible and context-specific methods, indicators, monitoring frequencies, etc. There is also the different purposes of the cycle and framework, reasons enough for Carden (Chapter 13) to state that: 'the self-assessment process is most effective when it is de-linked from the project cycle'.

The project cycle describes how a certain sequence of activities will, within a specific time frame, lead to pre-determined goals and objectives. Increasingly these dictates are transcribed into a 'logical framework' or one of its variations. Such frameworks are based on impartial knowledge and on assumptions that often turn out differently, particularly in participatory development. For example, in Brazil the assumption was made that a two-year old partnership between three organizations would have a clearly shared vision and goals, from which to derive indicators. When this proved incorrect, considerable time was needed at the onset of the PM&E work to clarify this vision, throwing the project out of kilter with its logframe (Chapter 5). Furthermore, as understanding grows and aspirations change, such visions are likely to be adjusted and refined. It is, in essence, a clash over locally emerging and fluctuating processes of development that respond flexibly to changing needs and priorities, versus streamlined, or rigid, externally imposed systems of information organization that emanate from higher levels and serve an internally integrating purpose.

Here is where Carden's concerns enter. The experiences of the IDRC in institutional self-assessment noted worries amongst the organizations involved that the assessment findings would influence ongoing funding. This concern about how powerful funding agencies will deal with honest, self-critical assessment also applies in more community-oriented PM&E efforts. How will they deal with negative news emerging from such monitoring efforts? For Carden, prior clarity about the purpose of the self-assessment is paramount to avoid the confounding of project cycles and self-assessment. In his example, recommendations for changing the organizations were important, while the funding agency was interested in the capacity building output and implementation of recommendations – but not in chastising the organizations involved. Hamilton *et al.* also note this tension. The funder's interest in performance accountability for internal information needs (to be reported on via a logframe) clashed with learning-oriented M&E not bound by a rigid framework. Symes and Jasser pick up on the difference between logframes as a mechanism for checking planning and PM&E as a process of experiential learning. Many stakeholders, they argue, find logframes alienating and far from logical – hence the need for alternative frameworks for programme planning into which PM&E can fit.

What are the options? One option is to develop simpler alternatives to existing frameworks. Many organizations have worked with slimmer frameworks. Redd Barna Uganda uses a two-layer hierarchy of goals and activities (Webare, 1997). Sidersky and Guijt centred their efforts around a series of diagrammatic 'objective trees' that formed the logic for structuring the indicators, while Espinosa's describes diagrams of development visions that led to project activities and indicators. Another option is offered by Ward, who views integration of PM&E with the project cycle as a product of a learning process. She has noted that CARE Zambia is, over time, becoming more systematic in their PM&E work, thus allowing for easier integration with systematic frameworks.

Two important questions need answers. First, are logical frameworks necessary for all projects and programmes, or are they more useful for some than for others? If the answer is 'no' then what are the alternatives? Second, how can learning-oriented principles, rather than performance-driven information needs, help to transform existing frameworks? Symes and Jasser argue that the logical framework is particularly problematic when building participation into a development process, as it is an alien way of tiered thinking. Alternatives could help maintain a focus on the primary stakeholders who are in danger of losing out to the heavy hand of the project cycle and a logical framework that does not follow *their* logic.

Roles and responsibilities

With more people involved, more tasks are needed and more confusion can arise as to who is responsible for which task. Clear allocation of core tasks can make or break PM&E. But for many, the novelty of PM&E means that roles are fuzzy and some tasks are not even known until after problems occur. Furthermore, the participatory aspect of PM&E means that roles shift – to which there may be some resistance. An organization's capacity to undertake PM&E depends on people's individual skills and mind-sets (especially willingness to change), but is also influenced by the dominating institutional culture (see Chapter 3).

The tasks relate, quite simply, directly to the core steps (see Box 15.1). However, what is often forgotten is that devolving parts of the process to a limited group of co-ordinators and/or drivers is fundamental, as total participation is impossible to achieve – not to mention, sustain. The stakeholders should, ideally, negotiate who is able and willing to be such a driver or part of the core team. In the USA the team was a mix of community members and academics (Chapter 9). In Bolivia and Laos, the researchers were the main drivers, while in Zambia this was a small group of project staff members (Chapters 4 and 11, respectively). Abes provides a clear example of how roles and responsibilities were divided amongst seven stakeholder groups (see Table 6.1 in Chapter 6). This way of 'unpacking' participation per group prior to starting can help avoid misunderstandings later on.

The negotiation over roles is not straightforward. Three aspects, in particular, need careful consideration in PM&E. The first is the comprehension of the tasks at hand. Without first-hand experience of what PM&E means, it is hard for people to imagine what certain tasks entail. This means they may abstain from involvement or leap in without thinking, only to confront problems later on. The second aspect is the problem of time and scope of responsibility. In the USA, one woman in a citizen learning team attended hundreds of meetings in one year. Few people would be able to invest this amount of time, and the time implications of each task must be made quite clear so that people know what they are signing up to do. Especially for large scale M&E work, the more complex the PM&E approach, the more likely that facilitators will be needed for each group. The third aspect is the need for flexibility. Continual re-negotiation of roles is needed as skills improve and people move on, or gain or lose interest. For example, Sidersky and Guijt describe how the initial passive involvement of community seed banks is growing into more proactive interest that will see the banks taking on new roles – and the NGO losing control.

A critical role referred to in many chapters is that of the facilitator. As in many other types of participatory development, PM&E relies heavily on strong facilitators. They need to understand both the practicalities and the principles. Some provide methodological ideas (see Chapter 5), while others take care of the details: 'Forest user groups need strong encourage-ment to adapt the indicators and pictures to suit their own information needs' (Chapter 2). But these facilitators are particularly essential as guardians of the core principles and aims, preventing the process from becoming mechanical and dominated by the vocal minority, and helping to negotiate differences (also see Chapter 16).

Levels of analysis

Organizations keen to pursue PM&E usually have no choice but to learn to work with several layers of information needs – information that aims to provoke social change cannot stay at the community level forever, nor will it always emerge from that level. Sampling may be one option for doing multi-level PM&E as it helps reduce the scale of the work. Rutherford's experience is one from a sample of ten regions in the USA where com-munity revitalization projects were funded. Likewise, Abes describes how in the Philippines his organization took a sample of 24 representative com-munities and leaders from the hundreds of graduates. With these leaders, they developed two indicator sets, one for individual leadership assessment and the second for community assessment. Hamilton *et al.* also separated the levels, and developed methods for different institutional levels. If com-parability is required over a large area, they stress the 'need [for] some degree of standardization of the indicators and methods used for assessing them'. However, they rightly caution that a more integrated system that covers a larger area could 'become mechanical and extractive' rather than something dynamic and adaptive to suit user needs.

The problems that arise from inter-level PM&E of incompatible data sets and faulty communication are often caused by trying to use one ap-proach to provide relevant information to multiple levels at the same time, or by trying to compare between areas or communities without some de-gree of standardization. A farmer wants field level information, NGO staff comparative community or district level, while funding agencies want total aggregate data. Rarely, if ever, can all these levels of information and units of analysis be catered for with one set of indicators or methods. Thus the question arises of how participatory indicator/method identification – and data analysis – can be, the higher up one goes. Who is involved in analysing and synthesising information at different levels? The further removed from local groups, the greater the difficulty of ensuring primary stakeholder involvement in selecting, collecting but also interpreting and using information. How much effort is invested to keep different groups within a community 'linked' to higher layers and, conversely, how much will policy makers be involved in grassroots M&E? (see Chapter 17).

Documentation and sharing

Documentation enables findings to be shared more easily and used for later comparison with new information. However, it can also become complicated when many participants and layers are involved, and when there are process as well as information needs. This issue is even more complex when local groups are involved in PM&E, as differences in communication styles, literacy and practice with formalized registering of information will need to be understood and accommodated. Methodologically, it is perhaps the least well implemented of the core steps of PM&E. The Philippines Workshop concluded that the lack of well-documented experiences in PM&E has been a limitation on sharing ideas about the process and impact of PM&E. Within each PM&E experience, a clear answer is needed to the question: 'For whom is documentation useful and/or necessary?' before tackling other questions relevant to documentation (see Box 15.3).

Espinosa provides some interesting insights into the role of documentation in a complex situation of three-tiered PM&E in Colombia. First, the indicators selected by a regional representative body are transformed into questions and converted into data forms. These 'fact sheets' are filled in by each community at large group meetings. The information is systematized at the community level and community specific, target

---

Box 15.3: Questioning the documentation

○ For whom is documentation useful or necessary – farmers, project staff, Northern donors or other projects?
○ How will documentation be used – to report to donors, for active use in planning, for scientific proof, to spread PM&E?
○ What will be documented – the process or the data, the mistakes or successes, the methods or the final analysis?
○ What form will documentation take – diagrammatic, written, numbers, tape recordings or video?
○ How often will documentation be shared – once a year, twice, every week?
○ Where will it be stored, and how will access to data and findings be managed – on computers or paper, in community halls or in the NGO/government office?

---

achievement data are set out in statistical tables. These tables are then returned to the assembly which further analyses the data at a more aggregate level. This analysis is then carried back to each community to compare and reflect further on 'the data and indicators of the [region] and the organization, from the family and community level up to the local and provincial level.' Thus, systematic sharing of recorded information allows the layers to keep in touch.

While not all experiences are as elaborate, many chapters hint at the multitude of possibilities for documenting the PM&E process, particularly data recording and sharing. Again, this raises the question of who participates in documenting, processing and using information (see 'Levels of analysis' discussed earlier). Ward mentions briefly the small-scale use of locally stored village and household record books, that was instigated by project staff. Abes writes that leaders are writing lesson focused reports alongside transcripts of open-ended discussions and stories. These are all coded, grouped and analysed, and then shared with the communities. For Lawrence *et al.* the matrix itself became the data record that they shared with others. But they caution that without discussion, it can easily revert to an extractive form rather than an analytical tool. For example, in Laos, farmers' evaluation were documented meticulously but with few explanations of why farmers rated changes differently. By contrast, in Bolivia the more haphazard approach provided better insights about farmer behaviour. Thus they stress the importance of understanding the institutional culture, as professionals in some contexts will tend towards some forms of documentation rather than others.

Special consideration for documentation is needed when working with groups – particularly when not all group members are literate. Lawrence *et al.* found the recording of information in larger group discussions difficult and requiring good skills. In the Philippines, heavy dependency on open-ended oral methods made subsequent transcription from tapes laborious, and led to mountains of raw data (Abes). That project has now planned for more training for local leaders on writing syntheses, and will employ a full-time data person. Hamilton *et al.* speak positively of the visualized forms that they use for 1,500 FUGs to record qualitative and relative changes. But they anticipate difficulties when they move towards more documentation of quantitative indicators. Torres also describes the importance of visual sharing of findings in public exhibitions, but they are also exploring verbal sharing of data that is 'comparable to the traditional way of presenting financial accounts in community assemblies'.

Documentation can easily disempower participants when, unlike the Colombia example, efforts are not made to share and use the data actively. Several authors note that in the data analysis stage – when documentation is used – participation reduces to a small group of people. Conscious efforts are needed to keep the documentation locally relevant and useful.

From M&E to learning and action

Participation of those usually excluded in designing and implementing M&E processes requires openness to new ways of learning about familiar contexts, to new types of indicators (or their absence) for established goals, and to new roles for established partners. The challenges lie neither with creating methods nor with perfecting indicators. More thorny questions relate particularly to acceptable levels of rigour, and with it developing complementary methods, applying multi-level PM&E, and linking PM&E to the ubiquitous project cycle that often still tries to dictate the pace of development. At the heart of the challenges lies the question of which objectives are more important: compliance and accountability, or learning and adaptation? And if it is to be learning, then we cannot avoid asking 'Learning for whom?' and 'Learning for what?'.

Many of the experiences here show that it does not have to be an 'either-or' situation. They also show that success requires more than a sequence of methods. These methods/methodologies do not necessarily lead to the organizational and institutional change that is needed in order to address emerging conflicts and sustain efforts. Strong convictions in the value of community involvement will be essential to overcome the inevitable obstacles. In the words of Rutherford: 'There was discussion as to whom the evaluation was for, what function it had. If it was not to strengthen the development process in McDowell County, then it was not worth doing.'

16

Laying the Foundation: Capacity Building for Participatory Monitoring and Evaluation[1]

DEB JOHNSON

Introduction

IT IS CLEAR from Chapters 14 and 15 that development practitioners and others interested in promoting and using participatory monitoring and evaluation (PM&E) are struggling with the need to distinguish how PM&E differs from 'conventional monitoring and evaluation (M&E)' and from other types of participatory approaches. It should be equally clear from these chapters that we are far from finding a singular discipline called PM&E. This is positive! We need a wide range and mix of concepts, methods, and definitions to fit an equally wide range and mix of uses, as 'development' is highly context-specific. This chapter strives to identify elements that ensure participants have both the *access* and the *ability* to participate in a PM&E process – because access and ability form the foundation for building PM&E capacity.

Access and ability are two sides of the same coin. If one has the access to participate in M&E but not the abilities to take advantage of that access, then the access is not an opportunity that can be tapped into. The reverse is also true; if one has the ability to contribute to M&E yet lacks the access, then the abilities are not assets that can be used. So, how do we define access and ability as the foundation for capacity building in PM&E?

Access is defined as the opportunity to participate in an M&E process that includes more than one stakeholder group. This implies that:

○ participants can physically participate in the process – simple things such as ensuring transport, providing basic materials such as pencils and paper if needed, and ensuring timely communication of meetings can assist the participation of stakeholders
○ participants are recognized as *bona fide* members of the process. There are plenty of examples where stakeholders are consulted during an M&E process, but their contributions are dismissed or considered less important than those of other stakeholders
○ participants understand the possible risks and benefits of the PM&E process so they can make informed decisions about where and how they want to be involved.

Ability can be defined as 'the skill or knowledge required to do something'. For PM&E this means the following:

○ participants have sufficient skills and knowledge of the PM&E terminology, approaches, methods, and tools, and analytical framework to contribute effectively to the process
○ participants change their attitudes, principles, and values. This is not limited to changing the attitudes of those in positions of power into accepting the views and contributions of others. People who have adapted to being marginalized can find it difficult to accept even small shifts of power, dismissing themselves before they even try (see Chapter 10)
○ participants have the time, financial, informational, and material resources needed to participate.

Obviously, there are overlaps between *access* and *ability* but, in general, attempts to increase access are focused on creating opportunities for participation within an M&E process, whereas attempts to increase ability are aimed at improving the skills and knowledge base of the stakeholder groups and individuals.

When and where does capacity building start?

Capacity building for PM&E starts at the very beginning, from the point of establishing the framework for a PM&E process. However, simply identifying the participants for PM&E does not necessarily ensure their access or ability to participate – there are many constraints when talking of building the capacity of a number of different stakeholder groups in M&E. Gaventa and Blauert touch upon some of the dynamics of power differences in Chapter 17 on 'scaling up' PM&E efforts. As a part of trying to level the inevitable power dynamics of participatory approaches, there is a need to try and collectively build participants' capacities so that there is mutual understanding and *agreement* concerning:

○ the language
○ the basic terminology to be used
○ the roles and responsibilities of those involved
○ the definition of layers of indicators
○ the risks and vulnerability of interaction
○ the different expectations.

After the PM&E process has been established, there is a continuing need to train new people entering the PM&E process and to increase the skills of those already involved in order to improve the process's ability to analyse and act on the lessons arising. Capacity building must be fluid and responsive, which makes it very difficult to prescribe what particular skills might be needed at specific times in the process. Different stakeholders bring different skills, capacities, expectations, and interests within a wide range of contexts and situations – all of which influence the capacity building needs. This chapter, therefore, offers insights on capacity building needs and concerns coming from the case studies and beyond.

What are the capacities to be built?

The first capacity that is required by a successful PM&E process is *accessibility*. Accessibility must be incorporated into the design, development, and implementation of the PM&E process in such a way that it seeks and encourages access by everyone. Access must be an integral part of the PM&E process before the PM&E facilitators worry about building the capacity of the participants.

This means that one of the first questions that needs to be answered is 'Why a *participatory* M&E process?' Answering this question will help identify who should be involved initially (knowing that this group should continually change as time goes on) and help define some of the initial agreements about principles, concepts, indicators, methods and tools for measurement, and uses of the learnings. The capacities to be built are:

○ an understanding of the conceptual background of monitoring, evaluation, and participation
○ specific PM&E skills such as the design and use of tools
○ proficiency in other essential skills such as literacy and negotiation that are necessary to further improve a participant's access to the PM&E process.

The extent to which any individual gains these capacities is dependent on his or her current and desired role in the PM&E process.

How are capacities built?

The intention of this chapter is not to overwhelm the reader but to stress that the capacities required are highly dependent on the reasons for and design of the PM&E process and the people to be involved. The types and levels of capacities required for establishing a PM&E process within individual institutions for their own learning, for instance, (Selener, 1997) will be very different from the institutionalization of PM&E for increasing transparency in the central and local governments of Mongolia (see Chapter 12).

The rest of the chapter closely examines ability and access as the basis of capacity building by first exploring the issue of access in terms of establishing a PM&E process that is accessible by all stakeholders (see 'Multiple stakeholders, different needs' below). It also identifies three main elements essential in building stakeholders' abilities to participate effectively in a PM&E framework process – training, experiential learning, and resources (see 'Key elements of strengthening abilities' below).

Multiple stakeholders, different needs

Since PM&E embraces the principles of wider inclusion of people in M&E processes, it must therefore be noted that different stakeholders frequently have differing expectations of PM&E and differing contributions that they can make. It also follows, therefore, that they have different access needs. In order to institutionalize a PM&E process, there is the formidable task of deciding where to start and with which stakeholder groups.

Many argue that capacity building in PM&E should start with those individuals and groups frequently excluded from M&E so that they have both the self-confidence and the skills to engage in evaluation dialogue (see Chapters 2, 3, 5 and 10). One of the workshop participants wrote:

'The findings of the World Neighbors evaluation shows how its development approach has increased local self-confidence, leading to greater self-initiated development based on local strengths. For example, villagers are doing research on drought-resistant seeds via government agricultural departments and other neighbouring villages. Other initiatives related to health no longer require intense inputs from the World Neighbors team.'

(Bandre, 1997)

Others point out the advantage of starting with the power groups (government agencies, wealthy individuals/groups, traditional leaders, etc.) to open the institutional context for the inclusion of marginalized voices and to increase their access to normally closed M&E processes (see Chapter 17).

Workshop experiences showed that it is not only important to think of capacity building in terms of 'with whom' but also in terms of 'where' to start. Sometimes it is not possible to develop a wider PM&E process at the beginning. Instead, individuals or organizations have slowly opened institutional access to PM&E by first introducing other participatory approaches before trying to move on to a PM&E process. At the workshop, it was recognized that there could be several predecessors to PM&E such as participatory monitoring, participatory evaluation, participatory impact assessment, and regular M&E processes.

Many participants at the Philippines Workshop further agreed that a participatory evaluation could lead to the institutionalization of a PM&E process but that this was not equivalent to a PM&E process. Many participants felt that if there was an opportunity to initiate a participatory evaluation, then it should be taken but with the longer vision of using the participatory evaluation as a basis for building capacity for a PM&E process. This is echoed by the Education for Life Foundation (ELF) as one of the organization's desired outcomes of a participatory impact evaluation of its leadership training:

'At the end, ELF's final goal with regard to this longitudinal impact evaluation is not primarily for improvements of the ELF programme and educational activities. ELF hopes that this evaluation will provide an opportunity for the leader-graduates to become aware of their progress and impact as well as identify gaps for improvements.'

(Abes, Chapter 6, this volume)

Varying levels of capacity

Each of the stakeholder groups involved in PM&E not only brings different expectations, they bring differing capacities and perspectives to contribute to the process. On the side of a community or a 'beneficiary group', their capacity to effectively negotiate access to the M&E process with other actors in the process can be greatly constrained by their limited power-base. Participants at the Philippines Workshop discussed how facilitators must recognize that in the case of development projects, community members or beneficiary groups are vulnerable as 'consumers' of the project. Although they might be invited to participate in a participatory activity, they are vulnerable to retaliation by stronger stakeholders who control the allocation of project resources.

In one workshop session, an example from Uganda was used as a discussion starter to illustrate how power dynamics frequently limit full access to M&E processes. In Uganda, an international non-governmental organization (NGO) wanted to carry out a participatory evaluation of its efforts in Uganda. The NGO works with a number of small, community-based groups throughout the country and, despite the invitation to participate in the evaluation, there were several issues that the community groups refused to discuss publicly as they were afraid they would lose their sole funding source. Recent history supported their fears, and the facilitators had to devise other means to ensure that attempts were made to address their concerns without exposing the groups to reprisal later. This constraint was also noted in a literature review by Estrella and Gaventa (1998).

> 'Many writers also acknowledge that the negotiation process of PM&E is a highly political exercise, which necessarily addresses issues of equity, power, and social transformation. Guba and Lincoln (1989) argue that the process of negotiation will either "enfranchise or disenfranchise" stakeholder groups in various ways, i.e., through the selective involvement of these stakeholders in the design, implementation, reporting, and use of evaluation.'

On the side of dominant PM&E stakeholders, their capacity or their willingness to share power and resources, such as information, allows alternative voices to be heard and incorporated into the process as an important influence on accessibility. There is increasing pressure coming from individuals, organizations, and donors to be seen to be participatory. However, unless participants are recognized as contributing members of the process, their contributions can be dismissed or considered less important than other stakeholders. This effectively blocks their access to the PM&E process because their participation is superficial. The CARE Zambia example, amongst others, illustrates the need for community participation to be more than simply data collection.

Another important influence on increasing the accessibility of PM&E to a wider number of stakeholders depends on the skills of the facilitators. Rutherford notes that PM&E processes are frequently too dependent on visionary, charismatic leaders alone. These leaders cannot keep the momentum of ensuring access to M&E going forever. These leaders are also usually limited in number, committed but usually overworked. One of the participants (Colin Kirk) noted:

'Participatory approaches in general, and PM&E in particular, require skilled and experienced practitioners and managers, preferably familiar with the local context. Personnel with skills in applying PM&E methods at the community level are often in short supply; people with PM&E skills relevant to institutional reorientation and change are even more scarce.'

Moreover, developing a capable 'learning team' requires bringing together a team of people who have different but complementary knowledge, skills and experiences (see Chapter 9). This may include government officials or staff, NGO staff, community representatives and other relevant actors who together can create a strong, diverse PM&E team and create access opportunities at many different levels (see Chapters 6 and 9).

Institutional environment

A supportive institutional environment is considered essential to ensuring initial and continued access to PM&E processes. There are arguments about whether PM&E can be effectively implemented in a *non-participatory* institutional setting (see Chapter 3), the primary concern being whether PM&E can be implemented in an institutional environment that does not embrace the values and principles of wider access and participation. Armonia and Campilan (1997) and Estrella and Gaventa (1998) uncovered a few examples where PM&E has been successfully implemented in a relatively non-participatory environment. They recognize, though, that access to PM&E processes is greatly improved where there is both the political will to support wider stakeholder access to M&E processes and the flexibility to explore alternative methods and indicators of success.

Institutional conceptualization of M&E has had a significant impact on the extent to which institutions will open these processes to other stakeholders. At the workshop, Anna Lawrence shared her experiences which compared the influence and impact that differing institutional contexts in Bolivia and Laos had on the ways the facilitators had to try and institutionalize PM&E:

'In neither Bolivia nor Laos are the collaborating research institutions accustomed to using PM&E. However, CIAT [Centre for International Tropical Agriculture] has a non-hierarchical structure that allows its staff considerable flexibility in working with farmers, and many of the field staff implicitly base their research on close knowledge of farmers' priorities and experience of previously introduced technology. In Laos, PM&E is more novel in the institutional culture and has had to be more formally integrated into work plans in order to fit institutional practice.'

As noted by Carden, the institutional attitudes and perceptions are affected by past experiences in conventional evaluation that is '. . . viewed largely as a policing mechanism and its implementation has largely been on a compliance basis.' If there is a continued focus on evaluation as a way to find fault and to place blame, then there will be a reluctance to include more people in the M&E process as people will feel vulnerable to attack.

Key elements of strengthening abilities

The previous section focused on ensuring access as one of the two important capacity-building aspects in laying the foundation for PM&E. The second important aspect to capacity building is strengthening the abilities of stakeholders to participate in M&E. Experiences coming from the Philippines Workshop fell into three major capacity-building elements that strengthen individual and institutional abilities to engage in PM&E. These three elements are:

○ formal trainings
○ experiential learning opportunities
○ availability of resources (see Table 16.1).

Table 16.1: Key elements of capacity building

Formal trainings	Experiential learning opportunities	Availability of resources
○ tools ○ conceptual/methodological issues (participation and M&E) ○ analytical framework ○ philosophical basis	○ exposure to participatory methods ○ incorporation of participation and M&E tools and methods into everyday activities ○ building from existing experience ○ values and principles	○ financial ○ human ○ information ○ materials

Each element has its own strengths and weaknesses in terms of building stakeholder abilities for PM&E, and in many ways they are inextricably linked. For example, a formal training setting is appropriate for introducing and explaining the tools to be used for monitoring, but it is not the most effective way to incorporate these tools into daily work activities. This is where hands-on experience in using and adapting the monitoring tools to the local context is essential. However, if the resources (financial, material, or human) for using the tools do not exist, then neither training nor hands-on experience will result in the tools being used.

Participants in the Philippines Workshop discussed several factors that contributed to, or constrained the effectiveness of, each element for capacity building. The following points are not meant to be a definitive list of factors, but instead are meant to provoke further thought and discussion.

Formal training

Training in a formal setting (resident or non-resident) is the most commonly identified capacity-building approach. It is the major focus and starting point for most projects and organizations desiring to establish a PM&E process. Training as an approach to building the abilities of stakeholders to participate in the M&E learning process is effective in quickly covering practical issues associated with PM&E. These practical issues include:

○ understanding the concepts of participation, monitoring, evaluation, and learning systems
○ skill building in how to use PM&E
○ tools and methods for measuring change.

Formal training can start to introduce the philosophical background and basis for *participatory* monitoring and evaluation. This will establish the groundwork for the changes in individual and institutional attitudes towards wider inclusion of people in the learning and decision-making processes.

However, to set the groundwork for attitude changes, formal training should be done in a context that embraces the principles and values of PM&E. The learning organization experience in CARE Zambia underlines this point by demonstrating how the commitment to PM&E needs to be found at all levels in the organization (see Chapter 11). Ward goes on to note that aspects of PM&E, such as principles and values of participation, cannot be taught during formal training if the trainees are not willing or if they are being forced to take the training.

As noted earlier, the commitment to establish a PM&E process does not automatically result in an understanding of the concepts of PM&E nor a change in attitudes (see Chapter 14). Creating a common language is an important first step in building team spirit and a sense of confidence as well as building common abilities of all stakeholders, because often language has been used to exclude people. The translation of PM&E terms into local language either before going to a village/locality or along with villagers/residents helps everyone (external facilitation team included) to better understand PM&E concepts, and starts the process of building a team (Bandre, 1997; Chapters 10 and 12, this volume).

One of the dangers of attempting to establish a PM&E process solely through formal training is that frequently there is no long-term ability or commitment to follow up the training (Chapter 6). This is especially important when using consultants or part-time resource persons to design the PM&E process and to conduct the training because they do not necessarily have the ability or commitment (in terms of funds and time) to continue to support the organizations or individuals involved to adapt, modify and institutionalize the process. It was further noted that demand-driven follow-up and appropriate timing for follow-up activities are crucial to ensuring that follow-up is effective (Chapter 6). One of the Philippines Workshop participants, Birendra Bir Basnyat, shared his experiences in institutionalizing PM&E processes within the Nepali Government and the support needed for linking experiential learning with formal training: 'One short training is not sufficient to bring out changes in thinking with regard to participatory process and to acquire well-grounded skills in participatory approaches.'

One of the methods used to bring together the strengths of both a formal training setting and an experiential learning opportunity is the 'workshop method'. In north-eastern Brazil, AS-PTA has used a series of workshops to form the basis of the PM&E process. The authors (Sidersky and Guijt) describe the method as the 'backbone' of the PM&E process since the discussion and analysis of the M&E data are done in a workshop setting that includes representatives of a number of stakeholder groups.

In Nepal, the Nepal–UK Community Forestry Project uses interactive, multi-stakeholder workshops for PM&E that allow for experience exchange, training, and other skill building. The project also made changes in its discussion methods, incorporating visual representations of indicators, to ensure non-literate participants have the ability to contribute to the PM&E process (Hamilton *et al.*).

Experiential learning

Several experiences found in this book have highlighted the importance of linking more formal training with 'hands-on' experiential learning as an approach to building capacity (Chapter 2, amongst others). There are many examples where the PM&E process was not established through formalized training but, instead, participation is built into existing M&E processes. Lawrence *et al.* noted that:

'In both projects (one in Bolivia and another in Laos), an iterative approach to the research process has incorporated stages of self-evaluation and learning, which led to local staff defining their own needs for PM&E.'

Experience is a necessary companion to training, though sometimes it is more difficult to arrange and organize. Experiential learning is seen as necessary to make the training practical for the participants and to give the individuals involved a sense of confidence in carrying out PM&E. It is crucial for putting the information coming out of formal training into the facilitators' and participants' normal context, making it easier to translate concepts, values and principles into practice. Furthermore, if a PM&E process is to be successfully integrated into everyday activities, many of the authors of the case studies stressed that it must be built from local forms and ideas of participation, co-operation, and solidarity (Chapters 4 and 8).

Mentoring, as a form of guided experiential learning, can be a very effective means for building stakeholder ability to participate in PM&E. PM&E facilitators work closely with stakeholders to establish a PM&E process within the normal context of the individual or group (see different examples in Chapters 7 and 10). Mentoring is important in the example of Laos noted by Lawrence *et al.* where the institutions involved have little exposure to participatory approaches and require much more guidance.

'While the two projects followed a similar research approach, local contexts required that the process be modified and adapted. Unlike the project in Bolivia, the institutions involved in Laos were not used to undertaking participatory research or evaluation and communication difficulties were much greater. Consequently, the process was led more by outside researchers, who supported project staff in developing tools.'

The incorporation of PM&E methods, tools, and values are tailored to the unique situation of each of the stakeholder groups. However, it is important to point out that mentoring can be a more resource intensive approach to building capacity – requiring an ongoing commitment of human and financial resources.

In some of the case studies, PM&E tools and techniques were introduced into participant's everyday settings or activities. This was accomplished by introducing participatory methodologies during regular staff training or activities, as well as incorporating participatory values into job performance evaluations (including that of supervisors in the case of mentoring) which greatly adds to project staff's learning (see Chapters 2, 3 and 5). One of the experiences arising during the Philippines Workshop illustrated the challenges of introducing 'participatory values' into staff job-performance when there is still reluctance on the side of the supervisors.

'When asked their personal views regarding the possibility of institutionalisation of the participatory approach with the Ministry of Agriculture (Nepal), [project staff] had mixed feelings. "Had we received the opportunity to learn about it earlier, we would have been different in our work." But the most difficult aspect for them was the lack of strong support and co-operation from their seniors. "When our seniors are not participatory, can you expect us to be participatory?" '

(Basnyat, 1997)

Other examples highlight the benefits of stakeholder participation in setting the baseline indicators for the PM&E process that provides the basic understanding and experience needed to follow up in the future (Chapters 9 and 11). Further to this, interactive gatherings are considered effective when participants develop their own style of working, i.e. developing their own timelines and tools for measuring change (Chapter 9), and when project staff work together with communities to establish baseline information, analyse farmer livelihoods, and better understand the issues and problems faced by communities (Chapter 11). These same examples highlight that success does not come immediately or completely. Ward recognized that the villagers are not fully involved in analysing information and using data as their own, and that field facilitators still needed support from higher level staff to apply participatory approaches and incorporate the learnings into their project activities.

Some examples took stakeholder participation further by creating multistakeholder M&E teams responsible for information analysis and action. In the McDowell County Enterprise Community programme, Rutherford noted that the inclusion of representatives from different stakeholders into a *learning team* was vital to the success of PM&E. As the learning team worked together, they became an effective research team that stayed with the process and were committed to the task. Although inclusion of local community members as part of the larger learning team is seen as essential to building their M&E abilities, one author noted that political and social conflicts can prevent the development of these evaluation teams (Chapter 3).

Resources

A lack of resources is frequently noted as one of the greatest constraints to building the abilities of stakeholders in PM&E. Resources, in this context, are not limited to funds but extend to human, information and material resources. The lack of skilled and trained facilitators, inadequate information (about PM&E, the local context, etc.) and insufficient materials are all constraints to building institutional and individual capacity in PM&E. Even something as simple as ensuring that stakeholders have pens, books, and other necessary materials for recording M&E information greatly helps improve accuracy, local ownership, and multi-level analysis of the information (Chapter 11). One of the workshop participants, Ashoke Chatterjee, noted that:

> 'Development Alternatives learned that before applying any methods, it was essential to have certain basic requirements in place: a sound information base (or a process of obtaining it), adequate techniques and tools, the right kind of motivation and expertise, and the *committed finances for a specific practical time frame*. Without these, it is virtually impossible for either the communities to involve themselves in meaningful ways or for a catalytic institution to retain credibility.'

There are significant costs associated with both formal training and experiential learning that must be recognized. These are in addition to the costs associated with the actual implementation of PM&E, though some of the capacity building is carried out during normal PM&E activities. Formal training can be organized externally (where participants travel and stay outside their homes) or within the local context of the group (if geographically defined). There are advantages and disadvantages to both types of formal training. The advantages of external training are: the participants are able to concentrate on the training; there can be an increased value given to the training; and the training can be done in a shorter period of time. The advantages of local training are: less costs needed for venue, transport, and accommodation for participants; the ability to draw different types of participants (e.g. women who may not be able to travel to external venues, etc.).

Experiential learning also requires a significant commitment of resources. As noted in the section on experiential learning, mentoring and other forms of 'on-the-job' capacity building demand a significant commitment of skilled human resources, which can sometimes be more difficult to find (see Chapters 9 and 3). Bringing together a number of the stakeholder groups to discuss the indicators, methods and tools to be used and to analyse the information gathered is seen as important to building their access and abilities in PM&E through an experiential learning approach. However, these meetings have a high cost in terms of financial, human, material and information resources.

Resource requirements are generally underestimated when agencies or individuals consider developing a PM&E process (Chapter 13). Since financial and human resources are usually scarce, outside resources must be sought. Those seeking funds and other outside resources are reluctant to make the process look prohibitively expensive in the beginning in order not to scare off potential investors. Therefore the tendency is to downplay the costs involved. However, the most hidden cost can be the substantial investment of human resources. This is most important to note when talking of incorporating marginalized groups. If talking of poor community members, one of the few assets they have is human resources (their time). A time-intensive PM&E process might exclude the very people it seeks to include simply because it is too costly for the participants.

Conclusions

As the applications of 'participatory monitoring and evaluation' vary greatly depending on the context and the intended outcomes, capacity-building efforts for PM&E must focus on the stakeholders' access and abilities to participate in a PM&E process. Access and ability are seen as inherently linked. Having access to an M&E process without having the abilities, in terms of the skills and resources needed to take advantage of that access, does not promote wider participation. This is also true if the abilities exist but the M&E process is not accessible.

Access and ability must also include the assurance that stakeholders are sufficiently informed about the possible risks and benefits of actively engaging in a PM&E process. When talking of risks, we must recognize that a M&E process that tries to bring other stakeholders into the learning and decision-making process can be perceived as a threat to the existing power dynamics (see especially Chapters 7 and 10). This point is further elaborated in Chapter 17 on scaling-up), but it is something that must be considered from the very beginning of establishing the process and building capacity for PM&E.

PM&E strives to be a process that includes a wide variety of people (both at an individual level and an institutional level) who have a diverse set of expectations and indicators, as well as different ways and means of recognizing success and failure. As such, building capacity for a PM&E process becomes very complex very quickly. However, building capacity for PM&E is not something that is accomplished overnight. Instead, PM&E capacity building should be seen as a process of laying foundations for lifelong learning.

17

Learning *to* Change by Learning *from* Change: Going to Scale with Participatory Monitoring and Evaluation

JOHN GAVENTA AND JUTTA BLAUERT

Introduction

PARTICIPATORY MONITORING EVALUATION (PM&E) is more than just a method or set of techniques. Like other processes of knowledge creation, it is also a deeply embedded social and political process, involving questions of voice and power. In aiming to privilege the voice of weaker or more marginalized groups, PM&E often raises sensitive (or threatening) questions about responsibility, accountability and performance (IIRR, 1998: 24; Whitmore, 1998). Negotiating and resolving these dynamics among differing groups towards learning and positive change is a difficult process, even at the level of a single project or community.

Increasingly, however, PM&E is going beyond the local community or project level. It is being used by institutions that operate at a larger scale, both geographically and in terms of programme scope. As several of the case studies in this volume suggest, PM&E is becoming an approach used for institutional accountability and organizational development, and, ultimately, for strengthening processes of democratic participation in the larger society. As it is being mainstreamed by government, non-governmental organizations (NGOs), donors or research agencies, PM&E highlights the complexity of social and power relationships amongst multiple stakeholders.

In this chapter, we briefly:

○ explore some of the social and political dimensions of PM&E, especially in relationship to scaling-up
○ address some of the uses and challenges of applying PM&E to encourage greater accountability of larger institutions, especially government
○ examine how PM&E can be used for institutional learning, and how institutional change is critical for the scaling-up of PM&E
○ identify some of the enabling factors that are necessary for using PM&E on a larger scale
○ provide some conclusions about the relationship of PM&E to the broader question of learning *from* change and learning *to* change.

Throughout, we will draw upon the case studies and previous chapters, as well as other experiences.

Scaling-up the PM&E process

Scaling-up of participation from the local level to a broader level has been a key theme for those concerned with participation in development during the 1990s[1] (see Blackburn with Holland, 1998; Edwards and Hulme, 1995; Gaventa, 1998; Holland with Blackburn, 1998). We have known for some time that high levels of participation on the ground can boost project performance. We have also discovered that participation holds promise outside the traditional project framework:

o in helping to inform national policy makers (Holland with Blackburn, 1998; Norton and Stephens, 1995; Robb, 1999)
o in large-scale government programmes (Bond, 1998; Hagmann et al., 1997; Korten, 1988; Thompson, 1995)
o in large-scale NGO service delivery programmes (Hinchcliffe et al., 1999; Korten, 1980)
o in the design and implementation of donor projects (Forster, 1998)
o as a fundamental ingredient of good governance in large public and private organizations (Gaventa and Valderrama, 1999; Lingayah and MacGillivray, 1999; Wheeler and Sillanpää, 1997; Zadek et al., 1997).

In 1998, at a workshop at the World Bank on 'Mainstreaming and up-scaling participation', a key lesson was that to be successful, large-scale participation must mean more than a focus on the role of the 'primary stakeholders', or those directly involved at the project level. Rather, there was a high degree of consensus on the need to focus on how participatory approaches were adopted and used by other stakeholders as well, i.e. donors, governments and other institutions that support development at the local level. A shift has thus taken place in our learning as participation goes to scale – from focusing on the involvement of primary stakeholders as the critical factor, to a growing appreciation of the need for broader institutional change, and the need to link actors at differing levels in participatory processes.

While the concern with the scaling-up of participation in development is now at least a decade old, most of it has been concerned with the processes of planning or implementation of projects – not with monitoring and evaluation. However, approaches emerging from the private sector are showing that large-scale institutions can often learn more quickly and effectively through the use of participatory evaluation and accounting approaches, such as social auditing (Zadek et al., 1997). Similarly, several of the cases in this volume have shown us how processes of PM&E that have developed at the community or project level are now being applied on a larger scale, to broader geographic areas, or to larger institutions, such as governments or donor agencies. For instance, in the Mongolia case study, PM&E is being used in a national poverty alleviation programme. We have seen examples of cases where PM&E is being adopted by large NGOs (e.g. CARE Zambia); by international research organizations (e.g. IDRC in Canada); in processes of local governance (e.g. Colombia and Ecuador), and by large donor agencies, such as in India where the Society for Participatory Research in Asia (PRIA) co-ordinated a process involving 23 voluntary health organizations, government and donors to evaluate the United States Agency for International Development's (USAID) national health programmes (Acharya *et al.*, 1997).

As at the local level, the practice of PM&E at large scale presents enormous challenges. Scaling-up PM&E with government and large-scale institutions may simply magnify issues of power, difference and conflict also found at the micro level. PM&E on a large scale involves many stakeholders, with differing levels of influence, differing reasons for involvement and differing indicators of success. Groups may be brought together who have little history of working together, little understanding of each other's needs and realities, and a history of suspicion, mistrust or conflict. Moreover, the policies, procedures, and systems within government agencies and other large institutions – many of which may tend to be more rigid and hierarchical – can also mitigate against the core principles of PM&E, which include sharing, flexibility, negotiation and learning.

In seeking ways to overcome these obstacles to PM&E practice, the case studies in this book reflect the broader literature on mainstreaming participation in suggesting that scaling-up implies at least two broad sets of changes in order to be effective:

○ first, it requires new kinds of relationships of accountability *amongst* and *between* stakeholders, and implies new forms of inter-organisational collaboration

○ second, it requires new forms of learning *within* institutions, large and small, in order to enable them to operate in a more participatory and flexible manner.

Not only are these conditions necessary for large-scale PM&E to be effective, but PM&E in turn, can contribute to these broader changes. We will discuss each of these sets of changes in turn.

Broadening the lens – changing the flow of accountability among stakeholders

Several of the case studies in this volume have alluded to the fact that concepts like 'monitoring' or 'evaluation' often have negative connotations for marginal or popular groups. In Mongolia, there is no equivalent word for monitoring, but it is often associated with other terms like 'supervision', 'surveillance', 'control' (Chapter 12). In Latin America, the understanding of evaluation is often associated with school exams and being checked on – not with a process of actual reflection and learning. Similarly, Symes and Jasser have pointed out that the Arabic word most commonly used for monitoring conveys a meaning related to 'controlling'. Many local projects which have been 'evaluated' think of it as the disempowering experience of being assessed and judged by others through a process in which they had little control.

PM&E attempts to change these more traditional understandings by means of a process that seeks to share control amongst various stakeholders – albeit not always equally. In so doing, PM&E attempts to

231

reverse the traditional processes of top-down monitoring and one-way accountability. In the Philippines Workshop, participants felt strongly that 'PM&E is not just about accountability *of* the community but accountability *to* the community' (IIRR, 1998: 32). A number of case studies illustrate ways in which the lens is being shifted (i.e. where PM&E tools, skills and processes are now being used by citizens and civil society organizations to monitor larger institutions – especially government – and to link differing stakeholders in new collaborative relationships), for instance:

○ In the Philippines, PM&E is being used by the Education for Life Foundation (ELF) to explore community indicators of democracy, within families, people's organisations, and local government. In other work in the Philippines, the *Ba*rangay *T*raining *Ma*nagement Project (BATMAN) – a coalition of approximately 45 NGOs including ELF – is using PM&E to develop citizens' indicators of participation, leadership and local governance. These indicators will be used by citizens and other civil society actors to examine the broader political institutions that affect their communities.

○ In Colombia, the Association of Indigenous Councils of Northern Cauca (ACIN), a community-based organization spanning over 13 municipalities and 90,000 members, has developed a monitoring and evaluation (M&E) system as part of the local and regional planning and development process, in which member communities define indicators based on their indigenous world views and cultural practices. In the process, the 'communities assess the work of their own institutions which are held liable in terms of fulfilling their commitments and responsibilities' (Chapter 7).

○ In the United States, citizen learning teams were formed to monitor the community impact of a national government programme, known as the Empowerment Zone programme, and to convey results to programme leaders at the local and federal level (Chapter 9).[2]

○ Similarly, in Ecuador, an NGO known as COMUNIDEC has developed a planning and PM&E process known as SISDEL (*Sistema de Desarrollo Local*, or Local Development System) which seeks to contribute to building alliances and coalitions amongst civil society organizations, the private sector and local municipalities. Among those items monitored are the extent to which inter-institutional agreements are themselves working, as well as the larger issues related to the policies and cultures of citizenship, management and collaboration (Chapter 8).

In other parts of the world, we have seen similar examples. In the United States, citizen monitoring has a long history as a means by which citizens assess – and attempt to hold accountable – government programmes (Parachini with Mott, 1997). More globally, the NGO Working Group on the World Bank has conducted a large-scale monitoring process to assess how effectively the Bank was implementing its own policies on 'participation' in local projects (Tandon and Cordeiro, 1998). The results then contributed to a dialogue between NGOs and Bank representatives on how participation could be improved.

In each of these cases, the process of PM&E attempts to contribute to new forms of governance,[3] involving greater transparency and more democratic involvement between citizens and the broader institutions that affect their lives (Gaventa and Valderrama, 1999). The usual relationships of 'upward' accountability – in which larger, more powerful institutions hold their grantees or operational staff to account – is broadened as local citizens and their organizations are using PM&E to demand and encourage greater responsiveness by public, private and NGO institutions through processes of 'downward' accountability, as well. However, accountability is a contentious concept. As it changes, issues of how to deal with power and conflict become critical concerns.

Managing power relationships

Whether in the locality, or when larger-scale institutions are involved, questions of who is accountable to whom, and who can voice concerns about performance, also involve questions of power. A pre-condition for meaningful participation is some degree of openness and a safe space for participants to articulate their views and concerns. These conditions may not readily exist. For instance, in the Palestine case study, community members were at first hesitant to speak out due to a history and culture of occupation, where 'the power of the gun appears far greater than that of the olive branch' (Chapter 10). In organizations that have traditionally operated through hierarchy, as in many government organizations, it may be difficult for those with less power to feel safe to speak out, and equally difficult for those in power to learn to listen to the views of those perceived as being 'below', as was mentioned in the Nepal example (Chapter 2). And, as the case in Mexico (Chapter 3) reminds us, often organizations that promote participatory evaluation 'out there' with communities in local projects, are hesitant to open up to an examination of their own power differences and dynamics.

At the same time, several of these case studies show that PM&E can sometimes become a means for attempting to redress power imbalances. For instance, in the use of PM&E by forest users groups (FUGs) in Nepal, women were able to challenge the FUG chairman and to demand more open accounting of the process to meet their needs and priorities (Chapter 2). In Colombia, Espinosa argues that doing M&E in public assemblies can also contribute to a more transparent process, in which (because many people are involved) it is more difficult for one individual or group to control the process. The PM&E process, he argues, also encouraged young people and others to emerge as new leaders, and thus served to weaken the influence of traditional politicians. Similarly, in the McDowell County example in the United States, Rutherford found that the experience of the learning team members contributed to greater self-confidence and skills, leading some to also get involved in new public leadership positions in the community.

Negotiating differences and conflict

Of course, not all PM&E processes are as successful as the illustrations given above. The cases in this volume have shown how in some circumstances the PM&E process can enable the voices and priorities of hidden stakeholders to emerge. When new actors enter a social process, they may articulate new views of reality and new priorities of what is important. But this very articulation may also lead to conflict. In some cases, the conflict may be extreme, including the use of violence as we saw in the case study from Colombia. More common is disagreement over what types of change are most important, and if and how they are to be attained.

While such conflict can paralyse a PM&E process, several of the cases in this volume also suggest that the opposite can occur: the very process of the PM&E can provide a framework and forum for discussing and managing different interests and priorities. Identification and use of indicators – sometimes, at least initially, in differing groups – offers a means for both improved communication and for negotiations amongst different actors. Participatory indicators allow focused presentation of views, and listening, rather than direct confrontation. In the Nepal case, for example, Hamilton *et al.* found that the process of developing indicators became a process in which the powerful and more vocal interest groups (in this case the men, and the more literate groups) tended to predominate. However, as the participants were given 'opportunities to articulate their views and needs through discussion, they [were] often supported by others with converging interests'. By presenting and clarifying interests in formalized discussion, conflicts were deliberated and often managed – especially if there was space in the process for the disadvantaged groups to articulate their concerns and to negotiate around them. Similar processes have been reported in projects in India and Ghana, in which the development of indicators and project plans initially in separate gender groups contributed to frameworks for understanding differences in the community (Shah, M.K., 1998).

Whereas conflict is often embedded in different social interests, it may also emerge or be reflected in the PM&E process – for example, around which indicators are to be used, which stakeholders to involve, or how to interpret and use findings. For instance, while local stakeholders may want to emphasize indicators that reflect the specificity or diversity of their situation, managers responsible for large-scale programmes may want indicators or data that allow them to generalize and compare across communities. These differences can be sorted out in several ways. In Latin America, the Grassroots Development Framework emerged through processes of negotiation around a common framework that aimed to reflect the needs and evaluations of different stakeholders while tracking change at various levels of impact (See Chapters 3, 7 and 8; see also Ritchey-Vance, 1998). Such negotiation is not always possible, though, and separate or parallel systems may be required. Hamilton *et al.* argue, for instance, that higher level institutions may need to be willing to hand over control of the process to local actors (in their case study, the forest users) and to develop their own complementary system if the local system does not meet their needs.

As noted earlier, resolving differences and negotiating conflicts is difficult in multi-stakeholder processes, whether at community or macro level. However, the workshop participants in the Philippines argued that expecting there to be complete agreement over the entire PM&E process from the beginning is unrealistic. More important, rather, is to identify areas of mutual agreement and then to proceed (IIRR, 1998: 69). Similarly, as Espinosa points out in the case of Columbia, 'consensus is not a precondition' for working together. Where these processes are appropriately managed, they can contribute to strengthened collaborative partnerships. In Ecuador, for instance, Torres finds that the PM&E process is being used by communities to negotiate and establish alliances with both the private sector and national government; to negotiate with government at regional and national levels for greater access to resources; and to contribute to consideration of new laws and policies. A note of caution, however: while PM&E contributes to negotiation and collaboration, it does not do away with the need for campaigning and advocacy work for democratic change, which may continue to involve conflict in order to raise issues effectively. 'Mediation processes between different conceptions . . . should not be confused with consensus, the amelioration of conflicting interests, or the alleviation of poverty' (Blauert and Zadek, 1998: 3).

Changing from within: PM&E *for* institutional learning

As we have suggested earlier, it is not sufficient to achieve mainstreaming of PM&E by promoting PM&E 'out there' – whether in smaller scale projects or in larger relationships between differing social actors. Learning to work across difference, to resolve conflicts, and to create new kinds of inter-institutional collaboration often requires institutions – whether NGO or public sector – to change internally as well. For change to occur, organizations and institutions need to learn what they have done well and what they have not, and how they are perceived by their stakeholders – as well as how they can appropriately respond by using this information to improve on institutional behaviour and performance. While learning is rarely easy, it can be aided by applying PM&E from within, to develop a systematic yet adaptive way of understanding what has or has not been achieved.

In 1980 David Korten wrote an influential article which articulated a learning process approach: 'The key [to achieving impact and competence . . . was] not preplanning, but an organization with a capacity for embracing error, learning with the people, and building new knowledge and institutional capacity through action' (1980: 480). Essential to organizational learning is understanding how knowledge is acquired, how the resulting information is shared and interpreted, and how effective organizational memory is. Thus, organizational learning at its most basic is both the detection and correction of errors, and the application by individuals within these organizations of the lessons learned. Such learning is not always conscious nor intentional. PM&E aims to make it more so.

In this vein, the organizational development literature of the 1980s and 1990s has argued[4] that a change in organizational practice is best achieved if individual change in attitude and behaviour is encouraged and provided with incentives, but also if the organization itself can learn in a way that corresponds to its prevailing organizational culture and needs. If this organizational culture is discriminatory and un-democratic, then 'working with' such a culture poses special challenges to PM&E approaches and practice. Some practitioners argue that working *with* is impossible in such cases, but that external lobbying needs to put pressure on the organization first. In the Philippines, the BATMAN programme decided to work mainly with local authorities where BATMAN NGO coalition members felt local authorities showed a sufficiently strong commitment to citizens' participation. By creating best practice examples, it is hoped that pressure can be put on other organizations to change. This approach is echoed in many of the benchmarking approaches used in corporate social responsibility work.

Where the organizational culture does provide openness to learning, two further elements are key to enable a sustained interest in it (rather than resistance to it): (i) initiating the process, and the approach, by identifying feasible 'entry points' of interest and opportunity for change; and (ii) keeping information and time involvement to a minimum to avoid people being overwhelmed and to allow them to feel safe with change. It is argued that creative learning can best take place by responding to – rather than fighting against – prevailing institutional culture, while also challenging people to change mental models and behavioural patterns.

In the first instance, PM&E may begin as a consultative practice to get information that is more accurate. However, such information may, in turn, point to further changes which are required in order to allow the organization to respond to the lessons learned. This 'ripple' effect from a PM&E process may take some staff by surprise. Currently, much PM&E practice is not initiated with this organizational change in mind. For many organizations, then, those first steps of a PM&E process can, if effectively used, represent a 'Trojan Horse'[5] in that by opening oneself up to multiple opinions, and taking first steps to correct one's actions, almost inevitably, larger questions are raised about organizational processes and internal democracy. We find, therefore, that it is often organizations that are living through key crisis points, or that already have developed a will to learn, that are the greatest risk takers in being creative in taking further steps towards greater public accountability.

The case studies in this volume have provided several examples of the use of PM&E to strengthen organizational learning. For instance:

○ in Palestine, Symes and Jasser guided the organization they were working in through the first hard steps of analysing their own internal procedures, rules and behaviour in order to balance the objectives of their participatory work in agricultural communities with practices within the organization to reflect the same openness to learning
○ CARE Zambia, as reported by Ward, pursued seven strategies for building a learning culture and practice within the organization. This included establishing a community monitoring system that has allowed staff to collaborate more directly with communities on how to strengthen their local institutions and make development programmes more effective
○ like public sector or donor institutions, development research agencies can also make use of self-evaluative processes to learn about how to improve the impact of their work. In his report on the Canadian development research agency, IDRC, Carden shows how the donor-initiated, institutional self-assessment work undertaken in some of the

research institutions that receive grants from IDRC required some degree of handing over of control of the internal change process to external partners.

The case studies do not suggest that there is any single approach to PM&E that enables or guarantees institutional learning in the most effective way, nor do they suggest that such learning always occurs. In fact, in some cases organizations may refuse to change in the light of difficult lessons. However, the case studies do suggest several common themes or lessons that may be useful in implementing a successful PM&E process for institutional learning. These include the importance of change and flexibility, ownership, internal accountability, and trust and trustworthiness.

Change and flexibility

Individual and organizational learning can take place where a process and a methodology is sufficiently adaptive to allow learning to be applied and, made tangible, almost immediately. One example of this openness to change that demonstrates an organization's willingness to learn is the flexible use of indicators – or even daring to move away from them into focusing on assessing critical changes without the quantification. Lawrence *et al.*, as well as Sidersky and Guijt, point to the utility of allowing indicators to change even from one year to the next, so as to incorporate learning into the planning cycle. This change in indicators in itself can demonstrate that those involved in the PM&E and planning systems are responsive to the lessons learned from previous cycles about new priorities or interests. Above all, the flexibility of 'champions' in the institution (see 'Leadership and champions' below) is of great importance in encouraging staff to dare to be transparent and to change: Carden describes this for research organizations, Ward for funding agencies and Abes for leaders of community-based organizations.

Building ownership

For institutions to change, individuals need to be motivated to apply learning – for which, it is recognized, a sense of ownership over a process and the results is essential. For this sense of 'ownership' to be anything more than participatory rhetoric, however, we argue that learning needs to recognize the *role and responsibility* of each individual, and the personal or collective *benefits or problems* to be expected. In contrast to conventional M&E, PM&E has the potential to enhance this sense of ownership amongst stakeholders both within the institution and outside.

With the recognition of the importance of who runs and owns the PM&E process, however, has also emerged a new role of the evaluator as facilitator (Guba and Lincoln, 1989). The facilitator is expected to recognize her or his subjectivity as well as that of the different stakeholders involved. This role also aims to build a sense of ownership over the process and outcome amongst stakeholders involved in any learning cycle, as well as to contribute to their learning. Mosse confirms this important role of negotiator and mediator, relevant also for the context of PM&E:

'Given multiple perspectives and agendas, the task of monitoring is no longer simply to manage impacts or outcomes. Rather, it must play a major role in creating a framework for negotiating common meanings and resolving differences and validation of approaches . . . The role of process monitors is then more of advocacy, facilitation or nurturing than analysis.'

(Mosse, 1998: 9)

Developing accountability within the institution

As the previous section pointed out, there is more to accountability than reporting to donors: accountability is increasingly recognized as relating not only to financial transparency, but also to learning about the social and economic impact of the organization's activities. This involves changing (and reversing) relationships amongst and between stakeholders – including those *within* the organisation. Accepting the responsibility to be accountable through dialogue and disclosure already implies a certain openness to learning. For institutions to change, actors internal to the organization also need to be willing to probe their own organization, recognize and discuss different 'hierarchies', be open about mistakes as well as successes, and, above all, know that the opinions expressed by them can lead to *internal* as well as *external* change.

For some organizations, accountability to differing stakeholders may lead to conflict due to differing expectations and requirements. NGOs and community-based organizations often find themselves suffering from multiple accountability pressures – the 'sandwich' phenomenon of being caught between the protocols and requirements of donors, and the needs and demands for accountability of the communities or groups with which they are working. Responding to demands for strategic accountability (wider impacts) over functional accountability (resource accounting) is still proving to be a challenge for these and other organizations (see Edwards and Hulme, 1995). Participants in the Philippines Workshop suggested several responses to this challenge, including:

○ piloting PM&E systems to persuade donors of their benefits, before taking them to a larger scale
○ developing complementary systems to meet differing needs, including complementing the logical framework with simplified frameworks that are more accessible to the community
○ combining participatory methods with traditional external evaluation activities
○ making donors more aware of the importance of people's indicators (IIRR, 1998: 50).

Trust and trustworthiness

For people to be open, and feel secure enough to learn and to share doubts about their own work, or ideas for future work, they need to have sufficient trust in their position as well as in their process of learning. Validating multiple perspectives – an essential characteristic of PM&E – is therefore crucial in making people feel more secure about expressing their analysis and concerns. Yet, trust requires more than 'permission' to give voice to opinions: actors that hold more structural, institutionalized power, (whether managers, donors or governmental agencies), need to start applying self-evaluation to themselves and to be transparent about their successes *and* shortcomings. This 'openness' beyond the act of simply recording or monitoring is, we argue, one of the first steps in establishing trust. Incorporating different stakeholders in dialogue-based appraisals of the *quality* of an organization's performance can also offer a way to establish trust, and, hence, the capacity to change – especially if the evaluation process is seen to lead to tangible action. This sense of sharing responsibility by seeing direct impact can, in turn, help build further relationships of trust, particularly by and for structurally weaker stakeholders such as operational or support staff in a bureaucracy or NGO, or villagers receiving grants from international donors.

Furthermore, trustworthiness of findings need to be proven in different forms to different stakeholders. Visualization can make findings more accessible to some people, whereas others may need short texts accompanied by substantial written back-up material to believe the conclusions and to take action. So, for instance, Sidersky and Guijt describe what information is considered sufficiently meaningful by farmers about soil improvements: for farmers to be willing to change their practice they need indicators about how many of their peer group ('small-scale farmers') have adopted a soil conservation practice, rather than whether the soil moisture content has increased. 'Scientific' proof is not sufficient – peer-group judgement is key for learning (and that is also how 'scientists' work!). In this vein, 'benchmarking' and external validation, in turn have become two M&E methods acknowledged to be of great use in PM&E processes for allowing inter-organizational trust and learning to take place.[6] In addition, it is the benchmarking that can entice an organization into action (appealing to competitiveness or its mission to improve on its impact) and into following up on evaluation results by knowing that it is being observed by other organizations that have collaborated in the external verification process.

For large institutions a systematic learning process needs to be in place that allows the management of extensive data emerging from an M&E process, and which permits the organization to have sufficient trust in the views received and to know that it can handle these in confidentiality, while also taking the key lessons 'out there' to share. Some of the most significant innovations in this regard are found where participatory methods and principles are being combined with conventional approaches to achieve systematic and effective learning within institutions, while enhancing accountability toward stakeholders outside the organization. Social auditing is one such approach.[7]

Enabling factors for scaling-up PM&E

The cases in this volume have given us some rich insights into scaling-up PM&E and its uses in contributing to new forms of institutional accountability, collaboration and learning. However, it would be misleading to suggest that PM&E can always be used successfully in these ways. The cases also offer lessons about the enabling conditions that may be necessary for scaling-up PM&E effectively.

Social and political context

The presence of many nationalities in the Philippines Workshop led to lively discussions about how differing social and political regimes may affect the potential of PM&E to lead to far reaching changes, and the strategies that might be used. For people to be able to raise questions about accountability or performance of others, the social and political context must be one in which there exists at least some level of political space that will allow people to participate and to voice their views and concerns about the project and institutional or social realities that affect them.

Many of the examples in this chapter of taking PM&E to scale are from contexts in which there is a certain degree of stability, an organized civil society, and a degree of institutional openness. Certainly, in cases of extreme conflict, or where there is a history of authoritarianism or a weak civil society, citizen monitoring of larger institutions may not be possible on a large scale – at least not openly. On the other hand, in some highly conflictual situations – e.g. over environmental issues, or in the case of violent human rights violations – well-organized advocacy for transparency and the respect of human rights has led large institutions to set in place some form of enhanced accountability mechanisms. In other cases, with strong government, or strong donor presence, participatory processes may be promoted, but from the top. While such interventions from above may create institutional openings for participation, using that space may still be difficult because of the lack of capacity or skills.

Enabling policies

Even where there is a sufficient degree of political openness, it still may be hard for local groups to engage in joint monitoring with government or other institutions without special enabling legislation or policies, which legitimate their involvement. Moreover, financial resources and scope for taking decisions need to be in place in order for people to participate in PM&E fully. In this volume, for instance, we find a number of examples where decentralization policies have mandated citizen involvement – not only in planning and implementation, but also in monitoring and evaluating performance.

As in many countries during the 1990s, in the Philippines the local government code of 1991 created legal space for POs (Peoples' Organizations) and NGOs to participate in local government, often bringing with them participatory skills they might have gained through project and advocacy work. Here, strong civil society, plus the enabling framework, have created the opportunity for NGOs and their coalitions, like the BATMAN Consortium,[8] to engage with local government – using participatory planning and

240

PM&E approaches not only for development projects, but also for strengthening local democratization and accountability.

Similarly, in both Bolivia and India, legislation allows for local committees to serve in a monitoring and watchdog role. While there is, so far, little evidence that these committees have developed the capacity and independence to do their job, there may be great potential if funding and capacity-building are also devolved. In Kerala, for instance, local 'vigilance' committees are empowered to sign off on local projects – inspecting both for quality and for proper use of funds – before final payments are made to contractors.

Local NGOs are beginning to explore how to strengthen these citizen monitoring-committees as a bottom-up device to ensure accountability (Intercooperation, 1999). And in the Indian state of Rajasthan, a women's led right-to-information movement has demanded transparency by local governments, especially by insisting that all local government expenditures be posted for everyone to see (Jenkins and Goetz, 1999).

Prior experience and capacity

Even with political space and enabling legislation, capacity is required to take PM&E to scale – both at the community level and with the larger institutions alike. In Chapter 16 Johnson elaborates on the requirements for capacity building for successful PM&E. Building such capacity needs time and the acceptance of trial and error; it also needs the presence of strong and creative institutions that are prepared to act as intermediaries.

Capacity refers also to the institutional capacity to participate. As the Brazil case suggested, it may be difficult to scale-up the PM&E process when the critical partners do 'not have a certain degree of institutional stability and maturity' (Chapter 5). Other cases point to the necessity of a certain level of institutional readiness or openness to take PM&E processes on board. Capacity, in turn, involves flexibility and creativity, not just efficiency. At the institutional level this also means examining the incentive structures that can reward team leaders, managers and operational staff for innovation, learning and adaptation.

Leadership and champions

Even where there is openness and capacity for change at various levels, the case studies have also recognized the need to count on a champion within the organization in order for PM&E to be effective and sustainable. Ward identifies the importance of management support in allowing staff in CARE Zambia to experiment with developing the new learning system, including making adjustments after errors. The work with farmer-to-farmer extensionists in Mexico (Chapter 3) relied a great deal on the donor's support for this experimental process and the wider objectives of enhancing learning and accountability skills – making the role of the donor even more critical in enabling the grantee to act on results. Yet, an external champion also needs an internal leader who takes on the risks involved in making his or her staff feel secure in opening themselves up to a more transparent critique. Such leaders will need to have relational skills as well as a strong value base to allow themselves to be appraised openly and to show the way in how to change in attitude and behaviour based on the lessons learned. Constructively critical, and encouraging, external support – including through supporting process consultancy formats or medium-term accompaniment – can thus be of great importance in enabling longer-term change to take effect.

Relying on champions, however, highlights a weak link in PM&E approaches. Champions can move on, or be replaced by their employers or constituency; champions can also start to use the new arena to build their own political stronghold, or close down the process when their own personal behaviour and performance is critically appraised. Carden refers to the problem of staff changes during a PM&E process in research institutions, where the departure of the senior manager can immediately interrupt or close down the process (see also Chapter 3). While in the case of a large organization, the existence of a broader institutional commitment could ensure that another person be appointed immediately, this might be different at the community level. Discussions in the Philippines Workshop pointed to cases where changes in village authorities could leave the PM&E process abandoned, with the risk of a new political faction in power not sharing the same interest, or new authorities not having yet acquired the necessary skills (IIRR, 1998: 47).

Strong champions for participation by primary stakeholders are sometimes individuals in large and powerful organizations, such as the World Bank. Whether in Mongolia or Guatemala, Mexico or Uganda, individuals in donor organizations have managed to cajole national institutions into daring to reform their practice of accountability, often making such reform part of loan agreements. Although such top-down conditionality may not be conducive to effective learning by state actors, it appears at present – as discussed earlier – to create a space within which civil society and advisory actors can move to ensure the development of participatory M&E practices that can enhance public sector accountability and citizens' monitoring.

Increased linkages and learning from others

A final factor to enable scaling-up of PM&E comes from the opportunity of learning from other organizations – especially those that have set new benchmarks for successful approaches to PM&E. Having 'role models' can allow an organization to compare and assess its own work within the specific context in which it operates and to learn from other perspectives. Institutions are increasingly recognizing the utility of linking with other organizations with specific skills, so as to complement their own expertise and to better use their own financial and human resources. In turn, one of the key challenges for future work raised at the workshop was the need for PM&E proponents to develop more systematic benchmarks or criteria for success to enable practitioners to learn from others in judging their own success.

Conclusions

The case studies in this volume have demonstrated the rapid spread and acceptance of PM&E practice across the globe. PM&E concepts and methods are being applied in almost every sector (health, agriculture, community development, local governance and more), in small and large organizations, and with a broad range of stakeholders and participants. Innovations in the field abound. The uses and methodologies of PM&E are increasingly varied, and, as we have seen, are moving from the project level and community level, to larger systems of governance and institutional learning and reform. The potential to continue to take PM&E to scale – to encourage its spread to yet further places and sectors, to be used by the mainstream as well as to challenge the mainstream, and to critique and learn from development practice – is enormous.

Yet, as we have also seen, the possibilities are not without pitfalls. As one participant at the Philippines Workshop put it, PM&E 'is a dream and a nightmare'. As with any approach, participatory processes can be misused, or become rigid and flat. PM&E is a social and political process, in which conflict and disagreements amongst stakeholders (over methods as well as broader social interests) can easily take over. Disagreements may exist over indicators of success, appropriate levels of rigour, the purposes of the PM&E process and the uses of its results. As the past few chapters have shown us, there is still much to be done – to strengthen the conceptual and methodological base of PM&E, to build human and institutional capacity for its use, to learn to negotiate the conflicts towards building collaborative action, and to apply it on a larger scale to issues of governance and institutional learning.

While the challenges are great, so are the stakes. Ultimately, asking questions about success, about impacts and about change is critical to social change itself. Learning from change is not an end itself, but a process of reflection that affects how we think and act to change the future. Learning *to* change involves learning *from* change: if we cannot learn effectively from our action, we cannot improve our understanding of the world, nor act more effectively on it. *Who* asks the questions about change affects *what questions* are asked, and whose realities are considered important. Who benefits from the questions – that is, who learns from the process – will affect who changes, who acts, and how. Learning *from* change means *changing who learns*, and looking at how differing stakeholders in change processes learn and act together.

Bibliography and references

Abbot, Joanne and Irene Guijt (1998) *Changing Views on Change: Participatory Approaches to Monitoring the Environment*, SARL Discussion Paper 2, London: IIED.

Acharya, B., Y. Kumar, V. Satyamurti and R. Tandon (1997) *Reflections on Participatory Evaluation – the Private Voluntary Organization for Health-II (PVOH) Experience*, Paper prepared for the 'International Workshop on Participatory Monitoring and Evaluation: Experience and Lessons', Cavite, Philippines, 24–29 Nov 1997.

Alcocer, Joel; Pilar Lizárraga; Jhonny Delgadillo *et al.* (1997) *Sondeo Sobre Utilización de Métodos Participativos de Monitoreo y Evaluación en Bolivia* (A Survey of the Practice of Participatory Monitoring and Evaluation Methods in Bolivia). Paper prepared for the 'International Workshop on Participatory Monitoring and Evaluation: Experience and Lessons', Cavite, Philippines, 24–29 Nov 1997.

Alexandra, J., S. Haffenden and T. White (1996) *Listening to the Land: A Directory of Community Environmental Monitoring Groups in Australia*, Fitzroy, Australia: Australian Conservation Foundation.

Amanor, Kojo (1990) *Analytical Abstracts on Farmer Participatory Research*, Agricultural Administration Unit, Occasional Paper 10, London: Overseas Development Institute.

Archarya, B., Y. Kumar, V. Satyamurti and R. Tandon (1998) 'Reflections on Participatory Evaluation – the PVOH –II Experience' in *Participation and Governance* Vol. 5, No. 12, pp. 11–16.

Archer, David (1995) 'Using PRA for a Radical New Approach to Adult Literacy', *PLA Notes* 23, pp. 51–56.

Archer, David and Sara Cottingham (1996) *REFLECT Mother Manual: Regenerated Freirean Literacy through Empowering Community Techniques*, London: ActionAid.

Armonia, Ricardo C. and Dindo M. Campilan (1997) *Participatory Monitoring and Evaluation: The Asian Experience*, Paper prepared for the 'International Workshop on Participatory Monitoring and Evaluation: Experience and Lessons', Cavite, Philippines, 24–29 Nov 1997.

Ashby, Jacqueline A. (1990) *Evaluating Technology with Farmers: A Handbook*, Colombia: IPRA projects, CIAT.

AS-PTA (1997) *Trajetória do Projeto Paraíba: Período 1993–1996*, (unpublished report), Solânea: AS-PTA.

AS-PTA, CTA-ZM, and IIED (1997) *Monitoramento Participativo da Agricultura Sustentável: Relatório do Terceiro Encontro na Paraíba*, (unpublished report), IIED/AS-PTA.

Aubel, Judi (1993) *Participatory Program Evaluation: A Manual for Involving Program Stakeholders in the Evaluation Process*, Senegal: Catholic Relief Services.

Avina, Jeffrey *et al.* (1990) *Evaluating the Impact of Grassroots Development Funding*, Issues in Grassroots Development, Monograph Series, Arlington: IAF.

Bajaj, Manjul (1997) *Revisiting Evaluation: A Study of the Process, Role and Contribution of Donor funded Evaluations to Development Organizations in South Asia*, Ottawa: IDRC.

Bandre, Paul (1997) *Participatory Self-Evaluation of World Neighbours, Burkina Faso*, Paper prepared for the 'International Workshop on Participatory Monitoring and Evaluation: Experiences and Lessons', Cavite, Philippines, 24–29 Nov 1997.

Basnyat, Birendra Bir (1997) *Can Participatory Monitoring and Evaluation Survive in a Government Organization? Lessons from Nepal*, Paper prepared for the 'International Workshop on Participatory Monitoring and Evaluation: Experiences and Lessons', Cavite, Philippines, 24–29 Nov 1997.

Bernard, Anne (1996) *IDRC Networks: An Ethnographic Perspective*, Ottawa: IDRC.

Blackburn, James and C. De Toma (1998) 'Scaling-Down as the Key to Scaling-Up? The Role of Participatory Municipal Planning in Bolivia's Law of Popular Participation', in J. Blackburn with J. Holland (eds) *Who Changes? Institutionalizing Participation in Development*, London: Intermediate Technology Publications.

Blackburn, James with J. Holland (eds) (1998) *Who Changes? Institutionalizing Participation in Development*, London: Intermediate Technology Publications.

Blauert, Jutta and Simon Zadek (1998) 'The Art of Mediation: Growing Policy from the Grassroots', in J. Blauert and S. Zadek (eds), *Mediating Sustainability. Growing Policy from the Grassroots*, West Hartford: Kumarian Press.

Blauert, Jutta and Simon Zadek (eds) (1998) *Mediating Sustainability: Growing Policy from the Grassroots*, West Hartford: Kumarian Press.

Bond, Richard (1998) *Lessons for the Large-Scale Application of Process Approaches in Sri Lanka*, Gatekeeper Series No. 75, London: IIED.

Booth, W. and R. Morin (1996) *Assessing Organizational Capacity Through Participatory Monitoring and Evaluation*, Handbook prepared for the Pact Ethiopian NGO Sector.

Boyett, J.H. and J.T. Boyett (1998) *The Guru Guide: The Best Ideas of the Top Management Thinkers*, New York: John Wiley & Sons.

Bunch, Roland (1982) *Two Ears of Corn*, Oklahoma: World Neighbors.

Campilan, Dindo (1997) 'Making Participatory Monitoring and Evaluation (PM&E) Work: Thirteen Vignettes from the Field', in *Self-assessment. Participatory Dimensions of Project Monitoring and Evaluation*, Los Baños, Philippines: UPWARD.

Campilan, D. and G. Buenavista (1997) 'Interfacing PM&E with the research and development process', in *Self-Assessment: Participatory Dimensions of Project Monitoring and Evaluation*, Los Baños, Philippines: CIP-UPWARD.

Campos, Jennie and Francois Praline Coupal (1996) *Participatory Evaluation*, Prepared for the UNDP (draft).

Carrasco, Hernán (1993) 'Democratización de los Poderes Locales y Levantamiento Indígena', in Nina Pacari, Ramón Valarezo Galo, Alberto Tatzo, *et al.* (eds) *Sismo Etnico en el Ecuador: Varias Perspectivas*, Quito: CEDIME-Abya Yala.

CEDRES (1997) *Auto-Évaluation Institutionelle du CEDRES*, Ouagadougou: Centre d'Études, de Documentation, de Recherches Économiques et Sociales de l'Universite de Ouagadougou.

Chambers, Robert (1992) *Rural Appraisal: Rapid, Relaxed and Participatory*, IDS Discussion Paper No. 333, Brighton: Institute of Development Studies.

Chambers, Robert (1994a) 'Participatory Rural Appraisal (PRA): Analysis of Experience', *World Development*, Vol. 22, No. 9, pp. 1253–68.

Chambers, Robert (1994b) 'Participatory Rural Appraisal (PRA): Challenges, Potential and Paradigm', *World Development*, Vol. 22, No. 10, pp. 1–17.

Chambers, Robert (1997) *Whose Reality Counts? Putting the Last First*, London: Intermediate Technology Publications.

Chambers, Robert (1997) 'Public Management: Towards a Radical Agenda', in Martin Minogue, C. Polidano and D. Hulme (eds) *Beyond the New Public Management: Changing Ideas and Practices in Governance*, Cheltenham: Edward Elgar.

Chambers, Robert and Gordon Conway (1992) *Sustainable Rural Livelihoods. Practical Concepts for the 21st Century*, IDS Discussion Paper No. 26, Brighton: Institute of Development Studies.

Chambers, Robert and Irene Guijt (1995) 'PRA – Five Years Later: Where Are We Now?', in *Forests, Trees, and People Newsletter*, No. 26/27.

CIRDAP (1996) *Institutional Self-Assessment of CIRDAP*, Dhaka: Centre on Integrated Rural Development for Asia and the Pacific.

CODESRIA (1997) *Report of the Auto-Evaluation 1996*, Dakar: Council for the Development of Social Science Research in Africa.

Community Partnership Center (1998) *Findings and Recommendations of the Community Partnership Center EZ/EC Learning Initiative*, Knoxville: University of Tennessee.

CONCERN Worldwide (1996) *Review of Participatory Monitoring and Evaluation*, mimeo.

Cornwall, Andrea, Irene Guijt and Alice Welbourn (1993) *Acknowledging Process: Challenges for Agricultural Research and Extension Methodology*, IDS Discussion Paper No. 333, Brighton: Institute of Development Studies.

Cornwall, Andrea and Rachel Jewkes (1995) 'What is Participatory Research?' *Social Science Medicine*, Vol. 41, No. 12, pp. 1667–76.

Cornwall, Andrea, John Gashigi, Charity Kabutha and Tilly Sellers (1997) 'A Report of the Participatory Process Evaluation of the Family Life Training Programme (FLTP)', a consultancy report for Kenya Government Programme with Support from Danida, 14–24 January.

Davies, R.J. (1998) 'An Evolutionary Approach to Organizational Learning: an experiment by an NGO in Bangladesh', in David Mosse, John Farrington, and Alan Rew (eds) *Development as Process: Concepts and Methods for Working with Complexity*, London: Routledge.

Davis-Case, D'Arcy and P. Grove (1990) *The Community's Toolbox: The Idea, Methods and Tools for Participatory Assessment, Monitoring and Evaluation in Community Forestry*, Community Forestry Field Manual 2, Rome: FAO.

Davis-Case, D'Arcy (1992) *Community Forestry: Participatory Assessment, Monitoring and Evaluation*, Rome: FAO.

de Raedt, Carol (1997) 'Project Monitoring and Evaluation: Does a Participatory Approach Make a Difference?', in *Self-assessment. Participatory Dimensions of Project Monitoring and Evaluation*, Los Baños, Philippines: UPWARD.

Diesing, Paul (1971) *Patterns of Discovery in the Social Sciences*, Chicago: Aldine Atherton.

Drinkwater, Michael (1994) 'Developing Interaction and Understanding: PRA and Farmer Research Groups in Zambia', in I. Scoones and J. Thompson (eds) *Beyond Farmer First: Rural Peoples' Knowledge, Agricultural Research and Extension Practice*, London: Intermediate Technology Publications.

Drinkwater, Michael (1997) *Household Livelihood Security in Southern and West African Regional Management Unit (SWARMU)*, Draft paper.

Edwards, Michael and David Hulme (eds) (1995) 'NGO Performance and Accountability: Introduction and Overview', in M. Edwards and D. Hulme (eds) *Non-Governmental Organizations – Performance and Accountability. Beyond the Magic Bullet*, London: Earthscan Publications.

Edwards, Michael and David Hulme (eds) (1995) *Non-Governmental Organizations – Performance and Accountability. Beyond the Magic Bullet*, London: Earthscan Publications.

Enriquez, Virgilio (1994) *From Colonial to Liberation Psychology: The Philippine Experience*, Manila, Philippines: De Lasalle University.

Estrella, Marisol and John Gaventa (1998) *Who Counts Reality? Participatory Monitoring and Evaluation: A Literature Review*, IDS Working Paper No. 70, Brighton: Institute of Development Studies.

Farrington, John and Adrienne Martin (1988) *Farmer Participation in Agricultural Research: A Review of Concepts and Practices*, Agricultural Administration Unit, Occasional Paper 9, London: Overseas Development Institute.

Feuerstein, Marie-Therese (1986) *Partners in Evaluation: Evaluating Development and Community Programmes with Participants*, London: Macmillan Education Ltd.

Ford, Richard (1994) *PRA for Monitoring and Evaluation: A Village Logbook from Ambodirafia, Madagascar*, Worcester, MA: Clark University and AF/FJKM.

Ford, Richard, Barbara Thomas-Slayter, Francis Lelo *et al*. (1996) *Conserving Resources and Increasing Production. Using Participatory Tools to Monitor and Evaluate Community-Based Resource Management Practices*, Worcester, MA: Center for Community-Based Development, Clark University.

Forster, Reiner (1998) *GTZ's Experience with Mainstreaming Primary Stakeholder Participation*, Contribution to the International Conference on 'Mainstreaming and Up-Scaling of Primary Stakeholder Participation – Lessons Learned and Ways Forward', Washington: World Bank, 19–20 Nov 1998.

Found, William C. (1995) *Participatory Research and Development: An Assessment of IDRC's Experience and Prospects*, Ottawa: IDRC.

Fowler, Alan (1997) *Striking a Balance: A Guide to Enhancing the Effectiveness of Non-governmental Organizations in International Development*, London: Earthscan Publications.

Fox, J.A and L.D. Brown (eds) (1998) *The Struggle for Accountability: The World Bank, NGOs, and Grassroots Movements*, Massachussetts: The MIT Press.

Gariba, Sulley (1995) *Participatory Impact Assessment as a Tool for Change: Lessons From Recent Experience in Poverty Alleviation Projects in Africa*, Paper presented at the Panel Session on Participatory Impact Assessment at the International Evaluation Conference, Vancouver, Canada, 1–5 Nov 1995.

Garvin, D. (1993) 'Building a Learning Organization', *Harvard Business Review*: July/August.

Gaventa, John (1998) 'The Scaling Up and Institutionalization of PRA: Lessons and Challenges' in J. Blackburn with J. Holland (eds) *Who Changes? Institutionalizing Participation in Development*, London: Intermediate Technology Publications.

Gaventa, J., V. Crccd, and J. Morrissey (1998) 'Scaling Up: Participatory Monitoring and Evaluation of a Federal Empowerment Program', in E. Whitmore (ed.) *Understanding and Practising Participatory Evaluation*, New Directions for Evaluation Series (80), San Francisco: Jossey Bass Publishers.

Gaventa, John and Camilo Valderrama (1999*) Participation, Citizenship, and Local Governance*, Background note prepared for workshop 'Strengthening Participation in Local Governance', Institute of Development Studies, Brighton, 21–24 June 1999.

Gohl, Eberhard, Dorsi Germann and Burkhard Schwarz (1996) *Participatory Impact Monitoring: Four Volumes: (1) Group-Based Impact Monitoring; (2) NGO-Based Impact Monitoring; (3) Application Examples; (4) The Concept of Participatory Impact Monitoring*, Braucschweig, Germany: GATE/GTZ.

Gonella, Claudia, Alison Pilling and Simon Zadek (1998) *Making Values Count: Contemporary Experience in Social and Ethical Accounting, Auditing and Reporting*, London: The Association of Chartered Certified Accountants/Institute of Social and Ethical AccountAbility/New Economics Foundation.

Gosling, Louisa and Mike Edwards (1995) *Toolkits: A Practical Guide to Assessment, Monitoring, Review and Evaluation*, London: Save the Children.

Greene, Jennifer (1994) 'Qualitative Program Evaluation: Practice and Promise', in N. Denzin and Y. Lincoln (eds) *Handbook of Qualitative Research*, Thousand Oaks, California: Sage Publications.

GTZ (1993) *Process Monitoring (ProM)*, Work Document for Project Staff, Bonn: GTZ/GATE.

GTZ (1996) *Process Monitoring (ProM)*, Work Document for project staff, Eschborn, Germany: Deutsche Gesellschaft für Technische Zusammenarbeit (GTZ) GmbH.

Guba, Egon and Yvonne Lincoln (1989) *Fourth Generation Evaluation*, London and California: Sage Publications.

Gubbels, Peter (1994) 'Farmer-First Research: Populist Pipedream or Practical Paradigm? A Case Study of the Projet Agro-Foresterie (PAF) in Burkina Faso', in I. Scoones and J. Thompson (eds) *Rural People's Knowledge, Agricultural Research and Extension Practice*, London: Intermediate Technology Publications.

Guijt, Irene (1998) *Participatory Monitoring and Impact Assessment of Sustainable Agriculture Initiatives: An Introduction to the Key Elements*, SARL Discussion Paper No. 1, London: IIED Sustainable Agriculture and Rural Livelihoods Programme.

Guijt, Irene and Pablo Sidersky (1996) 'Agreeing on Indicators', *ILEIA Newsletter* Vol. 12, No. 3, pp. 9–11.

Guijt, Irene and John Gaventa (1998) *Participatory Monitoring and Evaluation: Learning from Change*, IDS Policy Briefing 12, Brighton: Institute of Development Studies.

Guijt, Irene and Pablo Sidersky (1998) 'Matching Participatory Agricultural Development with the Social Landscape of Northeast Brazil', in F. Hinchcliffe, J. Thompson, J. Pretty *et al.* (eds) *Fertile Ground: The Impact of Participatory Watershed Development*, London: Intermediate Technology Publications.

Hagmann, J., E. Chuma, M. Connolly and K. Murwira (1997) *Propelling Change from the Bottom-up: Institutional Reform in Zimbabwe*, Gatekeeper Series No. 71, London: IIED.

Hamel, G. and C. Prahaled (1994) *Competing for the Future*, Boston: Boston Harvard Business School.

Hamilton, C., S. Hood and R.B. Shrestha (1998) *The FUG Planning and Self-evaluation Tool: A Guide for Rangers*, Nepal: Nepal–UK Community Forestry Project.

Harnmeijer, Joanne (1999) 'From Terms of Reference to Participatory Learning: Using an evaluation's creative space', *PLA Notes* 36, London: IIED.

Haylor G.S., A. Lawrence and E. Meusch (1997) *Identification of Technical, Social and Economic Constraints to the Rearing of Fish in Rice Fields in Lao PDR: Resource Management and Information Systems – A Situation Analysis*, Lao Rice–Fish Culture Project Report, Volume 3, University of Stirling.

Hiemstra, W., C. Reijntjes and E. van der Werf (eds) (1992) *Let Farmers Judge: Experiences in Assessing the Sustainability of Agriculture*, London: Intermediate Technology Publications.

Hinchcliffe, Fiona, John Thompson, Jules Pretty, Irene Guijt and Parmesh Shah (eds) (1999) *Fertile Ground: The Impacts of Participatory Watershed Development*, London: Intermediate Technology Publications.

Holland, Jeremy with James Blackburn (eds) (1998) *Whose Voice? Participatory Research and Policy Change*, London: Intermediate Technology Publications.

Holt-Giménez, Eric (1995) *The Campesino-a-campesino Movement: Farmer-led Agricultural Extension*, IIRR/ODI Workshop on Farmer-led Approaches to Agricultural Extension, Philippines, 17–22 July 1995.

Hope, Anne and Sally Timmel (1995) *Training for Transformation: A Handbook for Community Workers, Volumes 1–3*, Gweru, Zimbabwe: Mambo Press.

Horton, D. (1988) 'Disciplinary Roots and Branches of Evaluation: Some Lessons for Agricultural Research. Knowledge and Policy' in *The International Journal of Knowledge Transfer and Utilization*, Vol. 10, No. 4, pp. 31–36.

Horton, Doug, R. Mackay, S. Debela and M.M. Rahman (1997) *Assessing Organizational Performance and Institutional Impacts: The ISNAR Case*, Draft.

House, Ernest R. (1993) *Professional Evaluation: Social Impact and Political Consequences*, London: Sage Publications.

Howes, Mick (1992) 'Linking Paradigms and Practice: Key Issues in the Appraisal, Monitoring and Evaluation of British NGO Projects', *Journal of International Development*, Vol. 4, No. 4, pp. 375–96.

Humbert-Droz, Blaise (1992) *PIDOW Self-Evaluation: Main Features and Experiences*, Bangalore: Swiss Development Cooperation.

IDR and PRIA (1997) *Training Workshop on Monitoring Participation in World Bank Programmes, March 1997*, Institute for Development Research/Society for Participatory Research in Asia, mimeo.

IDS (1999) *Learning to Take Time and Go Slow: Mainstreaming Participation in Development and the Comprehensive Development Framework*, Report prepared for Operations Evaluation Department, World Bank (draft), Brighton: Institute of Development Studies.

IIED (1992) *New Horizons: The Social, Environmental and Economic Impact of Participatory Watershed Development*, Research Proposal, International Institute for Environment and Development, mimeo.

IIED (ed.) (1996) 'Participation, Policy and Institutionalization' *PLA Notes* 27, London: International Institute for Environment and Development.

IIED (ed.) (1998) 'Participatory Monitoring and Evaluation', *PLA Notes* 31, London: International Institute for Environment and Development.

IIED (ed.) (1998) 'Participation, Literacy and Empowerment', *PLA Notes* 32, London: International Institute for Environment and Development.

IIRR (1998) *Participatory Monitoring and Evaluation: Experiences and Lessons*, Workshop Proceedings, Cavite, Philippines: International Institute of Rural Reconstruction, Y.C. James Yen Center.

InterCooperation (1999) *Report of Workshop on Participatory Monitoring and Evaluation*, InterCooperation Kerala NGO Programme, 22–26 March.

ISEA (1998) *Social and Ethical Accounting, Auditing and Reporting: Concepts, Terminology and Glossary*, London: Institute of Social and Ethical Accountability.

Jackson, Edward T. (1995) *Participatory Impact Assessment for Poverty Alleviation: Opportunities for Communities and Development Agencies*, Paper presented at the Panel Session on Participatory Impact Assessment at the International Evaluation Conference, Vancouver, 1–5 Nov 1995.

Jackson, Edward T. and Yusuf Kassam (eds) (1998) *Knowledge Shared: Participatory Evaluation in Development Cooperation*, West Hartford: Kumarian Press.

Jenkins, R. and A.M. Goetz (1999) *Accounts and Accountability: Theoretical Implications of the Right-to-Information Movement in India*, Prepared for workshop 'Strengthening Participation in Local Governance', IDS, Brighton, 21–24 June 1999.

Johnson, Deb (no date) *Evaluation – A Participatory Relationship: Using PRA Tools and Techniques for Evaluation*, Discussion Paper, Oklahoma: World Neighbors.

Joshi A. and J.R. Witcombe (1996) 'Farmer Participatory Crop Improvement. II. Participatory Varietal Selection, A Case Study in India', *Experimental Agriculture*, Vol. 32, No. 4, pp. 461–77.

Kar, Kamal with S.N Datta, S. Goswami *et al.* (1997) *Participatory Impact Assessment of Calcutta Slum Improvement Project (February–May 1997)*, mimeo, New Delhi: Urban Poverty Office.

Kar, Kamal with S.N Datta, S. Goswami *et al.* (1997) *Participatory Impact Assessment. Calcutta Slum Improvement Project: Main Findings Report, Volume 1*, New Delhi: Calcutta Metropolitan Development Authority with the Urban Poverty Office and Department for International Development (DFID).

Karash, R. (1997) *Learning Organizations* in <tp//www.learning-org.com>.

Karna, A.L. (1997) *The Procedure Emerging in District Forest Offices for Bottom-up Planning*, NUKCFP Discussion Paper, Nepal: Nepal–UK Community Forestry Project.

Keane, Bernadette (1996) *Rural Appraisal Methods for Evaluating Alternative Agricultural Programmes: Utility for Stakeholders*, Manuscript of MAP programme working paper.

Korten, David (1980) 'Community Organization and Rural Development: A Learning Process Approach', *Public Administration Review*, September/October, pp. 480–511.

Korten, David (1988) 'From Bureaucratic to Strategic Organization' in D. Korten and F.F. and R.Y. Siy, Jr (eds) *Transforming a Bureaucracy: the experience of the Philippine National Irrigation Administration*, West Hartford: Kumarian Press.

Kottak, Conrad (1995) 'Cuando no se da Prioridad a la Gente: Algunas lecciones sociológicas de proyectos terminados', in Michael Cernea (ed.) *Primero la Gente: Variables Sociológicas en el Desarrollo Rural*, Mexico: Fondo de Cultura Económica.

Lawrence, Anna (1998a) 'Contours, Crops and Cattle: Participatory Soil Conservation in the Andean Foothills, Bolivia', *Agroforestry Forum*, Special Issue on Contour Hedgerows.

Lawrence, Anna (1998b) *Linking with Local Knowledge for Soil and Water Conservation in Bolivia*, Paper prepared for the Workshop on Participatory Natural Resource Management, Mansfield College, Oxford, 6–7 April 1998, AERDD Working Paper 98/4, University of Reading.

Lawrence, Anna, M. Eid and E. Sandoval (1997a) *Evolving Local Knowledge: Soil and Water Management in the Temperate Valleys of Santa Cruz*, AERDD Working Paper 97/9, University of Reading.

Lawrence, Anna with Miguel Eid and Osvaldo Montenegro (1997b) *Learning about Participation: Developing a Process for Soil and Water Conservation in Bolivia*, AERDD Working Paper 97/10, University of Reading.

Lee-Smith, Diana (1997) *Evaluation as a Tool for Institutional Strengthening*, Nairobi: Mazingira Institute.

Lightfoot, Clive, Mary Ann Bimbao, Peter Dalsgaard and R.S. Pullin (1993) 'Aquaculture and Sustainability through Integrated Resources Management', *Outlook on Agriculture* 22 (3), pp. 143–150.

Lincoln, Y. and E. Guba (1985) *Naturalistic Enquiry*, London and California: Sage Publications.

Lingayah, Sanjiv (1988) *Sustainable Development Indicators: Monitoring Change in the East Midlands*, Leicester: Environ and New Economics Foundation.

Lingayah, Sanjiv and A. MacGillivray (1999) *Working from Below. Techniques to Strengthen Local Governance in India*, London: New Economics Foundation.

Love, Arnold (1996) Knowledge for Empowerment, *Evaluation* 2: 3, pp. 349–61.

Lusthaus, Charles, G. Anderson and E. Murphy (1995) *Institutional Assessment: A Framework for Strengthening Organizational Capacity for IDRC's Research Partners*, Ottawa: IDRC.

Lusthaus, Charles, Marie-Hélène Adrien, Gary Anderson and Fred Carden (1999) *Enhancing Organisational Performance: A Toolbox for Self Assessment*, Ottawa: IDRC.

MacGillivray, A. and S. Zadek (1995) *Accounting for Change: Indicators for Sustainable Development* Vol. I, London: New Economics Foundation.

MacGillivray, A., C. Weston, and C. Unsworth (1998) *Communities Count! A Step-by-Step Guide to Community Sustainability Indicators*, London: New Economics Foundation.

Maharjan, M.R. (1997) *Self Monitoring and Assessment of Community Forestry using Picture and Symbols*, NUKCFP Discussion Paper, Nepal: Nepal–UK Community Forestry Project.

Manasan, R.G., E.T. Gonzalez and R.B. Gaffud (1999) *Towards Better Government: Developing Indicators of Good Governance for Local Government*, Manila,

Philippines: National Economic and Development Authority (NEDA) and United Nations Development Programme (UNDP).

Marsden, David and Peter Oakley (eds) (1990) *Evaluating Social Development Projects*, Development Guidelines No. 5, Oxford: Oxfam.

Marsden, David, Peter Oakley and Brian Pratt (1994) *Measuring the Process: Guidelines for Evaluating Social Development*, UK: INTRAC.

Marshall, G. (ed.) (1994) *The Concise Oxford Dictionary of Sociology*, Oxford: Oxford University Press.

Martínez, Luciano (1997) *Organizaciones de Segundo Grado, Capital Social y Desarrollo Sostenible*, Revista ICONOS, No. 2, Publicación de FLACSO-Ecuador.

Mayo, Ed (1996) *Social Auditing for Voluntary Organizations*, London: Volprof/New Economics Foundation.

McArthur Jr, Harold J. (1997) 'Participatory Monitoring and Evaluation: Passing Fad or the Logical Step in Research and Development Methodology?' in *Interfacing PM&E with the Research and Development Process: An Introduction'* in *Self-assessment: Participatory Dimensions of Project Monitoring and Evaluation*, Los Baños, Philippines: UPWARD.

Merrifield, Juliet, Alden Lancaster and Kristi Kirkham (1995) *Horizon's Participatory Evaluation Process*, Horizon Project Final Report, Maine: USA.

Minogue, Martin, C. Polidano and D. Hulme (eds) (1997) *Beyond the New Public Management: Changing Ideas and Practices in Governance*, Cheltenham: Edward Elgar.

Mitti, G., M. Drinkwater and S. Kalonge (1997) *Experimenting with Agricultural Extension in Zambia: CARE's Livingstone Food Security Project*, Agricultural Research and Extension Network Paper No. 77, London: Overseas Development Institute.

Mosse, David (1998) 'Process-oriented Approaches to Development Practice and Social Research' in D. Mosse, J. Farrington and A. Rew (eds) *Development as Process: Concepts and Methods for Working with Complexity*, London: Routledge/Overseas Development Institute.

MRDP (1995) *Village Evaluation of the Farm Level Forestry Project*, Vietnam Sweden Mountain Rural Development Programme, Vietnam: The Peoples Committee of Tuyen Quang Province and the Agriculture and Forest Department.

MRDP (1997) *Mountain Information Learning System: Province Level Training Document*, Vietnam Sweden Mountain Rural Development Programme, Vietnam: Programme Board Office.

Murphy, Josette (1993) 'Good Enough, Soon Enough: A User-Oriented Approach to Monitoring and Evaluation in Extension Agencies', *Rural Extension Bulletin* 1, April, pp. 4–8.

Nagel, Uwe Jens (1992) *Developing a Participatory Extension Approach: A Design for the Siavonga District, Zambia*, Berlin: Technical University, Center for Advanced Training in Agricultural Development.

Najam, Adil (1995) *Learning from the Literature on Policy Implementation: A Synthesis Perspective*, Laxenburg, Austria: IIASA (International Institute for Applied Systems Analysis).

Narayan-Parker, Deepa (1993) *Participatory Evaluation: Tools for Managing Change in Water and Sanitation*, World Bank Technical Paper No. 207, Washington, DC: World Bank.

NEF (1997) *Communities Count: Putting Local Indicators on the Map*, London: New Economics Foundation.

Noponen, Helzi (no date) *Participatory Monitoring and Evaluation – A Prototype Internal Learning System for Livelihood and Micro-Credit Programs*, Unpublished paper, Department of City and Regional Planning, University of North Carolina.

251

Norton, Andrew and T. Stephens (1995) *Participation in Poverty Assessments*, Environment Department Papers, Participation Series, Washington DC: Social Policy and Resettlement Division, World Bank.

NRI and University of Reading (1998) *A Methodological Framework for Combining Quantitative and Qualitative Survey Methods: Background Paper: Types of Combinations*, Report written for Department for International Development, Social Sciences Division, Natural Resources Institute, Chatham and Statistical Services Centre, University of Reading, Reading.

NUKCFP (1998) *NUKCFP: Some Concept Papers*, Project Report T/NUKCFP/18. Nepal: Nepal–UK Community Forestry Project.

Okali, C., J. Sumberg and J. Farrington (1994) *Farmer Participatory Research: Rhetoric and Reality*, London: IT/ODI.

Palestine Economic Pulse (1996/7), West Bank, Palestine: Palestine Economic Pulse.

PAMFORK (Participatory Methodologies Forum of Kenya) (1997) *Report of Workshop on Using Participatory Methodologies for Monitoring and Evaluation*, Nairobi, Kenya: South-South Sharing Forum.

Parachini, Larry with Andrew Mott (1997) *Strengthening Community Voices in Policy Reform: Community-based Monitoring, Learning and Action Strategies for an Era of Development and Change*, A special report for the Annie E. Casey Foundation (draft).

Pearce, John (1996) *Measuring Social Wealth: A Study of Social Audit Practice for Community and Co-operative Enterprises*, London: New Economics Foundation.

Peters, Tom (1992) *Liberation Management: Necessary Disorganization for the Nanosecond Nineties*, New York: Fawcett Columbine.

Petersen, P. (1995) *Diagnóstico Ambiental do Município de Remígio* (PB), (Unpublished report) Rio: AS-PTA.

Pfohl, Jacob (1986) *Participatory Evaluation. A User's Guide*, New York: Private Agencies Collaborating Together (PACT).

Pratt, B. and Boyden, J. (1985) *The Field Director's Handbook*, Oxford: Oxford University Press.

Pretty, Jules N., Irene Guijt, Ian Scoones, and John Thompson (1995) *A Trainer's Guide for Participatory Learning and Action*, London: IIED Sustainable Agriculture Programme.

Pretty, Jules; I. Guijt; J. Thompson and I. Scoones (1996) *Participatory Learning and Action. A Trainer's Guide*, London: IIED.

PRIA (1981) *Participatory Research and Evaluation: Experiments in Research as a Process of Liberation*, New Delhi: Society for Participatory Research in Asia.

PRIA (1995) *Participatory Evaluation: Issues and Concerns*, New Delhi: Society for Participatory Research in Asia.

Rahman, Muhammed Anisur (1990) 'Qualitative Dimensions of Social Development Evaluation', in David Marsden and Peter Oakley (eds) *Evaluating Social Development Projects*, Development Guidelines No. 5, Oxford: Oxfam.

Rai, R.K. (1998) 'Monitoring and Evaluating in the Nepal–UK Community Forestry Project', *PLA Notes* 31, pp. 37–43.

Rai, R.K. and C. Hamilton (1997) *A Report of a Workshop on FUG Self Monitoring and Evaluation at Chapgaire Tushepakha FUG, Bhojpur*, Field Report, NUKCFP, Nepal: Nepal–UK Community Forestry Project.

Rajakutty, S. (1991) 'People's Participation in Monitoring and Evaluation of Rural Development Programs: Concepts and Approaches', *Journal of Rural Development* (India) Vol. 10, No. 1, pp. 35–53.

Ramón, Galo and V.H. Torres (1995) *Informe de la Aplicación del Marco de Desarrollo de Base en el Ecuador*, Quito: COMUNIDEC.

Rasaily, R. and R. Shrestha (1997) *Awareness Raising Literacy Programme of Community Forestry for FUG Women at Rajarani Range Post, Dhankuta*, NUKCFP Discussion Paper, Nepal: Nepal–UK Community Forestry Project.

Raynard, Peter (1998) 'Coming Together. A Review of Contemporary Approaches to Social Accounting, Auditing and Reporting in Non-profit Organisations', *Journal of Business Ethics* Vol. 17, No. 13, pp. 1471–79.

Reckers, Ute (1996) *Participatory Project Evaluation: Allowing Local People to Have their Say. An NGO Guide for Community Driven Project Evaluation*, Environmental Liaison Centre International (ELCI) and United Nations Environment Programme (UNEP).

Ricafort, R.E. (1996) *People, Realities and Negotiations: Some Thoughts on Participatory Monitoring and Evaluation, Development Co-operation and Funding Organizations*, Unpublished report to the Institute of Development Studies, UK.

Ritchey-Vance, Marion (1998) 'Widening the Lens on Impact Assessment: The Inter-American Foundation and its Grassroots Development Framework – The Cone', in J. Blauert and S. Zadek (eds) *Mediating Sustainability: Growing Policy from the Grassroots*, West Hartford: Kumarian Press.

Robb, Caroline (1999) *Can the Poor Influence Policy? Participatory Poverty Assessments in the Developing World*, Washington DC: IBRD.

Roche, Chris (1993) 'Mali: "Auto-evaluation": An NGO Experience with Community-based Evaluation', in *Rural Extension Bulletin*, 1 April, pp. 27–33.

Roche, Chris (forthcoming) *Impact Assessment and Development Agencies: Learning How to Value Change*, Oxford: Oxfam.

Rodenburg, E. (1995). 'Monitoring for Sustainability', in T.C. Tryzna with J.K. Osborn (eds) *A Sustainable World: Defining and Measuring Sustainable Development*, Sacramento: International Centre for the Environment and Public Policy.

Rosen, Michael (1991) 'Coming to Terms with the Field: Understanding and Doing Organizational Ethnography', *Journal of Management Studies*, No. 28, Vol. 1, pp. 1–23.

Rubin, Frances (1995) *A Basic Guide to Evaluation for Development Workers*, Oxford: Oxfam.

Rudqvist, Anders and Prudence Woodford-Berger (1996) *Evaluation and Participation: Some Lessons*, A report prepared for the DAC Expert Group on Aid Evaluation, Dept. for Evaluation and Internal Audit, Swedish International Development Cooperation Agency.

Rugh, Jim (1992) *Self-Evaluation: Ideas for Participatory Evaluation of Rural Community Development Projects*, Oklahoma City: World Neighbors.

Rugh, Jim (1994) *Can Participatory Evaluation Meet the Needs of all Stakeholders? A Case Study: Evaluating the World Neighbors West Africa Program*, Paper to the American Evaluation Association Conference, Boston, 2–5 Nov 1994, Oklahoma: World Neighbors.

Rugh, Jim (1995) *Can Participatory Evaluation Meet the Needs of All Stakeholders? A Case Study: Evaluating the World Neighbors West Africa Program*, Discussion Paper, Oklahoma City: World Neighbors.

Rutherford, F. (1998) *McDowell County Action Network, Citizen Learning Initiative* (mimeo).

Rutherford, F. and H. Lewis (1997) *McDowell County, West Virginia Enterprise Community: A Report on the Learning Team's Assessment of EC Progress*, Knoxville: Community Partnership Centre, University of Tennessee.

Salewicz, Stephen and Archana Dwivedi (1996) *Project Leader Tracer Study*, Ottawa: IDRC.

Say, Rosalie and Lisa Singh (1997) *Are we on Track? A Case Study of CIRDAP's Institutional Self-Assessment* (draft), Dhaka: Centre on Integrated Rural Development for Asia and the Pacific.

Scott-Villiers, Patta (1997) *Consultative Skills for Participatory Monitoring and Evaluation, Course Programme*, Course Programme, Project Officer and Counterpart Workshop Part 1.

Scriven, Michael (1991) *Evaluation Thesaurus*, Newbury Park, CA: Sage Publications.

Scriven, Michael (1993) *Hard-won Lessons in Program Evaluation*, New Directions for Evaluation 58, San Francisco: Jossey-Bass.

Selener, Daniel (1997) *Participatory Action Research and Social Change*, Ithaca: Cornell University Press.

Selener, Daniel, with Christopher Purdy and Gabriela Zapata (no date) *Documenting, Evaluating, and Learning from our Development Projects: A Participatory Systematization Workbook*, Ecuador: IIRR.

Senge, Peter (1990) *The Fifth Discipline: The Art and Practice of the Learning Organisation*, London: Century.

Shah, Anwar (1998) 'Fostering Fiscally Responsive and Accountable Governance: Lessons from Decentralization' in R. Picciotto and E. Wiesner (eds) *Evaluation & Development. The Institutional Dimension*, New Brunswick: Transaction Publishers.

Shah, Meera K. (1998), 'Gendered Perceptions of Well-Being and Social Change in Darko, Ghana' and ' "Salt and Spices": Addressing Gender Issues in Participatory Programme Implementation in AKRSP, India' in I. Guijt and M. K. Shah (eds), *The Myth of Community: Gender Issues in Participatory Development*, London: Intermediate Technology Publications.

Shah, Parmesh, Girish Hardwaj and Ranjit Ambastha (1993) 'Gujarat, India: Participatory Monitoring. How Farmers, Extension Volunteers, and NGO Staff Work Together in Village-level Soil and Water Conservation Programmes', *Rural Extension Bulletin* 1, April, pp. 34–7.

Slim, Hugo and Paul Thompson (1993) *Listening for a Change. Oral Testimony and Development*, London: Panos Publications Ltd.

Sommer, Martin (1993) *Whose Values Matter? Experiences and Lessons from a Self-Evaluation in PIDOW Project, Karnataka, India, May–November, 1991*, Swiss Development Cooperation, Bangalore Field Office.

Soulama, S. (1997) *Auto-évaluation Institutionelle: Une Nouvelle Approche pour le Développement de la Capacité Organisationelle: Le Cas du Centre d'Études, de Documentation, de Recherches Économiques et Sociales (CEDRES) de l'Université de Ouagadougou (Burkina Faso)* (draft), Ouagadougou: Centre d'Études, de Documentation, de Recherches Économiques et Sociales de l'Université de Ouagadougou.

Srinivasan, Viji (1981) 'The Methodology of Participatory Evaluation', in W. Fernandes and R. Tandon (eds) *Participatory Research and Evaluation: Experiments in Research as a Process of Liberation*, New Delhi: Indian Social Institute.

Stephens, Alexander (1990) *Participatory Monitoring and Evaluation: A Handbook for Training Field Workers*, Bangkok: Regional Office for Asia and the Pacific (RAPA), FAO.

Swift, J (1989) 'Why are Rural People Vulnerable to Famine?', *IDS Bulletin*, Vol. 20, No. 2, pp. 8–15, Brighton: IDS.

Tallafer, Lily L. and P.E. Sajise (1997) *Self-direction Comes with Self-knowledge: SEARCA's Self-assessment Case Study*, (draft).

Tandon, Rajesh (1981) 'Participatory Evaluation and Research: Main Concepts and Issues', in W. Fernandes and R. Tandon (eds) *Participatory Research and Evaluation: Experiments in Research as a Process of Liberation*, New Delhi: Indian Social Institute.

Tandon, Rajesh and A. Cordeiro (1998) *Participation of Primary Stakeholders in World Bank's Project and Policy Work: Emerging Lessons*, Contribution to the International Conference on 'Mainstreaming and Up-Scaling of Primary Stakeholder Participation – Lessons Learned and Ways Forward', Washington DC, 19–20 Nov 1998.

254

Thompson, John (1995) 'Participatory Approaches in Government Bureaucracies: Facilitating the Process of Institutional Change', *World Development* Vol. 23, No. 9, pp. 1521–54.

Thompson, John and Jules N. Pretty (1995) *Sustainable Indicators and Soil Conservation: A Participatory Impact Study and Self-evaluation of the Catchment Approach of the Ministry of Agriculture, Kenya*, Paper to be submitted to the *Journal of Soil and Water Conservation*.

Topsoe-Jensen, Bente (1989) *Popular Participation, Monitoring and Evaluation in Integrated Rural Development. The Case of PDRI in Guinea-Bissau: Popular Participation Programme*, Working Paper No. 6, Development Studies Unit, Department of Social Anthropology, University of Stockholm.

UNDP (1990) *Workshop on Goals and Indicators for Monitoring and Evaluation for Water and Sanitation*, New York: UNDP–World Bank Water and Sanitation Programme.

UNDP (1997) *Who Are the Question-Makers? A Participatory Evaluation Handbook*, New York: Office of Evaluation and Strategic Planning, UNDP.

UNSCO (1996) *Economic and Social Conditions in the West Bank and Gaza Strip: Quarterly Report*, UNSCO Quarterly Report, Autumn 1996, Jerusalem: United Nations Special Co-ordinator in the Occupied Territories.

Uphoff, Norman (1988) Participatory Evaluation of Farmer Organizations' Capacity for Development Tasks, in *Agricultural Administration and Extension* 30, pp. 43–64.

Uphoff, Norman (1989) *A Field Methodology for Participatory Self-Evaluation of PPP Group and Inter-Group Association Performance*, Prepared for the People's Participation Programme of the UN Food and Agriculture Organization, Ithaca: Cornell University.

Uphoff, Norman (1991) 'A Field Methodology for Participatory Self-Evaluation', *Community Development Journal* Vol. 26, No. 4, pp. 271–85.

Uphoff, Norman (1992) *Participatory Evaluation of Rural Development Projects*, Monitoring and Evaluation Division, Report No. 0385, Rome: IFAD.

UPWARD (1997) 'Interfacing PM&E with the Research and Development Process: An Introduction', in *Self-assessment: Participatory Dimensions of Project Monitoring and Evaluation*, Los Baños, Philippines: UPWARD.

USDA, US Department of Agriculture (1994) *Building Communities Together: Rural Guidebook for Strategic Planning*, Washington, DC: USDA.

Uquillas, Jorge (1993) 'Research and Extension Practice and Rural People's Agroforestry Knowledge in Ecuadorian Amazonia', in T. Caldas *et al.* (eds) *Rural People's Knowledge, Agricultural Research and Extension Practice*, Latin America Papers, IIED Research Series Vol. 1, No. 4, pp. 69–88.

Wadsworth, Yoland (1991) *Everyday Evaluation on the Run*, Melbourne: Action Research Issues Association.

Walters, Hettie, Annet Hermans, Margreet van der Hel (1995) *Monitoring and Evaluation from a Gender Perspective: A Guideline*, The Hague: SNV.

Wang, Caroline, Yuan Yan Ling, and Fend Ming Ling (1996) 'Photovoice as a Tool for Participatory Evaluation: The Community's View of Process and Impact', in *Journal of Contemporary Health* 4, pp. 47–9.

Webare, Benon (1997) 'A bird in the hand is worth two in the bush. A report of the events of Phase 4 of the PRAP processes in Namagoma, Bweyo, Kizimiza and Lyakibirizi communities in Masaka and Sembabule Districts', Kampala, Redd Barna Uganda.

Webster's Ninth New Collegiate Dictionary (1983) Springfield, MA: Merriam-Webster Inc.

Welbourn, Alice (1993) *Notes for Christian Aid Staff on PRA Techniques of Potential Use for the JFS Burkina Faso Evaluation Exercise, June*, mimeo.

255

Wheeler, David and Maria Sillanpää (1997) *The Stakeholder Corporation: A Blueprint for Maximising Stakeholder Value*, London: Pitman Publishing.

Whitmore, Elizabeth (ed.) (1998) *Understanding and Practising Participatory Evaluation*, New Directions for Evaluation 80, San Francisco: Jossey Bass Publishers.

Wigboldus, Seerp, Maaike A. Wigboldus, Phauda S. Gurung, Prahlad B. Bhandari, Chandra K. Aryal, and Laxmi D. Khadka (1995) *Participatory Evaluation in Practice: NRMP's Experience in Community Capacity Development in Nepal*, Kathmandu: Nepal Resource Management Project (NRMP) and United Mission to Nepal (UMN).

Woodhill, Jim and Lisa Robins (1998) *Participatory Evaluation for Landcare and Catchment Groups: A Guide for Facilitators*, Australia: Greening Australia.

WWF/NEF (1997) *Signals of Success: A User's Guide to Indicators*, Godalming/London: World Wildlife Fund-UK/New Economics Foundation.

Zadek, Simon and R. Evans (1993) *Auditing the Market. A Practical Approach to Social Auditing*, London: New Economics Foundation.

Zadek, Simon and P. Raynard (1994) *Accounting for Change: The Practice of Social Auditing*, Working Paper, London: New Economics Foundation.

Zadek, Simon; P. Pruzan and R. Evans (1997) *Building Corporate Accountability: Emerging Practices in Social and Ethical Accounting, Auditing and Reporting*. London: Earthscan Publications.

Zaffaroni, Cecilia (1997) *El Marco de Desarrollo de Base: La Construcción de un Sistema Participativo para Analizar Resultados de Proyectos Sociales*, Montevideo: TRILCE/Fundación Interamericana/SADES.

Notes

Chapter 1

1. This chapter draws mainly from the literature review by Estrella and Gaventa (1998) produced in preparation for the Philippines Workshop on PM&E held in November 1997. Other literature reviews consulted included those from Latin America, Asia and Africa (see Alcocer *et al.*, 1997; Armonia and Campilan, 1997; PAMFORK, 1997). Special thanks to Deb Johnson and Irene Guijt for their extensive comments and support in the final writing of this chapter.
2. DFID was formerly the Overseas Development Agency or ODA.
3. Indicators are 'signals' that are used for simplifying, measuring and communicating important information (New Economics Foundation, 1997), and they reflect changes that occur as a result of a particular intervention. There are different types – namely *input, process, output* and *outcome* (or *impact*) indicators. Input indicators 'concern the resources (or activities) devoted to the project'. Process indicators 'monitor achievement during implementation and measure how resources are delivered'. Output indicators 'measure intermediate results, for example at a point when donor involvement in the project is close to complete'. Outcome indicators measure 'longer-term results of the project and after donor involvement is complete' (Walters *et al.*, 1995). In other words, 'outcomes' are the expected (but also unexpected) changes or impacts resulting from a particular intervention. 'Criteria' provide the set of broad guidelines for the selection of 'indicators'. Indicators are usually selected according to defined criteria, which reflect the priorities and objectives of the individuals, groups or organization that selects indicators.
4. These are described in a number of manuals and guidebooks on PM&E (see Aubel, 1993; Davis-Case and Grove, 1990; Feuerstein, 1986; Gosling and Edwards, 1995; GTZ, 1996; Hope and Timmel, 1995; Narayan-Parker, 1993; Pfohl, 1986; Pretty *et al.*, 1995; Rugh, 1995; Selener, n.d.; Stephens, 1990; Wadsworth, 1991; Walters *et al.*, 1995; Woodhill and Robins, 1998). There is also a forthcoming book on PM&E tools to be published by IIRR – as another output from the Philippines Workshop.
5. 'Methods' should be distinguished from 'methodologies' and 'approaches' – although these terms are sometimes used interchangeably. Methods are the specific tools and techniques used for data collection and information exchange – in other words, the 'how-to-do-its'. Methodologies define a particular approach. They orient the user by providing a framework for selecting the means to obtain, analyse, order and exchange information about a particular issue. They define what can be known or shared, as well as how that should be represented, and by and for whom this is done.
6. Some experiences in PM&E training include workshops conducted by several NGOs, namely ACORD, ActionAid, Oxfam, and Center of Concern (CONCERN, 1996). Recent experiences in training for PM&E have been conducted in Vietnam (see Scott-Villiers, 1997 for the training manual used). In 1998, IIRR offered an international course on PM&E.
7. Although these terms are often used interchangeably, 'institutions' shall be distinguished from 'organizations'. Drawing from Uphoff, 'An institution is a complex of norms and behaviours that persists over time by serving some socially valued purpose, while an organization is a structure of recognized and

accepted roles.' (1992, Fn1) Essentially, an institution can also be an organization, but an organization rarely is an institution. For instance, a traditional authority, such as an elders' council is an institution, but so is marriage. A school is an organization, but an education system is an institution. The World Bank is an organization, but has also become an institution for the norms and values it represents as much as for the influence it exercises.

Chapter 2

1. Many thanks to the entire project team for their support and time in developing the above processes and especially to Dr Hugh Gibbon for his guidance and his editorial input to this chapter. We are also indebted to the FUGs who have, more than anyone, steered the direction of the NUKCFP SM&E process.
2. This post-formation support typically includes: training on forest management, nurseries, record keeping/information management and conflict resolution.
3. These potential partners in the community development process include district and village development committees, the National Federation of Forest User Groups (FECOFUN), NGOs and international non-governmental organizations.
4. A bottom-up planning process guides the DFO's annual work programme: representatives of each FUG initially put forward the support they need at Range Post level meetings (see Footnote 9), which are then taken up at the district level through discussions with the DFO field staff. Finally, an area planning meeting at the project area level takes place to co-ordinate, budget and consider needs for support identified at district levels. For more details see Karna (1997).
5. We define 'change' throughout the chapter as 'institutional change', which refers to all key aspects of community forestry. These include institutional development, forest management, improvement in group management, community development, etc., in order to better meet the needs of local forest users.
6. Indicators are the means by which either improvement towards or achievement of a goal can be assessed.
7. 'Interest groups' are defined here as the various parties with differing needs and interests *within* a FUG.
8. Participatory learning and appraisal is both an approach and a set of tools to express concepts visually and to aid analysis.
9. A Range Post is the field administration unit of the DFO.
10. For instance, some FUGs may have four different income-generating activities (IGAs), while another may have none but have started a number of community-development activities. The current Health Check does not recognize these differences in scope or focus between the various FUGs. Nor can the Health Check show trends in individual activities of FUGs over time.
11. REFLECT stands for regenerated Freirean literacy through empowering community techniques, which combines PRA methods and Freirean Literacy principles. It was developed by Action Aid (see Archer, 1995).
12. Animators are usually members of the community and play an active role as community facilitators and motivators.
13. For instance, the Decision Making in SM&E method demonstrated the effectiveness of users developing their own pictorial codes of indicators, whilst during the Information Management Workshop, the strong linkages between goal formation, action planning, and monitoring and evaluation were seen as important.
14. A critical difference between the conventional M&E methods and the learning-orientated SM&E is that in the former approach the project and management level staff set performance criteria, whilst in the latter, the community forest institutions themselves determine their own goals and indicators of success.

Chapter 3

1. An earlier, shorter version of this chapter was presented with Eduardo Quintanar at the Biannual Oaxaca Studies Conference, Welte Institute-National Institute of Anthropology and History, August 1996, Oaxaca, and was published as an article in *Appropriate Technology*, 1997.

   An earlier version of this article in Spanish was published in: Blauert J. & S. Zadek (eds) *Mediación pasa la sustenabilidad: construyendo políticas desde las bases*, Plaza y Valdes/British Council/IDS/CIESAS, Mexico City pp. 147–172.

   A longer version of this same chapter was presented by Jutta Blauert both to the World Wide Fund (WWF) workshop on Appraisal, Monitoring and Evaluation Methodologies for ICDP in June 1997, Oaxaca, Mexico, and to the Second Latin American Conference on Evaluation Approaches for Rural Poverty Alleviation Projects, sponsored by PREVAL, Costa Rica, in November 1998. This chapter also draws on lessons summarized half-way through the fieldwork by Keane (1996).

2. The research and training work in the Mixteca was funded in part by WN, Central America and Oklahoma; and IFAD, Rome, as well as by a grant from the British Council Exchange Studentships for one collaborating researcher. The authors wish to thank these institutions and, above all, the staff of CETAMEX – collectively – for their collaboration and interest. This work owes most, however, to the hospitality and open minds of many of the villagers and the CETAMEX extensionists who participated in workshops and fieldwork.

   The research reported here was undertaken – as outside collaborators – by Jutta Blauert and the Methodologies for Participatory Self-Evaluation or 'MAP' team from 1995 onwards: Eduardo Quintanar in 1996, and Bernadette Keane in 1995, who took much of the brunt and pleasures of the first few months of work; and Miriam Watson, who collaborated for some months in 1996. Heidi Asjbornson is continuing to work with one of the NGOs in adaptations of M&E approaches in the forestry programme. The MAP work in early 1995 was a core part of a wider inter-institutional research effort with the collaboration of colleagues in other regions of Mexico from which it benefited, namely Lydia Richardson, Sabine Gündel, Simon Anderson and Eckart Boege. The fieldwork and programme design by Blauert was influenced strongly by the evolving parallel study group 'Mediating Sustainability' in London, as well as by the work of colleagues at the IIED (especially the New Horizons programme) and, centrally, the New Economics Foundation (NEF) social audit and indicator teams, Simon Zadek, Peter Raynard and Alex MacGillivray. Frequent, but still too rare, conversations with World Neighbors staff – Wilmer Dagen, Jethro Pettit and Deb Johnson – enlightened and encouraged the work along the way. A draft of this paper has been commented on by Ann Waters-Bayer, Peter Raynard and Osvaldo Feinstein, as well as by the review committee of the steering group that led the process of the PM&E workshop and subsequent publication. To all of them, particularly Marisol Estrella, sincere thanks.

3. To respect space restrictions in this chapter, we do not include initial work with Maderas del Pueblo del Sureste (MPS) that focuses more on social audit work than on indicator development, and which is currently awaiting funding to proceed further.

4. CETAMEX's group in this region is, as of 1998, a separate NGO, called CEDICAM.

5. Other participatory learning tools were also incorporated, including tools used for visioning and strategic planning.

6. Criteria or indicators that are negative are turned into positive statements to allow one to measure achievement against them; otherwise, any scoring is contradictory.

7. Farmer-to-farmer extension in resource-poor areas can take anything up to 20 years to show the scale of impact that common evaluation statistics consider of relevance!

Chapter 4

1. 'Participatory improvement of soil and water conservation in hillside-farming systems, Bolivia' is funded by DFID (UK) through the NRSP, Hillsides Production System, project R6638. 'Addressing technical, social and economic constraints to rice–fish culture in Laos, emphasizing women's involvement' is also funded by DFID through the Aquaculture Programme, project R6380CB. Carlos Barahona is working with project R7033, 'Methodological framework integrating qualitative and quantitative approaches for socio-economic survey work', funded by DFID NRSP Socio-Economic Methods. The views expressed here are those of the authors. We are grateful for feedback on the process through discussions with colleagues in CIAT and LFS.
2. A farming system constitutes all the productive and service components of the farm as managed by the farming household, and how these components interrelate.
3. Lawrence et al. (1997a); Lawrence (1998a, 1998b).
4. Haylor et al. (1997).
5. Other evaluation methods include: process documentation (of which this chapter itself is one output) and sponsoring workshops for sharing experience with other institutions. These experiences are ongoing and are described elsewhere (Lawrence et al., 1997b; Haylor et al., 1997).
6. Systems diagramming is a PRA tool that has been applied elsewhere to describe farming systems (Lightfoot et al., 1993).
7. Rice yields may have also increased because Mrs Nouna started adding fertilizer at the same time as she started fish culture.
8. It is generally difficult conceptually for farmers to set baseline values for fish and rice production or labour. When farmers do provide baseline values, our experience from other projects suggests that they tend to give them all the same value (such as 0 in a control plot). It would then be very problematic to ask a farmer to represent all of these factors with piles of stones *before* trials are conducted. It is much more straightforward to ask about impact after the trials; to represent change with 'before' and 'after' scores.
9. However, women may have greater difficulty developing their own forms, as they are less literate than most men in this part of Bolivia. Hence, as more women participate in the project, the use of matrices for easy recording of information will be more appropriate.
10. We are now in the second year of the project.
11. Ranks only represent the relative position of each criterion with respect to the set of criteria under consideration, i.e. which one comes first, second, etc. On the other hand, scores provide a measurement of how important each criterion is with respect to a continuous scale of priority (implicitly) agreed by the farmers and researchers during their discussions. Based on the scores, it is possible for farmers or researchers to derive ranks.

Chapter 5

1. The participatory monitoring work on which this chapter is based was funded by DFID (UK) through the Socio-Economic Methodologies component of the Natural Resources Systems Programme (grant R6547). Projeto Paraíba is funded by: ICCO (Interchurch Organisation for Development Co-operation –

Netherlands); EC (Commission of the European Union); MLAL (Movimento Laici per America Latina – Italy) with MAE (Ministero degli Affari Esteri – Italy); Kellogg's Foundation (USA); and the Biodiversity project with CIC (Centro Internazionale Crocevia – Italy). The writing of this chapter was also supported through a Visiting Fellowship at the Department of Forestry, Australian National University, Canberra.

2. AS-PTA staff. We would also like to acknowledge contributions by Maria Paula C. de Almeida, José C. da Rocha, Marilene Nascimento Melo (AS-PTA staff) and leaders of the Sindicatos of Solânea and Remígio.

3. Assessoria e Servicos a Projetos em Agricultura Alternativa with headquarters in Rio de Janeiro, and field offices in Pernambuco (Recife), *Paraíba* (Esperança) and *Paraná* (União da Vitória) States. Since the mid 1980s, this NGO has been working with agroecology, family agriculture and sustainable development. Its activities focus around field research and the extension of appropriate technology for small-scale producers, networking, and advocacy.

4. Centro de Tecnologias Alternativas – Zona da Mata is a local NGO which works along similar lines to AS-PTA but in the Brazilian state of Minas Gerais.

5. This means gathering or collecting in areas with natural vegetation, for construction and fuelwood, fodder, and fruit.

6. *Animadores* are union members who dedicate an important part of their time to sustainable agriculture activities. They organize meetings and learning trips, visit experimenting farmers, train seed bank members, etc. They receive a small salary from the STR (see Footnote 7) for this – with the help of Projeto Paraíba funds.

7. STR: Sindicato de Trabalhadores Rurais, or Rural Worker's Union, are independent membership organizations that operate at municipal level and are federated at state and national levels. Members are usually poorer farmers and issues tackled are often highly political and related to farmers' rights.

8. EMATER: Empresa de Assistência Técnica e Extensão Rural/Paraíba.

9. Irene Guijt has been the facilitator throughout.

10. This happened through a process of eliminating duplicate cards and identifying how the different objectives from the three groups were linked.

11. Possible methods are (from Guijt and Sidersky, 1998): bio-physical measurements, forms*, diaries, photographs (or video), maps*, transects, well-being or social mapping*, impact flow diagrams*, systems diagrams, matrix scoring, relative scales and ladders*, ranking and pocket charts*, calendars, daily routines, institutional diagrams, network diagrams, dreams realized, critical event analysis, case studies, participatory theatre. (Those with an * were discussed at the workshop.)

12. Sometimes when a farmer has no seed at sowing time, he or she agrees to share half the harvest with the seed provider, regardless of other costs (land, labour, etc.).

13. A kind of approximate contour planting, based on visual assessments of contours.

14. For example, in one of the two communities, farmer adoption of contour ploughing was partly a result of dissemination efforts that had inadvertently triggered the unplanned, quick uptake of animal traction by farmers. A local leader, who was a keen experimenter and active disseminator, had taken the initiative to use his own animals in demonstration trials that were part of the contour planting training. As he knew that the animals were unable to plough up and down steep hills, he expected it would reinforce the message to farmers to plant along the contour lines. He also knew that farmers in that area faced a labour shortage, thus making animal traction more appealing. Thus, once farmers learned about the possibility of hiring the services of other farmers with

261

draught animals, the contour planting message was 'adopted' on a wide scale as part of an overall change in land preparation.
15. Only one of the two communities involved in these discussions had been monitored the year before with participatory mapping.
16. Traditionally, STRs focus their efforts on the legal rights of small holders or landless farmers, not on more practical aspects of rural livelihoods such as farming techniques, co-operative action, marketing and buying, etc.
17. Even if we have not yet managed to get direct involvement of funding agencies in discussing what information needs they have and how to incorporate that into our monitoring process.

Chapter 6

1. The *barangay* is the smallest unit of governance in the Philippines.
2. Experiences from the second year (1997) and the third year (1998) of the impact evaluation are still being synthesised and written up. The final impact evaluation report is forthcoming.
3. Two leader-researchers were assigned per *barangay* visited.
4. We hope to publish the entire output of the evaluation research by the end of 1998. The findings will also be published in popular form by 1999 and will involve leader-researchers in the writing process.

Chapter 7

1. The first, shorter, version of this chapter was translated from the Colombian Spanish by staff at PREVAL, Costa Rica, whom the author wishes to thank. Other material was translated by the editorial team.
2. Various territorial entities exist within Colombia: *la vereda, el cabildo, el municipio, la zona* or *provincia*. The *vereda* is the smallest local unit, a group of which makes up a *cabildo* or a *municipio*. In some cases, a *cabildo* may equally be considered a *municipio* or a municipality; in other cases, a *municipio* consists of several *cabildos*. A *zona* ('zone') or *provincia* ('province') is made up of a group of *cabildos* or *municipios*.
3. Presently, the index of unsatisfied basic needs remains high, with average life expectancy at only 40 years old.
4. The development plans are a means through which national resources and functions are allocated to local authorities (municipalities and *cabildos*) under the national decentralization law. In Colombia, 20 per cent of tax revenue is returned to local authorities in this way.
5. Valuable support in helping communities use the GDF has been provided by Gloria Vela from the Inter-American Corporation for Development and Social Responsibility based in Quito, Ecuador.

Chapter 8

1. The GDF or the 'cone' is a system for reporting results of social projects (and is described in detail in Chapter 3). It prioritizes beneficiary participation in constructing and implementing the M&E system as the basis for developing their own self-evaluation mechanisms, and can thus be used in a participatory fashion well beyond the actual needs of donor-reporting requirements. It also promotes innovations that seek to adapt it to specific contexts in different countries (see Zaffaroni, 1997; see also Chapters 3 and 7 in this volume).
2. Administrative divisions in rural Ecuador are as follows: province (*provincia*), municipality (*cantón*), parish (*parroquia*), borough (*barrio*), parish association (*junta parroquial*).

3. 'Concertation', or *concertación*, is a word that is much used in Latin America, expressing a process and a meeting 'space' – not always formalized – for different actors in the policy or development arena sharing their views, negotiating actions and resources, with the aim of reaching agreement and of leading to collaborative action. This process, and these 'spaces' do not necessarily imply reaching a consensus, however.
4. This is an Ecuadorian network composed of NGOs, municipalities and grassroots organizations committed to local development. It shares methodologies, jointly analyses and systematizes their experiences, engages in debates and coordinates projects.
5. The documentation concerning experiences contributes to the academic curriculum of the School for Management and Local Development of the Universidad Politécnica Salesiana, which offers a degree course with an alternative programme requiring only part-time attendance. It is intended for local development agents who desire to professionalize their activity.

Chapter 9

1. Thanks to Helen Lewis and the members of the McDowell County Learning Team members who helped to write the original report on which this chapter is based.
2. For further information on the national dimensions of this project, see Gaventa, Creed and Morrissey (1998). This chapter focuses on the local experience in McDowell County.
3. In total there were four broad goals but the team decided initially not to assess the fourth, 'Sustainable Community Development', because the EC programme had just begun and no immediate development changes could be measured at that time. As enough work has now been done to begin to show measurable impacts, the team intends to evaluate this goal during their second round of research scheduled for March 1999.
4. This raised questions such as: 'Were organisations and citizens informed on the progress of McCAN activities? Did McCAN clearly communicate with the projects it funded, and with the public? Did EC-supported projects begin to communicate with each other?'
5. For instance: Did McCAN encourage projects to develop innovative and creative solutions to problems? Did McCAN formally collaborate with a diverse group of organizations and projects? Were lasting alliances developed from these collaborations?

Chapter 10

1. The term 'PPM&E' is used throughout the chapter to mean 'Participatory Planning, Monitoring & Evaluation'.
2. The 'Green Line' is the Armistice Line drawn in 1949 between the areas under control of Arab and Jewish forces after the 1948 War.
3. Despite its limitations, we use the term 'community' to refer to the different groups of people that PARC works with.

Chapter 11

1. Other training included group management, financial management and record keeping, amongst others.
2. Interviews were carried out by trained VMC members.

3. These terms have been translated from the various local languages spoken by participants.
4. However, a field visit in March 1997 revealed that in at least two of the pilot villages, record books containing documented household information were considered village property and were used as a village registry.

Chapter 12

1. Additional refinements were made by an external M&E expert based in Thailand.
2. M&E findings revealed that people required further training in business practice and marketing. It was also observed that the four-year loan periods and the soft terms of repayment did not encourage financial discipline.
3. Thanks to Robin Mearns, from the Rural Development and Natural Resources Sector Unit at the World Bank, for this new information.

Chapter 13

1. Presented at the Participatory Monitoring and Evaluation Workshop, IIRR, Manila, November 1997. Portions of this chapter were also presented at the annual meeting of the Quebec Evaluation Society, November 1997.
2. Senior Programme Officer, IDRC (Canada). Thanks are due to Terry Smutylo and Cerstin Sander, Evaluation Unit, IDRC and Charles Lusthaus and Marie-Hélène Adrien, Universalia Management Group, for their input and collaboration and to Karen McAllister, IDRC, for presenting the chapter as a paper at the IIRR workshop in Manila, November 1997. The views expressed are those of the author and do not necessarily reflect those of the Centre.
3. In the development of this framework we have used the words 'institution' and 'organization' interchangeably; we have not attempted to differentiate the two. Webster's Ninth New Collegiate Dictionary defines an institution as, 'A significant practice (viz. a legal system) and as an established organization'.
4. The cases will be published by IDRC and can be obtained through the Evaluation Unit.
5. 'Readiness' refers to the clarification of the evaluation's primary purpose and the identification of the main actors to be involved in the process, through an examination of factors such as culture, leadership, resources, vision, strategy, and systems.
6. The case examples presented in the following sections are taken from, Charles Lusthaus et al., Enhancing organizational performance, (in press ms p. 15).

Chapter 15

1. Although it was considered impractical to include all groups, each group should be given the option to get involved.
2. This is based on Woodhill and Robins (1998); Guijt (1998); Community Partnership Center (1998); NEF (1997); IIRR (1998).

Chapter 16

1. Many thanks to Mallika Samanarayake and Catherine Blishen for reviewing and commenting on this chapter.

Chapter 17

1. Scaling-up, or upscaling [of participation] we generally define as 'an expansion which has a cumulative impact' (Blackburn with Holland, 1998:1). More specifically, it refers to (i) an increase in the number of participants or places in which participation occurs (the quantity dimension) and to (ii) 'scaling out . . . i.e. the expansion of participation from one activity, such as appraisal, to the involvement of people throughout the whole development process in a way that increases their empowerment' (Gaventa, 1998: 155). The challenge of effective scaling-up is to increase numbers without undermining quality. For a broader literature summary see IDS (1999).
2. See also Gaventa, Creed and Morrissey (1998).
3. Governance has been described by some authors as 'both a broad reform strategy, and a particular set of initiatives to strengthen the institutions of civil society with the objective of making government more accountable, more open and transparent, and more democratic.' (Minogue *et al.*, 1997:4)
4. The literature is extensive; some examples are: Chambers (1997); Fowler (1997); Peters (1992); Senge (1990).
5. Thanks to Irene Guijt for this point.
6. See Pearce (1996); Gonella *et al.* (1998); Zadek *et al.* (1997) for processes and experiences in using benchmarking and external verification for social auditing.
7. Social auditing examines the social and ethical impact and behaviour of the organization from two perspectives: from the inside – assessing performance against its mission statement or statement of objectives; and from the outside: using comparisons with other organizations' behaviour and social norms. By listening to and reporting the assessment of an organization by its stakeholders the social audit will: provide feedback about areas in which the organization is failing to meet stakeholders' expectations and its own stated objectives; and account for its performance to a wider range of interested people than simply those who have invested capital (e.g. funders) (Gonella *et al.*, 1998; Mayo, 1996; Raynard, 1998; Zadek and Evans, 1993).
8. The BATMAN Consortium is also known as the Barangay-Bayan Governance Consortium.

Author details

Roy V. Abes works as a research and evaluation officer of Education for Life Foundation (ELF), an NGO working for grassroots leadership formation in the Philippines. ELF believes that grassroots leaders have a crucial role in empowerment and democratization. As an advocate and practitioner of participatory approaches, Roy's current interest is in helping translate grassroots leaders' personal empowerment into organizations and eventually towards community empowerment through participation.

Carlos Barahona is a statistician and agronomist interested in the integration of quantitative and qualitative methodologies for research, monitoring and evaluation. He is working on developing methodologies that incorporate statistical principles into participatory methods and allow for the generalization of results. He has worked in Central America, Bolivia, Malawi and the UK.

Jutta Blauert is a fellow at the Institute of Development Studies at the University of Sussex in the UK. She is a rural sociologist, having worked mostly in the areas of environmental sociology and sustainable agriculture and rural development in Latin America. Previously, she undertook research and teaching on these subjects at the Institute of Latin American Studies of London University. In Mexico she is attached to the Research and Postgraduate Studies Center in Social Anthropology (CIESAS) in Oaxaca. Her current research work focuses on accountability and participation, based on participatory evaluation and monitoring approaches in the context of natural resource management at project and policy levels.

Dindo M. Campilan is a social scientist at the International Potato Center (CIP). He is the co-ordinator of CIP's Users' Perspectives With Agricultural Research and Development (UPWARD), a Philippines based Asian network for participatory research and development in root-crop agriculture. He has a Ph.D. (Communication and Innovation Studies) from Wageningen University, The Netherlands.

Fred Carden Ph.D., is Senior Specialist in Evaluation at the International Development Research Centre (Canada). He has extensive experience in international development research and has written in the areas of evaluation, international co-operation and environmental management. He has taught and carried out research at York University (Canada), the Co-operative College of Tanzania, the Bandung Institute of Technology (Indonesia) and the University of Indonesia. He holds a Ph.D. from the Université de Montréal and a Masters in environmental studies from York University. His current research interests include evaluation tools and methodology development, participatory monitoring and evaluation, and organizational assessment.

Ruben Dario Espinosa Alzate is part of an inter-disciplinary group of consultants known as CODACOP, which supports women's organizations, indigenous communities, and farmers' groups. He acts as a facilitator for the Local Government and Development initiative of the Association of Indigenous Cabildos (ACIN) in seven municipalities of the Northern Cauca, a region that is socially and economically important in Colombia. His interests lie in contributing to the development of participatory monitoring and evaluation methodologies that strengthen community practices of local democracy, and promoting the study of factors that help ensure the successful implementation of decentralization policies in favour of local development in Latin America.

Marisol Estrella is a research associate at the Institute for Popular Democracy (IPD) based in Manila, Philippines. Her interest in participatory research, monitoring and evaluation evolved when she was a graduate student at the University of Sussex, UK, where she obtained her Master's degree in 1997. Her research interests and advocacy efforts currently focus on participation and local governance, in areas that relate to local development planning and budgeting, poverty monitoring, and local environmental policy.

John Gaventa is a fellow with the Participation Group at the Institute of Development Studies, University of Sussex (UK). A political sociologist and adult educator by background, he has over 20 years experience in using participatory methods of research and education for development in both the North and South. He also has written widely on issues of participatory research, power, empowerment and participation. Prior to coming to IDS, he served as the Director of the Highlander Center and of the National Learning Initiative at the University of Tennessee in the United States.

Davaa Gobisaikhan is a Mongolian national who studied economics at the Trade Union Institute in Moscow. He graduated from the institute in 1984 with a diploma in economics. He worked for the Confederation of Mongolian Trade Unions as an economist from 1984–1993. He took up his current position as the Financial Officer of the Poverty Alleviation Programme Office in 1995.

Irene Guijt was, until recently, a research associate for the Sustainable Agriculture and Rural Livelihoods Programme at the International Institute for the Environment and Development (IIED). After obtaining degrees in tropical land and water use engineering, she worked on diverse aspects of participatory resource management in Brazil, eastern and western Africa, south Asia, and Australia. Her interests and publications relate to gender and environment policies and methodologies, local level valuation of wild resources, participatory monitoring, and institutionalizing participatory planning. She recently worked as a visiting research fellow in the School of Resource Management and Environmental Science (ANU) Canberra, where she developed and taught a course in Participatory Resource Management. Key publications have been *Participatory Learning and Action: A learner's guide* and *The Myth of Community: gender issues in participatory development*. Her recent work with IIED and International Union

267

for the Conservation of Nature on participatory monitoring and organizational learning for collaborative resource management is also the focus of her Ph.D. research.

Clare Hamilton is currently working in a community forestry project in Nepal. It is a process project, which makes issues of who is learning and how the learning influences working practices central to its approach. Clare's interests include learning processes, forms of participation and audio-visual forms of communication and analysis.

Graham Haylor is a consultant and research lecturer in aquaculture systems at the Institute of Aquaculture, University of Stirling, and has worked extensively in Europe, Asia and Africa. He has co-ordinated research projects in India, Laos, Sri Lanka and Pakistan, as well as contributing to projects in Bangladesh.

Sibongile Hood has worked with participatory approaches in the area of natural resource management over many years in both tropical and temperate, and rural and urban environments. She initially studied agroforestry but shifted her focus from the biological to more social processes, with the realization that this approach was an essential element for the success of any environmental project. She is currently working in the UK, using participatory techniques for watercourse development in the Mersey Catchment.

Sa'ed Jasser is an economist with a Ph.D. from the Moscow Academy of Science. He has been working with the Palestinian Agricultural Relief Committees (PARC) for seven years and has extensive experience in research, needs assessment and evaluation. Committed to the use of participatory approaches in development, Sa'ed has been involved in setting up a PME system in PARC and facilitating a participatory strategic planning process. He is currently working on setting up a PME network in Palestine, and on a study of gender relations and decision making in Palestinian rural areas.

Deb Johnson is currently working in eastern and Southern Africa as a director of Sikiliza International, Ltd, based in Kampala, Uganda. She has been involved in using and promoting participatory approaches for a number of years, first as a nutritionist/nutrition educator in Niger, then as a development communication associate with World Neighbors based in Oklahoma City, USA. She has worked in Asia, Africa, Latin America, and North America. Her work with Sikiliza International, Ltd has offered her the opportunity to become more involved in decentralization and governance issues.

Anna Lawrence is a research fellow at the Agricultural Extension and Rural Development Department of the University of Reading, UK. She collaborates in research projects in South America and Asia relating to participatory management of natural resources, with a particular interest in conservation through use of biodiversity.

Maksha Maharjan is currently working as a community forestry advisor in the Nepal–UK Community Forestry Project (NUKCFP), Nepal. Her main roles and responsibilities include the following: formulating and integrating macro- and micro-level community forestry policy; developing strategies to enhance community forestry in Nepal; supporting forest users groups in building capacity for sustainable community forest management, among others. Her interests focus on participatory self-monitoring and evaluation in community forestry in the developing countries.

Alexander Menamkart is a Canadian economist who has specialized in developmental economics and co-operative credit. He obtained his Ph.D. in economics and social sciences from the University of Fribourg, Switzerland in 1975. He has been working in Ulaanbaatar, Mongolia since April 1997 as Programme Management Adviser for the National Poverty Alleviation Programme of Mongolia under a UNDP–UNV contract.

Eric Meusch, after a short period of working for the collaborative project in Laos, continued working in Savannakhet Laos with the AIT Aqua Outreach Program as an advisor to the newly established Regional Development Committee for Livestock and Fisheries in Southern Laos (RDC). The RDC is a regional government organization in Laos working as a co-ordinating body for development issues in the livestock and fisheries sectors. Eric is currently the Program Unit Manager/Senior Adviser to the AIT Aqua Outreach Unit in Cambodia, where he works with the Aquaculture Office in the Department of Fisheries in Phnom Penh. The outreach programme is supporting the Aquaculture Office in the development and co-ordination of sub-national networks, management systems and techniques for improved small-scale aquatic resources management. The programme focuses on food security and alleviation of rural poverty.

Eduardo Quintanar is a Mexican and a veterinarian medic (*medico veterinario zootecnista*). He has a postgraduate degree in Integrated Rural Development in the University of Laval in Quebec, Canada. He is a researcher in the Environmental Study Group within the Natural Resource Management Program. He is presently working in farmers' experimentation research using participatory methods and in the area of natural-resource management, with a focus on livestock.

Raj Kumar Rai is currently working in the Nepal–UK Community Forestry Project as a community forestry officer. He provides support to strengthen capacities of the government forestry staff and forest user groups; facilitates training and workshops; supports forest user groups' networks; and works to develop resources related to participatory monitoring and evaluation at the community level. Before joining the NUKCFP, he was involved in community mobilization in agricultural research and rural development.

Leela Rasaily has been working as a community forestry officer in Nepal–UK Community Forestry Project since 1994. Recently she has assumed the responsibility as community forestry adviser in the NUKCFP. Through her work she has gained experience in group management, gender and development, participatory monitoring with women's groups, networking, and facilitation. Before joining the NUKCFP, she worked with non-governmental organizations as an assistant researcher, HIV/AIDS awareness communicator, literacy co-ordinator. She holds a Master of Arts in Sociology.

Frances Patton Rutherford was the co-ordinator of the Citizen Learning Team in McDowell County, West Virginia. She has also worked for many years in the county as a community organizer, educator and health worker. Currently, she is working as Executive Director of the grassroots organization Big Creek People in Action. The daughter of a coalminer, she was born and raised in the county. Her husband, by the way, is an excellent bluegrass and country musician!

Ram Bahadur Shrestha is a community development facilitator with an educational background in sociology. Her main interests are in participatory development approaches, especially participatory monitoring and evaluation. Her experiences are in community forestry, community health and development.

Pablo Sidersky currently holds the position of regional director of the NGO AS-PTA, entailing institutional responsibilities as well as the supervision of three projects/programmes. His main interests concern exploring new ways of seeing and understanding rural extension and research.

Janet Symes is a community development specialist focusing on participatory approaches to development. She has worked with a variety of community organizations including women's groups in Kenya, a labour and community coalition in West Virginia, USA and community development trusts in northern England. She has been working with the Palestinian Agricultural Relief Committees since 1994 where she has been developing participatory methods for planning, monitoring and evaluation, setting up a PME system within the organization and facilitating strategic planning and the introduction of gender approaches. She has carried out research on gender relations and decision making in Palestinian rural areas.

Victor Hugo Torres D. is currently involved in researching methodologies pertaining to participatory monitoring and evaluation in Ecuador. He is a consultant for rural water and sanitation systems for the World Bank, and facilitates in the Forests, Trees and Communities Programme sponsored by the FAO.

Penelope Ward is the Programme Co-ordinator of CARE South Africa's Institutional Strengthening Programme. This programme involves establishing partnerships with local service organizations to strengthen the capacity of civil society networks. Currently, she is facilitating a series of household-livelihood security assessments to develop strategies that will address issues prioritized by the partner organizations, such as staff development, improving project impact or increasing management effectiveness.

Index